How to use your tastecard...

A tastecard membership gives you 50% off the total food bill or 2 meals for the price of 1 at all 4000+ participating restaurants. What's more; you can always order from the full a la carte menu, so your choice will not be restricted.

tastecard is primarily a web and mobile solution based product – these forms of new media allow us to keep you informed of our ever expanding restaurant portfolio, something that is impossible to do in print. We are adding hundreds of new restaurants to the club every single week and our website is updated daily, so please always reference www.tastecard.co.uk or any of our mobile applications in order to search for participating restaurants, current offers, details of how to use your membership, tastecard news and much more.

The rules of taste are simple

- Search our website, phone applications or mobile site to find a restaurant
- IMPORTANT: If the telephone icon is shown you must make an advance booking, mentioning taste
- Enjoy your meal
- Present your tastecard upon arrival at the restaurant when requesting the bill to receive either 50% off the total food bill or 2 meals for the price of 1

Note: 50% off the total food bill means that multiple diners receive a 50% discount on food with just 1 tastecard. Please check the individual restaurants on the website for maximum numbers per tastecard.

2 meals for the price of 1 is across all courses ordered; the cheapest or equivalent dish of each course being free. This is an offer for 2 people only.

Key to icons on tastecard.co.uk

- **50%** — The restaurant offers taste members 50% off the total food bill
- **241** — The restaurant offers 2 for 1 meals (across all courses ordered)
- You must telephone in advance and mention taste
- **4** — The number denotes the maximum number of people per taste booking
- **FRI✗** — The taste offer is not available on Friday Evenings
- **SAT✗** — The taste offer is not available on Saturday Evenings
- **1st** — The restaurant is a 'first visit only' restaurant
- **U** — The restaurant is an 'unlimited usage' restaurant
- The tastecard offer is not available during December

Note: The Christmas Period, Bank Holidays and 'celebration days' such as Valentine's Day, New Year's Eve, Mother's and Father's Day are extremely busy for our restaurants. We therefore ask that you check the website or call the restaurants to ensure that you can use your card on these days.

GW01337059

Welcome to the dining revolution

tastecard.co.uk

taste is an online product which is ever-evolving, with all current offers at participating restaurants detailed on the website.

With great new restaurants being added every day, www.tastecard.co.uk provides a comprehensive portfolio of restaurants, illustrating where you can enjoy the benefits of your tastecard.

Our website also features all participating restaurants, full in depth write-ups, member recommendations, image galleries, location maps and much more. You can search by postcode or area, cuisine, Friday and Saturday evening availability and a whole host of other criteria. Londoners can also search by tube station or London landmark in addition to the standard search function.

You can also get great new restaurants emailed to your inbox by signing up to our newsletter; and have exclusive offers made available to you by becoming a fan of our facebook page and following us on twitter.

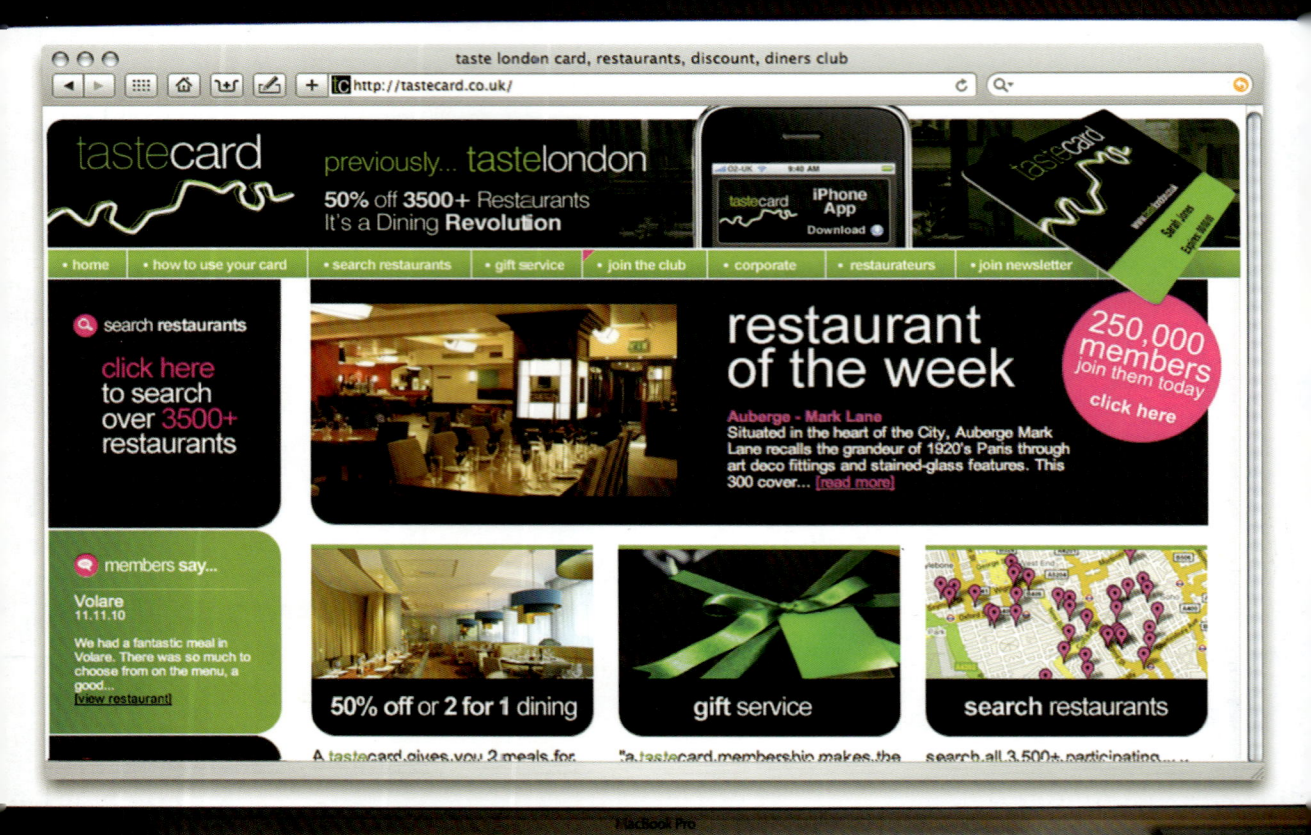

online

Advanced search
Narrow your search down to a particular cuisine, offer availability, average price or type of offer availability.

Search facility
Use the postcode search facility to list restaurants from a particular postcode.

You can also do a quick search by restaurant name, nearest tube station or famous landmark

Results
Your results will be displayed in distance from your search. Click each restaurant for its full page entry on the site

Map
Pins correspond to your results and show the restaurants' locations

Restaurant Pages
Each restaurant has its own page on the tastecard site, with numerous photographs, full write-up, reviews, map and directions

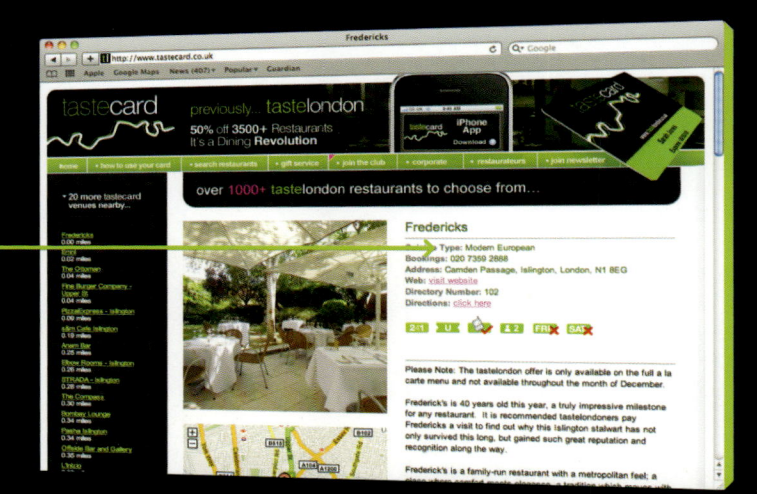

The tastecard gift service

Why not treat someone special in your life to a tastecard, a truly unique gift that they will use all year round?

The recipient will receive their taste directory and card wrapped with a personalised gift tag message attached. You can have their pack delivered to you so that you can hand it over personally, or alternatively have it delivered directly to them on a set date.

With taste now nationwide there has never been a better time to buy, or be bought, a tastecard.

To purchase a taste gift membership please visit tastecard.co.uk or call 0800 5677 241

Corporate Memberships

taste works with many organisations helping them to add real value to their company benefits package. Below are just a sample of our 100s of current clients.

'taste cards continue to be one of the most popular employee benefits we have on offer at Cancer Research UK. It is such excellent value for money and the taste team are so friendly and efficient – we love working with them!'

Angela De Ath, Reward Analyst, HR
Cancer Research UK

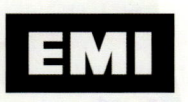

EMI · UBS · eurostar · CNBC · Harrods
Lovells · City of London · DTZ · Macquarie · Bank of England · Universal · Sony Music · MTV Music Television
NBC Universal · Fremantle Media · Berwin Leighton Paisner · Harvey Nichols · Cancer Research UK · London Stock Exchange
Warner · BBC · getty images · LexisNexis · BMA
WestLB · IPC Media · mace · informa · FORTIS
telegraph media group · london.gov.uk · Kingsley Napley · LOVEFiLM.COM · Pershing
mediabrands · PRS for Music · SUNGARD · QAS · ProcServe · NYK Line · DDB · Islington · City of London
bestinvest · Hill & Knowlton · Marubeni · emap advertising · NHS Central London Community Healthcare · OMD · Octopus · Eisai
withers LLP · lewis silkin · BRISTOWS · SAGE Publications · CBS Interactive · marcus evans · cohn & wolfe
IQPC · JWT · novae · streetcar · Turner · King Sturge · ZenithOptimedia · visit Britain
kfh.co.uk · Waterstone's · monster · Diabetes UK · endemol · Southwark Council · Live Nation · IoE London · The Peverel Group
Moody's · Chantrey Vellacott DFK · Munich RE · LexisNexis · The Spectator · Ask Jeeves · Orrick · Algorithmics
ascent media · ticketmaster · EUROSPORT · DIESEL · phd · NYK Logistics · British Horseracing Authority · Knight Frank · OLSWANG
hachette UK · kcc.ac.uk · Huntress Group · Mitsui Sumitomo Insurance · incisive media · Reed Business Information

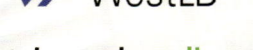

For further information please visit tastecard.co.uk, email benefits@tastecard.co.uk or call 0800 5677 241

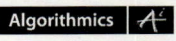

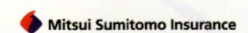

PUT A SMILE ON YOUR MUG!

taste are delighted to be supporting Macmillan Cancer Support as their chosen charity for the next 12 months.

taste will be running a number of campaigns over the coming 12 months, during which £5 will be donated to Macmillan for every promotional membership sold.

Get together with friends, family and colleagues and raise some money (and a smile) for people affected by cancer. The World's Biggest Coffee Morning is held on Friday, 24 September, but you can hold your event at any time of the year.

Register now at
www.macmillan.org.uk/coffee
or call **0845 602 1246**
quoting NA12

An estimated 2.6 million people got together last year to help make a huge difference to people affected by cancer. You can be part of this too, by bringing your friends together to help raise over £8m for Macmillan.

Hold your own (traditional or with a twist) coffee morning event and make it a good day for you and a good day for people affected by cancer.

Get involved and put a smile on your mug for Macmillan. Register today.

WE ARE MACMILLAN. CANCER SUPPORT

WORLD'S BIGGEST COFFEE MORNING

Macmillan Cancer Support, registered charity in England and Wales (261017) Scotland (SC039907) and the Isle of Man (604). MAC12839 March 2010
Printed on recycled paper. Please recycle

taste on the move

If you are out and about, we have a host of mobile solutions to enable you to get full use out of your tastecard...

Mobile Apps
We currently have an iPhone and Android App allowing users of these two platforms a speedy and in-depth referencing tool. You can download the tastecard App from the relevant App Stores.

Mobile Website
For other 'smart-phone' users, we have a mobile site: www.tastecard.co.uk/mobile The site allows you to search using a specific area or postcode, or use the 'near me' function to find participating restaurants in your vicinity. You can also view offers and call restaurants directly from the web page.

Non-Smart Phone
If you do not have a 'smart phone' you can text **TASTE** to **80182** for the nearest restaurants to you - texts are charged at 25p each.

All our mobile solutions are constantly updated with new restaurants and offers, so wherever you are you can always get full use out of your tastecard!

How the taste directory works

Volume 6 of the tastecard directory is split into 9 specific areas of the UK and Ireland. Each area will have a number of featured restaurants first, to give you a taste of those that are on offer, followed by a more comprehensive listing of restaurants, in alphabetical postcode order. The restaurant listings will begin with a selection of some of the national chain restaurants that we work with, followed by a breakdown of each area. It is important to note that not all restaurants participating in taste are featured in this guide, but can be found at www.tastecard.co.uk and the information is only correct at time of print.

London	24
South East	62
South West	90
Central England	100
Wales	114
North West England	120
North East & Yorkshire	140
Scotland	160
Eire & Northern Ireland	170

Contents

National Restaurant Chains

As well as working with 1000s of independently owned restaurants throughout the UK and Ireland, we are also pleased to bring you the fantastic taste discount at many popular high street venues.

Your tastecard can be used at:

- CAFÉ ROUGE — RESTAURANT BAR CAFE
- BELLA ITALIA — Caffe · Bar · Ristorante
- LIVEBAIT — FRESH FISH AND SEAFOOD
- PIZZA EXPRESS
- CAFFÈ UNO
- PREZZO
- gbk (gourmet burger kitchen)
- TIFFINBITES
- LIVEBAIT — FRESH FISH AND SEAFOOD
- tigertiger
- Fine Burger Co.
- All Star Lanes
- La Tasca — SPANISH TAPAS BAR & RESTAURANT
- STRADA
- Sargam Swadesh
- BARCELONA TAPAS BAR Y RESTAURANTE
- Belushi's — www.belushis.com
- rbg BAR & GRILL
- Ashöka RESTAURANTS
- The GRAND UNION BAR · GRILL
- FIRE & STONE — Deliciously different pizzas
- bertorelli EST. 1913
- Jongleurs Comedy Clubs
- Azzurro ITALIAN BAR · KITCHEN
- BRASSERIE GÉRARD — SIMPLE FRENCH FOOD
- HENRY'S CAFÉ BAR

La Tasca

SPANISH TAPAS RESTAURANT AND BAR

La Tasca

For many people, La Tasca was the 'missing piece of the jigsaw' for taste – a chain of hugely popular tapas restaurants which have proved a massive hit since becoming part of the Dining Revolution.

Welcome to La Tasca….where sun, sea, sangría and sizzling Spanish tapas are the order of the day – close your eyes and you can almost imagine that you're in Spain.

Now, there's no need for day-dreaming, since La Tasca, the authentic Spanish tapas restaurant and bar group, is offering taste members a fantastic 50% off its 'Tapas to Share' menu. With over 30 tapas dishes to choose from, including the classic chorizo in red wine and tasty calamari rings, you can experience the true taste of Spain for less – the moment you step inside La Tasca.

La Tasca – Spain is closer than you think!

PizzaExpress

The largest chain of restaurants in the UK, PizzaExpress joined taste in January 2008, since when it has proved a huge hit with our members.

Peter Boizot started the first PizzaExpress in London, 1965. However his first taste of pizza was in 1948 whilst in Northern Italy. From there, he found himself in Germany where he witnessed pizzaiolos dressed in blue and white striped shirts tossing the dough high into the air. This was accompanied by opera, classical and jazz music all played off a juke machine.

On returning to London and finding no good pizzas, Peter invested in a Signora Notaro oven from Italy, got an exclusive deal with London's only mozzarella maker, Margaret Zampi and took over her ailing pizza shop, PizzaExpress. Soon a second restaurant was opened and the beginnings of PizzaExpress started...

National Restaurant Chains

National Restaurant Chains

gourmet burg

gbk

gbk has become the quintessential lunch spot for tastecard members, receiving rave reviews from cardholders throughout the UK.

The idea for Gourmet Burger Kitchen originated in New Zealand. Where once the traditional burger was seen purely as a fast food option, gourmet burgers have knocked tradition on the head. Gourmet Burger Kitchen has created a nutritious, sophisticated product using the best and freshest ingredients available.

What makes gbk burgers different?

The Gourmet Burger Kitchen menu has been consulted on by leading New Zealand and London based chef Peter Gordon. His involvement has been key in creating the menu.

"I love the concept of taking something simple like a burger and expanding its potential - giving it a distinct, cutting edge flavour" - Peter Gordon

The menu offers classic flavour combinations such as Chicken, Camembert and Cranberry, and Beef, Avocado and Bacon. It then goes one step further with exciting new burger combinations such as Chorizo and Sweet Potato or Lamb and Minted Relish. The specially developed GBK sauces and relishes help to define each burger.

Not just any ingredients will do, Gourmet Burger Kitchen uses only the best ingredients available to create each burger. The oversized sourdough buns are baked each morning by their artisan baker. The Aberdeen Angus Scotch Beef, fresh English chicken and fresh vegetables are delivered each day. Gourmet Burger Kitchen uses only 100% Aberdeen Angus Scotch Beef which is sourced from fully traceable grass reared animals.

A place to eat and relax

The GBK premises reflect the simplicity of the operation. The décor is clean, crisp and fresh. The kitchen is clearly visible - watch while you wait, see what you eat, enjoy the creation.

STRADA
Cucina Italiana

STRADA

Part of the Tragus Group of restaurants; STRADA joined taste in November 2009, to be followed in January 2011 by the other members of the Tragus Group; Cafe Rouge and Bella Italia.

Strada is your ideal dining destination, serving simple, freshly prepared Italian dishes using the finest seasonal produce. The menu offers hand stretched pizzas, fresh pasta salads, risotti and grilled meat and fish dishes, together with an exclusive Italian wine list.

The contemporary restaurants offer a sophisticated ambience that's perfect for a leisurely lunch, a romantic dinner with that special someone, or a celebration with friends.

National Restaurant Chains

National Restaurant Chains

...ron pressé · paté · menthe · olives

CAFÉ ROUGE
RESTAURANT BAR CAFÉ

Cafe Rouge

Joining in January 2011, and one of the most recent additions to tastecard, Cafe Rouge's involvement in taste was met with great excitement from our members on Facebook and followers on Twitter.

Café Rouge is the UK's premier French restaurant brand with a broad offer of classic French dishes and wines. With over 120 restaurants across the UK you'll not have to go far to experience the warm Parisien charm that makes Café Rouge such a popular choice.

The menu offers the some favourite French classics, with onion soup, mussels and chicken liver parfait all on offer. You can then move on to smoked Toulouse sausages and mash, pan fried smoked haddock fishcake with a lemon butter sauce or beef Bourguignon. But steaks are what Café Rouge are proud of. Offering some interesting traditional French cuts such as the Bavette marinated in rosemary and garlic to give that true Gallic experience!

National Restaurant Chains

PREZZO

Prezzo

One of our longest serving partners, Prezzo continues to receive rave reviews from our members all over the UK.

The chefs at Prezzo use the finest seasonal products available, many of which are imported directly from Italy.

The original Prezzo opened in the heart of London's West End in New Oxford Street in November 2000, since then, their team of chefs have worked hard to develop a fabulous menu. The menu includes a wide variety of delicious antipastic, as well as pizza, pasta, risotto, grilled meats, fresh salads and frequently changing specials. Prezzo remain committed to using only the highest quality produce.

It is policy, where possible, to seek to restore particularly impressive buildings or sites of local interest.

National Restaurant Chains

BELLA ITALIA
Caffe • Bar • Ristorante

Belle Italia

Joining in January 2011 and also part of the Tragus Group; Bella Italia is set to become a firm favourite amongst taste members.

Visit Bella Italia and let Italy inspire you! With a great selection of pizza, pasta, salads, and grill dishes, there is always a choice to suit everyone's taste! Enjoy familiar Italian favourites in with a lively atmosphere and a heavy dose of Italian hospitality.

Whether you're popping in for breakfast and a cappuccino, a light lunch with friends, or dinner with the family, you'll find a warm welcome awaits you at Bella Italia.

National Restaurant Chains

London

London

Frederick's
Modern European — 020 7359 2888

Camden Passage, Islington, London, N1 8EG

Frederick's is 40 years old this year, a truly impressive milestone for any restaurant. It is recommended taste members pay Frederick's a visit to find out why this Islington stalwart has not only survived this long, but gained such great reputation and recognition along the way.

Frederick's is a family-run restaurant with a metropolitan feel; a place where comfort meets elegance, a tradition which moves with the times. Frederick's has grown up with Islington; it is at the heart of the famous Camden Passage antiques quarter, and a step away from the bustle of Upper Street. It also couldn't be more convenient for Sadler's Wells, The Almeida and King's Head theatres, the Screen on the Green Cinema and the Business Design Centre.

Frederick's main dining area is the Garden Room, an airy yet intimate space beneath a spectacular vaulted glass roof. It overlooks the patio and garden, which are open for drinks and dining whenever it is warm enough.

The bar at Frederick's is the perfect place to meet up or drop into: drinks, coffee and snacks are served throughout the day. And for those with business or celebrations to attend to, Frederick's offers stylish but welcoming private rooms.

Almeida
French — **020 7354 4777**

30 Almeida Street, London, N1 1AD

Almeida offers traditional and delectable French cuisine to a rather groovy part of north London. Almeida certainly more than compliments the bustling Islington restaurant scene, as well as having an appeal for foodies throughout London.

The restaurant is located just a stones throw from Upper Street, at 30 Almeida Street just opposite the Almeida Theatre and has a simple but contemporary interior design which was conceived by Terence Conran.

Almeida has also become renowned for its revival of trolley service; there is a trolley of charcuterie featuring home made rillettes, terrines and pates. In addition, a trolley of tarts provides a tempting end to meals.

Marco
British — 020 7915 2929

Stamford Bridge, Fulham, London, SW6 1HS

Nestled just off Fulham Road in this fashionable district of West London, MARCO is a collaborative effort between restaurateur Marco Pierre White and Roman Abramovich fusing culinary delights from both sides of the Channel.

Building on the success of his previous restaurants the Marco Pierre White name has become synonymous with a superior culinary experience and MARCO as the newest addition does not disappoint. Style and elegance combine to make this the perfect dining experience for any occasion.

Rivington Grill
British — 020 8293 9270

178 Greenwich High Road, London, SE10 8NN

Housed in the Greenwich Picturehouse building, The Rivington Bar and Grill serves back-to-basics British food.

The bar offers terrific cocktails and all-day dining - the perfect place to chill and meet friends. But it's the main restaurant we want to focus on here - flooded with natural light, the whitewashed walls and stripped wooden floors creating a cool and relaxed dining space.

The Rivington Bar and Grill's menu is carefully compiled using the best seasonal produce available, sourced from small suppliers in and around the British Isles. Traditional favourites includes dived Lyme Bay scallops with squash and black pudding; Hereford rib eye with chips; the all-day breakfast and the delicious bread and butter pudding.

London

London

Mint Leaf
Indian — 020 7600 0992

Angel Court, London, EC2R 7HB

Mint Leaf Lounge is recognised as both stylish and contemporary and brings a sense of elegance and sophistication to the Indian restaurant scene here in the City of London.

'Namaste', which means 'welcomes the divine in you', exquisitely sums up what is so special about this place. You will experience the finest food, which perfectly combined with the ancient traditions and authentic flavours of India, fused exotically with a unique ethnic edge. All served to you with a style of service rooted in the finest eastern traditions.

The opulent main restaurant area is defined by a maze of dark wooden partitions in American black walnut and contrasting with cream leather seating designed to seat 90 guests for dinner.

Acorn House
British — 020 7812 1842

69 Swinton Street, London, WC1X 9NT

Positioned on the corner of Grays Inn Road and Swinton Street, Acorn House Restaurant is a five-minute-stroll from Kings Cross and St. Pancras mainline railway station, and a ten-minute walk from Holborn and Angel tube and is the most important restaurant which has opened in London for years. The reason for this is that Acorn House is London's first truly environmentally sustainable restaurant, it is an exciting venture offering exceptional quality food with a fresh, seasonally evolving menu and every aspect from design through to delivery aims to be environmentally conscious and sustainable.

The calibre of food and service at Acorn House aims to draw customers from surrounding areas as a "destination restaurant". Local residents and workers now have the option of a stylish, modern and health-conscious eatery which is affordable, whilst being absolutely delicious, and there is always the added bonus that you can leave the restaurant with a clear conscience knowing you have done your bit for the environment.

London

London

Smithfield Bar & Grill
Fusion— 0870 442 2541

2-3 West Smithfield, London, EC1A 9JX

Situated opposite London's most famous meat market, Smithfield Bar and Grill is a popular lunchtime restaurant and post-work destination for local City slickers.

The interior reminds us of a sleek Manhattan steakhouse with its dark wood, shimmering chandeliers and sexy curved leather booths. During the day it's ideal for a quick burger between meetings, while in the evening the excellent cocktails and live music make it a great choice for after-work dinners and dates. As you would expect given the location, the menu is a meat-heavy mix of first class steaks and fish. Adventurous diners can tuck into grilled ostrich and seafood fans will love the lobster with garlic butter.

Whatever your preference, you won't leave hungry!

Madsen
International — 020 7225 2772

20 Old Brompton Road, London, SW7 3DL

A unique dining experience in South Kensington...

The climate, landscape and coastal waters of Scandinavia have given rise to a unique food culture. The light, the long growing season and the wide open spaces create a cuisine shaped by the environment itself: healthy, natural, and infused with taste.

This is the background for Madsen, a new Scandinavian restaurant in South Kensington.

Here, you'll find food that's simple and straightforward, yet full of character. Blending the traditional with the modern, you can enjoy dishes prepared with a variety of fresh, seasonal ingredients, brought to your table without fuss and unnecessary adornment.

Food as it should be.

Indian Zing
Indian — 020 8748 5959

236 King Street, London, W6 0RF

Lauded by press from the FT and the London Evening Standard, to Tatler magazine, Indian Zing is an elegantly simply restaurant, headed up by acclaimed chef owner Manoj Vasaikar.

Manoj's name has become synonymous with some of the most creative and exciting Indian cooking and his impressive CV includes time spent in some of the best Indian restaurant kitchens in Mumbai and London.

Expect thoroughly modern Indian food, which nevertheless does not abandon its robust sub-continental roots. Try the Lamb Dhansak with dill, pumpkin, aubergine, tamarind, fenugreek and lentils - a parsee favourite in Mumbai; or Prawn and Aubergine Kharkhatla, both showing an admirable lightness of touch.

Don't forget to check out the interesting fusion desserts - tandoori figs and apple crumble, which comes with a hot mango and ginger coulis in place of English custard, or multi-grained masala bread and butter pud.

Bombay Bicycle Club
Indian

Located in Balham, Hampstead and Holland Park – see listings for details

The Bombay Bicycle Club was a stylish gathering place on the Indian sub-continent where colonial officers would take trips and country picnics, always with delicious food. Like Kava Khanna (teahouses), it was a place to catch up on local gossip and events of the Raj, at its height in 1895. Today, the Bombay Bicycle Club is known for the best Indian Cuisine in London.

The first Bombay Bicycle Club Restaurant opened in Nightingale Lane, Clapham, over 20 years ago and is a regular favourite of many of London's top chefs and restaurant critics. A further two restaurants were opened in Holland Park and Hampstead offering the finest dining experience north of the river.

The award winning food in the restaurants is the philosophy of creating simple, yet fresh and inventive Indian food, using raw ingredients of the highest quality that is fundamental to The Bombay Bicycle Club. The dish of your choice is always freshly cooked to order and the food is spicy and aromatic but not searingly hot, unless requested otherwise, allowing you to taste each flavour within these fragrant dishes.

London

Kettners
French — **020 7734 6112**

29 Romilly Street, Soho, London, W1D 5HP

Kettner's is a legendary venue, first opened by Auguste Kettner, chef to Napoleon III in 1867. It was a favourite of Edward VII, Lillie Langtry and Oscar Wilde, and pays homage to theatre in its striking and stylish refurbishment.

Kettner's informal all-day Brasserie serves meals for all pockets and moments, from a casual lunch to a theatre supper or a special occasion. The menus draw on some retro classics of French cuisine, while introducing fresh new Mediterranean flavours and modern European dishes.

The Pudding Bar is about French fun with a twist and is open for tea, a light lunch, an informal rendez-vous or a late night treat. The large marble 'bar' is decked daily with an ever changing array of homemade treats, cakes and tarts and the Brasserie meals are also served in this area of the venue.

Kettner's incorporates many other spaces, including The Champagne Bar and The Apartment Cocktail Bar, where customers can continue an evening out or enjoy a leisurely drink prior to dining.

Both of these spaces, as well as various private rooms and the original 'Cabinets Particuliers' which have been restored, plus a complete party floor, can be hired for special bespoke events.

Kettner's has warmth and a sense of bonhomie that only the best brasseries possess and is well worth a visit for a truly unique experience.

Whitechapel Gallery Dining Room

British — 020 7522 7896

77-82 Whitechapel High Street, London, E1 7QX

The Whitechapel Gallery Dining Room offers a stylish and intimate dining experience, championing British ingredients using local seasonal produce in an eclectic and interesting way. Their fabulous evening a la carte menu is 'short and sweet' but changes and evolves on a regular basis reflecting the best of the season.

Awana
Malaysian — 020 7584 8880

85 Sloane Avenue, London, SW3 3DX

London's first high-end Malaysian restaurant has brought a spring to the step of this under-represented style of Asian cuisine. Awana allows you to explore exciting new tastes and flavours as you celebrate the diversity of the Malaysian food culture. The cuisine is inspired by the street food of Malaysia and offers you the opportunity to enjoy the variety and incredible depth of exotic flavours native to this very beautiful part of the world.

The decor draws inspiration from the traditional Malaysian teak house adding lush silk panels and delicate glass screens to a dark wood interior. Awana is a large, modern space predominantly made of teak, softened with burgundy leather chairs and spot lighting. It divides comfortably into a medium-sized dining area, a funky cocktail bar and at the back, through the restaurant, a smart satay bar designed specifically for solo diners.

belowzero
Modern European — 020 7478 8910

31-33 Heddon Street, London, W1B 4BN

belowzero restaurant + lounge and ABSOLUT ICEBAR London are, quite literally, London's coolest venues!

Once you have experienced the freezing temperatures of ABSOLUT ICEBAR (made of crystal clear ice and kept at -5 degrees year-round), warm up with the fantastic and well-priced modern European a la carte menu. After dinner, sink into the bed-like upholstery and relax with a cocktail & chilled out music, in the belowzero lounge.

Located on bustling, vibrant Heddon Street (just off Regent Street) in the former wine vaults for the British monarchy, belowzero is a luxurious, stylish restaurant & lounge bar and the perfect place to enjoy fine food with excellent service in warm, sumptuous surroundings. belowzero is open for lunch and dinner, ideal for a shopping break or the start to a great night out.

belowzero is a wonderful addition to taste, and we would recommend that all members visit as soon as possible!

London

supperclub
International — 020 8964 6600

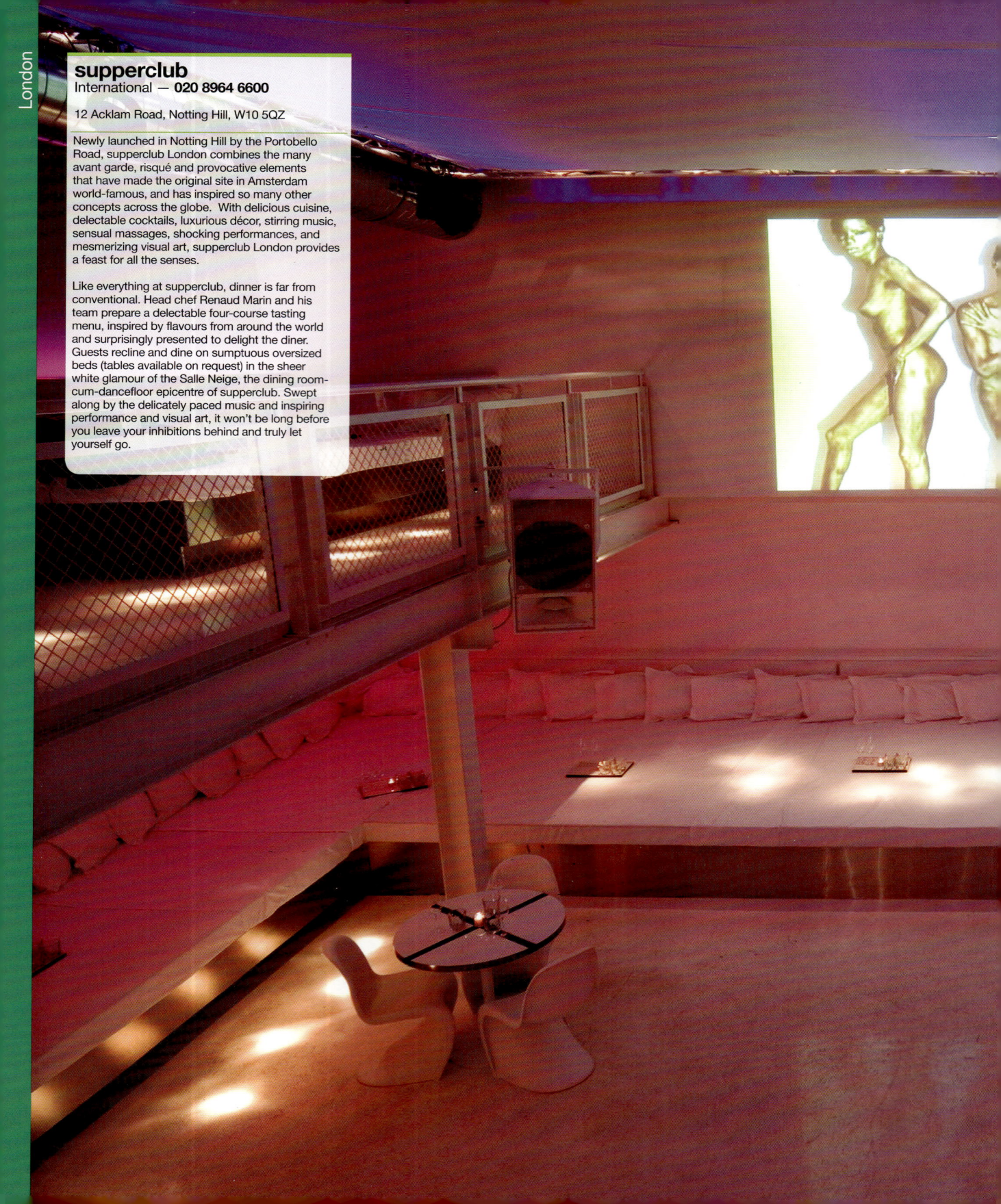

12 Acklam Road, Notting Hill, W10 5QZ

Newly launched in Notting Hill by the Portobello Road, supperclub London combines the many avant garde, risqué and provocative elements that have made the original site in Amsterdam world-famous, and has inspired so many other concepts across the globe. With delicious cuisine, delectable cocktails, luxurious décor, stirring music, sensual massages, shocking performances, and mesmerizing visual art, supperclub London provides a feast for all the senses.

Like everything at supperclub, dinner is far from conventional. Head chef Renaud Marin and his team prepare a delectable four-course tasting menu, inspired by flavours from around the world and surprisingly presented to delight the diner. Guests recline and dine on sumptuous oversized beds (tables available on request) in the sheer white glamour of the Salle Neige, the dining room-cum-dancefloor epicentre of supperclub. Swept along by the delicately paced music and inspiring performance and visual art, it won't be long before you leave your inhibitions behind and truly let yourself go.

108 Marylebone Lane
British — 020 7969 3900

108 Marylebone Lane, London, W1U 2QE

108's bar is a relaxed space ideal for informal dining, after-work drinks or pre-dinner aperitifs. The brasserie adjoins the bar and is a buzzy space.

The menus are designed to reflect seasonality of produce and change every couple of months. Specials change daily and are designed with a fast turnaround in mind Where ever possible produce and goods are sourced from local Marylebone businesses. They provide the area with a rich and plentiful supply of stunning produce and it is 108's pleasure to help provide them with another platform to sell and promote their products within a village setting.

The food philosophy is simple. Great ingredients are used to create simple, classic dishes. Local suppliers include the acclaimed and award-winning La Fromagerie, The Ginger Pig and Biggles Sausages.

London

The Bollo
International — 020 8994 6037

13 Bollo Lane, Chiswick, London, W4 5LR

The Bollo is a fine quality Gastro Pub with a great atmosphere and delicious food, situated on Bollo Lane in Chiswick.

The pub is consistently praised by local residents for the high quality of their menu.

The Butcher & Grill
British

Located in Wimbledon and Battersea, see listings for details

Dominic Ford (former supremo of Harvey Nics's extensive restaurant operations, including the Oxo Tower) and Paul Grout (an upmarket butcher of over 20 years' standing) have teamed up to launch Butcher and Grill.

The Butcher and Grill is a unique combination of a Modern Butcher Shop, an informal Restaurant, serving all the produce from the shop, and a casual bar serving coffee and patisserie in the morning during the week and full breakfast at the weekends.

The absolute focus of 'The Grill' is on the quality of the produce from the Butcher counter and good service in simple surroundings.

Customers have the option of making their selection from the butcher counter or by choosing their preferred cut from the menus. The menu comprises of top quality cuts of meat, simply grilled or roasted and a choice of potato dishes, vegetables or salad. In the winter months there is a range of slow braises and stews.

The key emphasis in 'The Butcher' is the quality of product, sourcing, preparation and customer service. Wherever possible, meat has been be sourced through British Farms, with great care taken to establish the integrity of the producer and the meat. Beef, lamb, coming mainly from Highfields Farm in East Sussex, pork, Sausages, veal, offal, poultry and game is available, along side home-cooked meats, pies and pates and a small selection of oils, mustards and pickles.

Meat and Poultry is prepared to a very high standard in both English and French cuts. The butchers are trained to offer the best advice on seasonality and the quality of specific products of that day, enabling customers to make an informed decision on every purchase.

London

Le Chardon
French

Located in Dulwich and Clapham, see listings for details

Robert Benyayer, owner of Le Chardon, first came to London in 1984 from Cannes in the south of France. Shops and restaurants have always run in the family and with years of chef experience in Cannes and catering in the French army, Robert came to work in London at the Claridges Hotel and then finally took the plunge and opened his own restaurant in 1997.

The restaurants are particularly famed for their seafood, amongst others, and the seafood platter – Plateau de Fruit de Mer certainly does not disappoint. The homemade foie gras terrine with brioche and sweet chutney will have you travelling from miles around and you will be hard pushed to find one better, or indeed, homemade.

With exceptional authentic, fresh, innovative food, attentive service and the knowledge of experienced chefs and staff, one thing is for certain when you visit Le Chardon; you will defiantly feel as though you have just experienced something very special and it will soon become a favourite.

Central London

Sfizio Caffe Bar & Pizzeria - Italian 0207 831 1888
35-37 Theobald's Road, London, WC1 X8SP

PizzaExpress Coptic Street - Pizza 0207 636 3232
30 Coptic Street, London, WC1A 1NS

Truckles - International 020 7404 5338
Off Bury Place, Bloomsbury, WC1A 2JR

Kingsley Two Brasserie, The Kingsley by Thistle - International 0871 376 9006
Bloomsbury Way, London, WC1A 2SD

merkaba - International 0203 004 6021
11-13 Bayley Street, Bedford Square, London, WC1B 3HD

Creation Restaurant & Bar - Fusion 0207 637 3477
Kenilworth Hotel, 94-97 Great Russell Street, London, WC1B 3LB

Malabar Junction - Indian 0207 580 5230
107 Great Russel Street, London, WC1B 3NA

Landseer British Kitchen - British 0207 347 1222
The Bloomsbury Hotel, 16-22 Great Russell Street, London, WC1B 3NN

Tea and Tattle - British 0772 219 2703
41 Great Russell Street, London, WC1B 3PE

Bloomsbury Street - Modern European 020 8817 0944
9-13 Bloomsbury Street, London, WC1B 3QD

Hason Raja Indian and Bangladeshi Restaurant - Indian 0207 242 3377
84 Southampton Row, Holborn, London, WC1B 4BB

All Star Lanes Holborn - American 0207 025 2676
Victoria House, Bloomsbury, London, WC1B 4DA

PizzaExpress - Southampton Row - Pizza 0207 430 1011
114-117 Southampton Row, London, WC1B 5AA

Bloomsbury Kitchen and Bar @ Bloomsbury Park - British 0871 376 9007
126 Southampton Row, London, WC1B 5AD

Fitzroy Doll's Restaurant at The Hotel Russell - British 0207 837 6470
Russell Square, London, WC1B 5BE

Number Twelve Restaurant & Bar - Italian 020 7693 5423
12 Upper Woburn Place, London, WC1H 0HX

The Harrison - British 0207 278 3966
28 Harrison Street, London**, WC1H 8JF**

Bloomsbury Lanes - American 0207 183 1979
Basement of Tavistock Hotel, London, WC1H 9EU

gbk - Brunswick - Antipodean 0207 278 7168
44/46 The Brunswick Centre, London, WC1N 1AE

STRADA - Brunswick Centre - Italian 020 7278 2777
15-17 The Brunswick Centre, Marchmont Street, London, WC1N 1AF

Salaam Namaste - Indian 0207 405 3697
68 Millman St, London, WC1N 3EF

PizzaExpress High Holborn - Pizza 0207 831 5305
99 High Holborn, London, WC1V 6LF

The Pakenham Arms - British 0207 837 6933
1 Pakenham Street, London, WC1X 0LA

Chutney Raj - Indian 0207 8311149
137, Gray's Inn Road, London, WC1X 8AU

Mediterraneo - Italian 020 7837 5108
112 King's Cross Road, King's Cross, WC1X 9DS

Thai Aubergine - Thai 0207 278 7555
109 King's Cross Road, London, WC1X 9LR

Acorn House Restaurant - British 0207 812 1842
69 Swinton Street, London, WC1X 9NT

The Hercules Pillars - British 0207 242 2218
18 Great Queen Street, Holborn, WC2 5DG

The Terrace Lincoln's Inn Fields - Caribbean 0207 430 1234
Lincoln's Inn Fields, Holborn, WC2A 3LJ

Bhatti - Indian 0207 831 0817
37 Great Queen Street, London, WC2B 5AA

Tandoori Nights - Indian 0207 831 2558
35 Great Queen St, London, WC2B 5AA

Sway - Modern European 0207 404 6114
61-65 Great Queen Street, London, WC2B 5DA

Los Locos - Mexican 0207 379 0220
24-26 Russell Street, Covent Garden, London, WC2B 5HF

Belushi's Covent Garden 0207 240 3411
9 Russell Street, Covent Garden, London, WC2B 5HZ

Guanabara - Brazilian 020 7242 8600
Parker Street, London, WC2B 5PW

PizzaExpress Bow Street - Pizza 0207 240 3443
9-12 Bow Street, Covent Garden, London, WC2E 7AH

Café Rouge - French 020 7836 0998
34 Wellington Street, Covent Garden, London, WC2E 7BD

Livebait Covent Garden - Seafood 0207 836 7161
21 Wellington Street, Covent Garden, London, WC2E 7DN

Fire & Stone Covent Garden - Italian 0844 371 2550
31/32 Maiden Lane, Covent Garden, London, WC2E 7JS

Jewel Covent Garden - Modern European 020 7845 9980
29-30, Maiden Lane, London, WC2E 7JS

La Tasca Covent Garden - Spanish 020 7240 9062
23-24 Maiden Lane, Covent Garden, London, WC2E 7NA

gbk Covent Garden - Antipodean 0207 240 9617
13-14 Maiden Lane, London, WC2E 7NE

Roadhouse - American 0207 240 6001
35 The Piazza, Covent Garden, London, WC2E 8BE

Navajo Joe - South American 0207 395 5802
34 King Street, Covent Garden, London, WC2E 8HN

Palm Court Brasserie - Modern European 0207 240 2939
39 King Street, Covent Garden, London, WC2E 8JS

Henrys Cafe Bar Covent Garden - International 020 7379 1871
5 - 6 Henrietta Street, Covent Garden, London, WC2E 8PS

Cafe Pasta Garrick Street - Italian 0207 497 2779
2-4 Garrick Street, London, WC2E 9BH

Le Garrick - French 0207 240 7649
10 Garrick Street, Covent Garden, London, WC2E 9BH

Bertorelli Covent Garden - Italian 0207 836 3969
44a Floral Street, London, WC2E 9DA

Cafe des Amis - French 0207 3793444
11-14 Hanover Place (off Long Acre Lane), London, WC2E 9JF

The Long Acre - Fusion 0207 520 6920
1-3 Long Acre, London, WC2E 9LH

Café Rouge - French 0207 434 2635
43 Charing Cross Road London, WC2H 0AP

Listings are for ILLUSTRATIVE PURPOSES ONLY, please visit www.tastecard.co.uk for participating restaurants and offers | 45

London

Patterson's - British
4 Mill Street, London, W1S 2AX
0207 499 1308

Artisan - Modern European
Mayfair, London, W1S 2YF
0207 629 7755

Chor Bizarre India's Restaurant - Indian
16 Albermarle St, Mayfair, London, W1S 4HW
0207 629 9802

Dover Street - French
8-10 Dover Street, Mayfair, London, W1S 4LQ
0207 491 7509

Elysee Restaurant - Greek
13 Percy Street, London, W1T 1DT
0207 636 4804

Jerusalem - Modern European
33/34 Rathbone Place, London, W1T 1JN
0207 255 1120

PizzaExpress Charlotte Street - Pizza
7-9 Charlotte Street, London, W1T 1RB
0207 580 1110

Bertorelli Fitzrovia - Italian
19 Charlotte Street, London, W1T 1RL
0207 636 4174

Costa Dorada - Spanish
47-55 Hanway Street, London, W1T 1UX
0207 631 5117

Stef's - Italian
3 Berners Street, London, W1T 3LD
0203 073 1041

Ragam - Indian
57 Cleveland Street, London, W1T 4JN
0207 636 9098

Charlotte Street Blues - American
74 Charlotte Street, London, W1T 4QH
0207 580 0113

Amaretto Restaurant - Italian
116 Tottenham Court Road, London, W1T 5AJ
0207 387 6234

Aston Bar & Restaurant - British
130 Tottenham Court Road, London, W1T 5AY
0207 388 4131

Archipelago - International
110 Whitfield Street, London, W1T 5ED
0207 383 3346

Agra Restaurant - Indian
135-137 Whitfield St, Soho, London, W1T 5EL
0207 387 8833

Jetlag Bar and Restaurant - International
125 Cleveland Street, London, W1T 6QB
0203 370 5838

Café Rouge - French
264/267 Tottenham Court Road, London, W1T 7RH
0207 631 3075

PizzaExpress Barrett Street - Pizza
21-22 Barrett Street, London, W1U 1BF
0207 629 1001

La Tasca James Street - Spanish
30-34 James Street, West End, London, W1U 1ER
0207 486 3314

Made in Italy James Street - Italian
50 James Street, London, W1U 1HB
0207 224 0182

Auberge St Christopher's - International
6-8 St. Christopher's Place, London, W1U 1ND
0207 486 5557

deVille - British
The Mandeville Hotel, Mandeville Place, London, W1U 2BE
0207 935 4040

108 Marylebone Lane - British
108 Marylebone Lane, London, W1U 2QE
0207 9693 900

Levant - Lebanese
76 Wigmore Street, Jason Court, London, W1U 2SJ
0207 224 1111

PizzaExpress Thayer Street - Pizza
13-14 Thayer Street, London, W1U 3JS
0207 935 2167

STRADA Marylebone - Italian
31 Marylebone High Street, London, W1U 4PP
020 7935 1004

Colony Bar and Grill - International
7-9 Paddington Street, London, W1U 5QH
0207 935 3353

Original Tagines - North African
7a Dorset Street, London, W1U 6QN
0207 9351545 / 07878 364408

PizzaExpress Baker Street - Pizza
133 Baker Street, London, W1U 6SF
0207 486 0888

gbk Baker Street - Antipodean
102 Baker Street, London, W1U 6TL
0207 486 8516

STRADA Baker Street - Italian
100 Baker Street, London, W1U 6TW
020 7935 7071

Hardy's - Modern European
53 Dorset Street, London, W1U 7NH
0207 935 5929

ON ANON - Fusion
London Pavillion, Piccadilly Circus, London, W1V 9LA
0870 777 7080

Villandry Bar - International
170 Great Portland Street, London, W1W 5QB
0207 631 3131

Palms of Goa - Indian
160 New Cavendish Street, London, W1W 6YR
0207 580 6125

Shikaras Restaurant - Indian
65 Great Titchfield Street, London, W1W 7PS
0207 636 6555

Melito Pizza - Pizza
12 Great Castle Street, London, W1W 8LR
0207 636 6560

Nuocmam - Vietnamese
35 Great Portland Street, London, W1W 8QQ
0207 631 2080

86 St James - British
86 St James Street, London, SW1A 1PL
0207 747 1185

One Twenty One Two - British
The Royal Horseguards, 2 Whitehall Court, London, SW1A 2EJ
0207 451 9333

The Tattershall Castle - British
Victoria Embankment, Whitehall, London, SW1A 2HR
0207 839 6548

La Tasca Victoria - Spanish
6, Cathedral Walk, London, SW1E 5JE
0207 828 5515

PizzaExpress 154 Victoria Street - Pizza
154 Victoria Street, London, SW1E 5LB
0207 828 1477

PizzaExpress 85 Victoria Street - Pizza
85 Victoria Street, London, SW1H 0HW
0207 222 5270

City Cafe - Modern European
30 John Islip Street, London, SW1P 4DD
0207 932 4600

Altitude 360 - British
29th Floor Millbank Tower, 21 - 24 Millbank, London, SW1P 4QP
0845 500 2929

PizzaExpress Mill Bank - Pizza
25 Mill Bank, London, SW1P 4QP
0207 976 6214

Spicy World - Indian
76, Wilton Road, London, SW1V 1DE
020 7630 9951

Spicy World - Indian
1 Gillingham Street, London, SW1V 1HN
0207 630 9668

Prezzo Victoria Buildings - Italian
4 Victoria Buildings, 22 Terminus Place, London, SW1V 1JR
020 7233 9099

Chimes - British
26 Churton Street, Pimlico, London, SW1V 2LP
0207 821 7456

PizzaExpress Pimlico - Pizza
46 Moreton Street, London, SW1V 2PB
0207 592 9488

The Akbar - Indian
147 Lupus Street, London, SW1V 3HD
0207 630 1919

48 | Listings are for ILLUSTRATIVE PURPOSES ONLY, please visit www.tastecard.co.uk for participating restaurants and offers

Café Rouge - French 020 7931 9300
Victoria Place Shopping Centre, Buckingham Palace Rd, London, SW1W 9SJ

Prezzo Victoria Place - Italian 0207 828 5199
Unit CY7 Victoria Place Shopping Centre, Buckingham Palace Road, SW1W 9SJ

The Talbot Belgravia - British 0207 2351639
1-3 Little Chester Street, London, SW1X 7AL

Satori Robata Knightsbridge - Japanese 0207 235 1943
28-30 Knightsbridge, London, SW1X 7JN

Chicago Rib Shack - American 0207 591 4664
145, Knightsbridge, London, SW1X 7PA

Off The Hook @ The Paxton's Head - International 0207 589 6627
153 Knightsbridge, London, SW1X 7PA

One O One - Seafood 0207 2907 101
101 Knightsbridge, London, SW1X 7RN

Beit Eddine - Lebanese 0207 235 3969
8 Harriet Street, Knightsbridge, SW1X 9JW

Langtry's Restaurant - British 0207 201 6619
21 Pont Street, London, SW1X 9SG

Prezzo - Haymarket - Italian 020 7839 1129
Kinghouse, 8 Haymarket, London, SW1Y 4BP

PizzaExpress Haymarket - Pizza 0207 930 8044
26 Panton House, London, SW1Y 4EN

Mint Leaf Restaurant & Bar - Indian 0207 930 9020
Suffolk Place, Haymarket, London, SW1Y 4HX

Planet Hollywood - American 0207 2871000
57-60 Haymarket, London, SW1Y 4OX

Tiger Tiger - Modern European 0207 930 1885
29 The Haymarket, London, SW1Y 4SP

Jom Makan - Malaysian 0207 925 2402
5-7 Pall Mall East, London, SW1Y 5BA

Getti Jermyn Street - Italian 0207 734 7334
16/17 Jermyn Street, London, SW1Y 6LT

PizzaExpress Shrewsbury - Pizza 01743 354 647
55 Mardol, London, SY1 1PP

City of London

Barbican Tandoori - Indian 0207 7964 499
55 Aldersgate, Barbican, London, EC1A 4LA

The Distillers - British 0207 600 2705
Smithfield Market, 64-66 West Smithfield, London, EC1A 9DY

Smithfield Bar and Grill - Fusion 0870 442 2541
2-3 West Smithfield, London, EC1A 9JX

Kurz & Lang - German 020 7993 2923
1 St. John Street, Smithfield, EC1M 4AA

PizzaExpress Clerkenwell - Pizza 0207 253 7770
1 Clerkenwell Road, London, EC1M 5PA

Anexo - Spanish 0207 250 3401
61 Clerkenwell Road, London, EC1M 5PT

Neo Barbican - International 0207 726 8925
14-17 Carthusian Street, Barbican, London, EC1M 6AD

Malmaison Bar & Brasserie - British 0207 012 3700
18-21 Charterhouse Square, London, EC1M 6AH

PizzaExpress Cowcross Street - Pizza 020 7490 8025
26 Cowcross Street, London, EC1M 6DQ

Ortega Smithfields - Spanish 0207 253 1612
55 Charterhouse Street, London, EC1M 6HA

Beduin - Spanish 0207 336 6484
Charterhouse Street, Smithfields, London, EC1M 6HA

Fluid - Japanese 0207 253 3444
40 Charterhouse Street, London, EC1M 6JN

Clerkenwell House - International 020 7404 1113
23-27 Hatton Wall, London, EC1N 8JJ

The Green - British 0207 490 8010
29 Clerkenwell Green, London, EC1R 0DU

54 Pinang - Malaysian 0207 336 0603
54 Farringdon Road, London, EC1R 3BL

Coach and Horses - Modern European 0207 278 8990
26-28, Ray Street, Clerkenwell, EC1R 3DJ

Dollar Grills and Martinis - American 0207 278 0077
2 Exmouth Market, Farringdon, London, EC1R 4PX

Sade Restaurant - Turkish 0207 833 1111
21 Exmouth Market, London, EC1R 4QD

Cinnamon Tree - Indian 0207 837 6000
14 Exmouth Market, Islington, London, EC1R 4QE

The Ambassador - Modern European 0207 837 0009
55 Exmouth Market, London, EC1R 4QL

STRADA Exmouth Market - Italian 020 7278 0800
8 - 10 Exmouth Market, London, EC1R 4QR

Cafe VN - Vietnamese 0207 278 4123
144 Clerkenwell Road, London, EC1R 5DP

Offside Bar and Gallery - British 0207 2533306
271-273 City Road, London, EC1V 1LA

Bavarian Beerhouse Old Street - German 0207 608 0925
190 City Road, London, EC1V 2QH

Darbucka - Lebanese 0207 490 8772
82 Basemenbt St John Street, Clerkenwell, London, EC1V 4JZ

Renaissance - Italian 0207 7130409
316 St John Street, Islington, London, EC1V 4NT

120 Central Brasserie at Thistle City Barbican - Modern European 0871 376 9004
Central Street, Clerkenwell, London, EC1V 8DS

Regency Indian Cuisine - Indian 0207 336 8636
96 Old Street, London, EC1V 9AY

Thai Thai East - Thai 0207 490 5230
110 Old Street, London, EC1V 9BD

Bogayo - North African 0207 012 1226
320 Old Street, London, EC1V 9DR

Monsieur M Restaurant - Asian 0207 613 4094
380 Old Street, Shoreditch, London, EC1V 9LT

Piya Piya - Thai 0845 4751971
1 Oliver's Yard, City Road, London, EC1Y 1HQ

Davy's at Exchange Square - British 0207 256 5962
2a Exchange Square, London, EC2A 2EH

The Flying Horse - British 0207 247 5338
52 Wilson Street, London, EC2A 2ER

The Hoxton Pony - British 0207 613 2844
104-108 Curtain Road, London, EC2A 3AH

Listings are for ILLUSTRATIVE PURPOSES ONLY, please visit www.tastecard.co.uk for participating restaurants and offers

London

The Comedy Cafe - International
66/68 Rivington Street, London, EC2A 3AY
020 7739 5706

Elbow Rooms Shoreditch - International
97-113 Curtain Road, Shoreditch, EC2A 3BS
020 8305 3082

Favela Chic
91-93 Great Eastern Street, London, EC2A 3HZ
0207 6134228

Lena - Italian
66 Great Eastern St, Shoreditch, London, EC2A 3JT
020 7739 5714

Cantaloupe - Modern European
35-42 Charlotte Road, Shoreditch, London, EC2A 3PD
0207 729 5566

PizzaExpress Curtain Road - Pizza
49-51 Curtain Road, London, EC2A 3PT
0207 613 5426

Little Hanoi - Oriental
147 Curtain Road, Shoreditch, EC2A 3QE
0207 729 6868

Yard Al Rollo - Pizza
140 Tabernacle Street, London, EC2A 4SD
0207 336 7758

The Bathhouse Venue - British
7-8 Bishopsgate, Churchyard, London, EC2M 3TJ
0207 920 9207

Tsuru Sushi - Japanese
Unit 3, 201 Bishopsgate, London, EC2M 3UG
0207 377 1166

PizzaExpress Bishopsgate - Pizza
232-238 Bishopsgate, London, EC2M 4QD
0207 247 2838

Kenza Restaurant & Lounge - Lebanese
10 Devonshire Square, London, EC2M 4YP
0207 929 5533

Henrys Cafe Bar City - International
4 London Wall Building, Blomfield Street, London, EC2M 5NT
020 7614 0075

Mehek - Indian
45 London Wall, Moorgate, London, EC2M 5TE
0207 588 5043

La Tasca Broadgate - Spanish
16 Eldon Street, City Of London Broadgate, London, EC2M 7LA
0207 256 2381

The Wall Bar - Modern European
45 Old Broad Street, London, EC2N 1HU
0207 5884845

Mint Leaf Lounge & Restaurant - Indian
Angel Court, London, EC2R 7HB
020 7300 0992

Off The Wall Bar and Restaurant - British
7-9 Copthall Avenue, London, EC2R 7NJ
0207 562 3060

The Livery - International
130, Wood Street, London, EC2V 6DL
0207 6009 624

City Pipe - Modern European
31-33 Foster Lane, Off Cheapside, London, EC2V 6HD
0207 606 2110

Goldfish City - Chinese
46 Gresham Street Bank, London, EC2V 7AY
0207 726 0308

PizzaExpress -Russia Row - Pizza
8 Russia Row, London, EC2V 8BL
0207 600 2232

PizzaExpress London Wall Alban Gate - Pizza
125 Alban Gate, London, EC2Y 5AS
0207 600 8880

Wood Street - Modern European
Corner of Wood Street & Fore Street, Barbican, London, EC2Y 5EJ
0207 256 6990

PizzaExpress - London Wall Salisbury House - Pizza
Salisbury House, London Wall, London, EC2Y 5HN
0207 588 7262

Amber - Fusion
1 Ropemaker Street, London, EC2Y 9AW
0870 7777080

The Cuban City - Cuban
Citypoint, One Ropemaker Street, London, EC2Y 9AW
0207 253 2202

Cuban Bar - Cuban
Citypoint, 1 Rope Maker St, Moorgate, EC2Y 9AW
0207 256 2202

Barcelona Tapas Bar and Restaurant Beaufort House - Spanish
Unit 1, Beaufort House, 15 St Botolph Street, EC3A 7DT
0207 377 5111

Hemingways - Modern European
19 Bevis Marks, London, EC3A 7JB
020 7220 7170

Barcelona Tapas Bar & Restaurant Lime Street - Spanish
24 Lime Street, London, EC3M 7HS
0207 929 2389

Kasturi Restaurant - Indian
57 Aldgate High Street, London, EC3N 1AL
0207 480 7402

Abbey - British
30-33 Minories, London, EC3N 1DD
020 7488 1918

Jamies The Minories - British
119-112 The Minories, London, EC3N 1DR
0207 709 9900

Corney & Barrow Jewry Street - Modern European
37 Jewry Street, London, EC3N 2EX
0207 680 8550

Addendum - Modern European
1 Seething Lane, London, EC3N 4AX
0207 977 9500

PizzaExpress Byward Street - Pizza
1 Byward Street, London, EC3R 5AS
0207 626 5025

gbk Tower Bridge - Antipodean
Unit 2A, Tower Place, London, EC3R 5BU
0207 929 2222

Agenda - International
Minster Court, 3 Mincing Lane, London, EC3R 7AA
0207 929 8399

Bertorelli Mincing Lane - Italian
15 Mincing Lane, London, EC3R 7BD
0207 283 3028

Auberge Mark Lane - International
56 Mark Lane, City of London, EC3R 7NE
0207 480 6789

Franco's - Spanish
1a Pudding Lane, London, EC3R 8AB
0207 929 3366

PizzaExpress Leadenhall, Pizza
20-22 Leadenhall Market, London, EC3V 1LR
0207 283 5113

Abacus - Fusion
24 Cornhill, London, EC3V 3ND
020 7337 6767

PizzaExpress New Fetter Lane - Pizza
1 New Fetter Lane, London, EC4A 1AN
0207 583 8880

Bertorelli Fetter Lane - Italian
1 Plough Place, Fetter Lane, London, EC4A 1DE
0207 842 0510

Volupte - Fusion
9 Norwich Street, London, EC4A 1EJ
0207 831 1622

The White Swan - International
108 Fetter Lane, London, EC4A 1EN
0207 242 9696

The Chancery - British
9 Cursitor Street, London, EC4A 1LL
0207 831 4000

PizzaExpress St Brides Street - Pizza
7/9 St Brides Street, London, EC4A 4AS
0207 583 5126

Wine Tun - British
2-6 Cannon Street, London, EC4M 6XX
0207 248 3371

Terranostra - Italian
27 Old Bailey, London, EC4M 7HS
0203 201 0077

Jamies Fleet Place - British
1 Fleet Place, Holborn Viaduct, London, EC4M 7RA
0207 236 4262

gbk St Pauls - Antipodean
Unit 4 Condor House, St Pauls Church Yard, London, EC4M 8AL
0207 248 9199

50 | Listings are for ILLUSTRATIVE PURPOSES ONLY, please visit www.tastecard.co.uk for participating restaurants and offers

PizzaExpress - St Paul's - Pizza　　　　　　　　　0207 248 9464
Condor House, London, EC4M 8AY

Mustard Bar Lounge & Restaurant - International　020 7236 5318
2 Old Change Court, Peters Hill, St Pauls London, EC4M 8EN

Barcelona Tapas Bar & Restaurant Well Court - Spanish　0207 329 5111
13 Well Court, Off Bow Lane, London, EC4M 9DN

Jamies Bar Groveland Court - British　　　　　0207 248 5551
5 Groveland Court, London, EC4M 9EH

Sri Thai - Thai　　　　　　　　　　　　　　　0207 827 0202
Bucklesbury House, 3 Queen Victoria Street, London, EC4N 4TQ

Apt - Fusion　　　　　　　　　　　　　　　　0870 777 7080
Aldermary House, 10-15 Queen Street, London, EC4N 1TX

@15 - British　　　　　　　　　　　　　　　0207 717 0088
15 Abchurch Lane, London, EC4N 7BW

Bar Capitale - Pizza　　　　　　　　　　　　020 7248 3117
Unit 6 The Concourse, 1 Poultry, London, EC4N 8AD

Swithins Restaurant - Seafood　　　　　　　0207 623 6853
21-23 St Swithins Lane, London, EC4N 8AD

The India - Indian　　　　　　　　　　　　　020 7248 5855,
21 College Hill, London, EC4R 2RP

Northbank Restaurant - British　　　　　　　0207 329 9299
Millennium Bridge, One Paul's Walk, London, EC4V 3QH

Carter Rooms - British　　　　　　　　　　　0207 236 4441
56 Carter Lane, London, EC4V 5EA

The Albion - British　　　　　　　　　　　　0207 583 0227
2/3 New Bridge Street, London, EC4V 6AA

The Class Rooms - Modern European　　　020 7822 2330,
26, Tudor Street, London, EC4Y 0AY

Punch Tavern - British　　　　　　　　　　　0207 353 6658,
99 Fleet Street, London, EC4Y 1DE

East London

Hayfield Masala - Indian　　　　　　　　　　0207 001 1582
156 Mile End Road, London, E1 4LJ

Reema Balti House, - Indian　　　　　　　　　0207 655 4544
48 Hanbury Street, London, E1 5JL

s&m Cafe Spitalfields - British　　　　　　　020 7247 2252
48 Brushfield Street, London, E1 6AG

Bundu Khan - Indian　　　　　　　　　　　　020 7375 2595
43 Commercial Street, London, E1 6BD

Scarlet Dot - Indian　　　　　　　　　　　　0207 375 0880
4 Crispin Square, Crispin Place, London, E1 6DW

Fire & Stone Spitalfields - Italian　　　　　　0844 371 2554
4 Horner Square, Old Spitalfields Market, London, E1 6EW

gbk Old Spitalfields Market - Antipodean　　0207 422 0052
5 Horner Square, London, E1 6EW

Le Bouchon Breton - French　　　　　　　　0800 0191 704
8 Horner Square, Old Spitalfield Market, London, E1 6EW

STRADA Spitalfields - Italian　　　　　　　　020 7247 4117
88 - 90 Commercial Street, London, E1 6LY

The Light Bar & Restaurant - International　0207 247 8989
233 Shoreditch High Street, London, E1 6PJ

The Drunken Monkey - Chinese　　　　　　0207 392 9606
222 Shoreditch High St, London, E1 6PJ

Saffron - Indian　　　　　　　　　　　　　　0207 2472633
53 Brick Lane, London, E1 6PU

Sheraz Bangla Lounge - Indian　　　　　　　0207 247 5755
13 Brick Lane, London, E1 6PU

Shampan - Indian　　　　　　　　　　　　　0207 375 0475
79 Brick Lane, London, E1 6QL

The Famous Curry Bazaar - Bangladeshi　　020 7375 1986
77, Brick Lane, London, E1 6QL

All Star Lanes Brick Lane - American　　　020 7426 9200
91 Brick Lane, London, E1 6QL

Muhib Indian Restaurant - Indian　　　　　0207 247 7122
73 Brick Lane, London, E1 6QL

Bengal Cuisine - Indian　　　　　　　　　　0207 377 8405
12 Brick Lane, London, E1 6RF

Cafe Naz - Indian　　　　　　　　　　　　　0207 247 0234
46-48 Bricklane, London, E1 6RF

Cinnamon Brick Lane - Indian　　　　　　　0207 377 5526
134 Brick Lane, Aldgate, London, E1 6RL

Mango - Indian　　　　　　　　　　　　　　0207 247 9686
90 Brick Lane, Shoreditch, London, E1 6RL

Monsoon Restaurant - Indian　　　　　　　0207 375 1345
78 Brick Lane, London, E1 6RL

Papadoms - Indian　　　　　　　　　　　　0207 377 9123
94 Brick Lane, London, E1 6RL

Brick Lane Clipper - Bangladeshi　　　　　　0207 377 0022
104 Brick Lane, Shoreditch, London, E1 6RL

The Brickhouse - Modern European　　　　0207 247 0005
152C Brick Lane, London, E1 6RU

City Spice Brick Lane - Bangladeshi　　　　0207 2471012
138 Brick Lane, London, E1 6RU

Nazrul Restaurant - Indian　　　　　　　　　0207 247 2505
130 Brick Lane, London, E1 6RU

Sheba Brick Lane - Indian　　　　　　　　　0207 247 7824
136 Brick Lane, London, E1 6RU

Sajna - Indian　　　　　　　　　　　　　　　0207 392 2100
30 Osborn Street, London, E1 6TD

Cafe Suki - Modern European　　　　　　　0207 456 1067
12 Obsourn St, London, E1 6TE

Kapok Tree - Fusion　　　　　　　　　　　　0207 377 1797
12 - 20 Osborn Street, London, E1 6TE

Whitechapel Gallery Dining Room - British　0207 522 7896
77-82 Whitechapel High Street, London, E1 7QX

Cafe Spice Namaste - Indian　　　　　　　0207 488 9242
16 Prescot St, London, E1 8AZ

The River Lounge - Modern European　　　0207 7024588
50 St Katharines Way, St Katherines Dock, London, E1W 1L A

The Brasserie at the Tower - International　0871 376 9036
St Katharine's Way, London, E1W 1LD

Copyright - International　　　　　　　　　0207 488 9000
110 Pennington Street, St. Katherine's, London, E1W 2BB

PizzaExpress Wapping - Pizza　　　　　　　0207 481 8436
78-80 Wapping Lane, London, E1W 2RT

Listings are for **ILLUSTRATIVE PURPOSES ONLY**, please visit www.tastecard.co.uk for participating restaurants and offers | 51

London

Cafe River Spice - Indian 0207 488 4051
83-85 Wapping Lane, London, E1W 2RW

Kiismat Diner, - Indian 0207 613 2220
267 Bethnal Green Road, London, E2 6AH

Mai'da Indian Eatery - Indian 0207 739 2645
148-150 Bethnal Green Road, London, E2 6DG

Almoj Restaurant - Lebanese 0207 729 8200 / 0795 696 1305
388 Hackney Road, London, E2 7AP

Agra Tandoori - Indian 0207 613 2613
277 Hackney Rd, London, E2 8NA

Zeera Indian Cuisine - Indian 0208 983 3111
South Side Mile End Park, 554 Mile End Rd, London, E3 4PL

Fat Cat Cafe Bar - Fusion 0208 983 4353
Bow Wharf, Grove Rd, London, E3 5SN

Thai Room - Thai 0208 880 6500
G2-G7 Bow Wharf, 221 Grove Road Bow, London, E3 5SN

PizzaExpress Chingford - Pizza 0208 529 7866
45-47 Old Church Road, London, E4 6SJ

The Old Ship - British 0208 986 1641
2 Sylvester Path, London, E8 1EN

Cirrik - Hackney, Turkish 0208 985 2879
1 - 3 Amhurst Road, Hackney, London, E8 1LL

La Vie En Rose - French 0207 249 9070
2 Broadway Market, Hackney, E8 4QJ

Zuma Rocks - African 0208 536 9903
512 Lea Bridge Road, London, E10 7DT

Amurg Restaurant - Eastern European 0208 556 9602
579 High Road Leytonstone, Waltham Forest, Greater London, E11 4PE

La Tasca Canary Wharf - Spanish 0207 5319990
Hertsmere Road West India Quays, Canary Wharf, London, E14 4AE

Bar 38 - British 020 7515 8361
Unit C, West India Quay, London, E14 4AX

VIA - British 0207 5158549
2 The Port East Building, Hertsmere Road, London, E14 4AY

Manhattan Bar and Terrace @Marriott Hotel - International 0207 093 1000
22 Hertsmere Rd, Canary Wharf, London, E14 4ED

Curve Restaurant and Bar - Seafood 0207 517 2808
22 Hertsmere Road, London, E14 4ED

Gourmet Pizza Canary Wharf - Pizza 0207 345 9192
18-20 Mackenzie Walk, 20 Cabot Square, London, E14 4PH

Café Rouge - French 020 7537 9696
29-35 Mackenzie Walk, 10 Cabot Sq, Canary Wharf, London, E14 4PH

PizzaExpress Canary Wharf - Pizza 0207 513 0513
Cabot Place East, 2nd Floor, London, E14 4QT

Brodies - British 0207 719 0202
43 Fishermans Walk, Canary Wharf, London, E14 5HD

gbk Canary Wharf - Antipodean 0207 719 6408
Unit 24 Jubilee Place, Canary Wharf, London, E14 5NY

Indiana Restaurant - Indian 0207 987 2576
129 Salmon Lane, London, E14 7PG

Dockmaster's House - Indian 0207 345 0345
1 Hertsmere Road, London, E14 8JJ

Clifton Docklands - Indian 0207 001 2999
32 Westferry Road, Isle of Dogs, London, E14 8LW

Azura - British 0207 987 2050
Radisson Edwardian New Providence Wharf, 5 Fairmont Avenue, E14 9PQ

Caribbean Scene Family Stratford - Caribbean 02085 228 660
Gerry Ruffle Square, Stratford, E15 1BG

PizzaExpress Stratford East - Pizza 0208 534 1700
Theatre Square, London, E15 1BX

The Upper Deck Restaurant & Bar - Modern European 0207 055 1942
7 Western Gateway, Royal Victoria Dock, London, E16 1AA

Docklands Bar & Grill - British 0207 055 2119
Royal Victoria Dock, Western Gateway, London, E16 1AL

Caribbean Scene - Caribbean 0845 371 8000
17 Western Gateway, Royal Victoria Dock, London, E16 1AQ

Fine Burger Company ExCel Exhibition Centre - British 020 7069 4823
Royal Victoria Docks, 1 Western Gateway, London, E16 1XL

Custom House Pub and Kitchen - International 0207 474 0011
272-283 Victoria Dock Road, Custom House, London, E16 3BY

Bhangra Beat South Woodford - Indian 0208 989 8909 / 0208 989 0911
49 Chigwell Road, South Woodford, London, E18 1NG

Parade Gastro Bar - British 0208 530 2010
17 Electric Parade George Lane, South Woodford, London, E18 2LY

PizzaExpress South Woodford - Pizza 0208 924 4488
76 High Road, London, E18 2NA

Prezzo South Woodford - Italian 020 8559 0192
98-106 High Road, South Woodford, Essex, E18 2QH

North London

PizzaExpress Islington - Pizza 0207 226 9542
335 Upper Street, Islington, London, N1 0PB

Emni - Indian 0207 226 1166,
Upper St, London, N1 0PD

Almeida - French 0207 3544777
30 Almeida Street, London, N1 1AD

Public House - Modern European 0207 359 6070
54 Islington Park Street, London, N1 1PX

STRADA Islington - Italian 020 7226 9742
105-106 Upper Street, Islington, London, N1 1QN

Cafe La Davina - Italian 0208 616 4149
134 Upper Street, Islington, London, N1 1QP

Grand Union Bar and Grill Islington - American 020 7226 1375
153, Upper Street, Islington, London, N1 1RA

Pasha Islington - Turkish 0207 226 1454
301 Upper Street, Islington, London, N1 2TU

Fine Burger Company Upper St - British 020 7359 3026
330 Upper St, Islington, London, N1 2XQ

Zigni House - African 0207 226 7418
330 Essex Rd, London, N1 3PB

Jay Restaurant 0207 359 4118
366-368 Essex Road, London, N1 3PD

Puji Puji Restaurant - Malaysian 07952 674 626
122 Balls Pond Road, Islington, London, N1 4AE

Bacchus Pub and Kitchen - Modern European 0207 613 0477
177 Hoxton Street, London, N1 6PJ

52 | Listings are for **ILLUSTRATIVE PURPOSES ONLY**, please visit www.tastecard.co.uk for participating restaurants and offers

London

The North Star - British 0207 354 5400
188 - 190 New North Road, Islington, London, N1 7BJ

Fredericks - Modern European 020 7359 2888
Camden Passage, Islington, London, N1 8EG

s&m Cafe Islington - British 020 7359 5361
4-6 Essex Road, Islington, London, N1 8LN

Elbow Rooms Islington - International 020 8305 3082
89-91 Chapel Market, Islington, N1 9EX

Anam Bar - International 020 7278 1001
3 Chapel Market, Islington, London, N1 9EZ

Bombay Lounge - Indian 07771 720 793
3 Penton Street, London, N1 9PT

Darjeeling Indian Restaurant - Indian 0208 347 7666 / 0208 340 8404
25 Aylmer Parade, Aylmer Road, London, N2 0PE

Clissold Arms - British 0208 444 4224
105 Fortis Green, East Finchley, London, N2 9HR

Dudley's Pancake House Stroud Green - British 0207 281 5437
119 Stroud Green Road, London, N4 3PX

The Triangle - Fusion 0208 292 0516
1 Ferme Park Road, Crouch End, N4 4DS

Iznik - Turkish 0207 704 8099
19 Highbury Park, Islington, London, N5 1QJ

Juniper Dining - International 0207 288 8716
100 Highbury Park, London, N5 2XE

Capri - Italian 0208 341 7327
256 Archway Road, Highgate, London, N6 5AX

PizzaExpress Highgate - Pizza 0208 341 3434
30 High Street, Highgate, London, N6 5JG

Café Rouge - French 020 8342 9797
6-7 South Grove, Highgate, London, N6 6BP

STRADA Highgate - Italian 020 8347 8686
4 South Grove, Highgate Village, London, N6 6BS

Dastarkhan Restaurant - Middle Eastern 0754 521 1010
203 Holloway Road, Islington, London, N7 8DL

Pradera - Spanish 0208 340 9400
14 High Street, Hornsey, N8 7PB

gbk Crouch End - Antipodean 0208 347 5241
45 Topsfield Parade, Tottenham Lane, London, N8 8PT

Rhythm Bar - Caribbean 0208 342 8822
29 Park Road, Crouch End, London, N8 8TE

PizzaExpress Muswell Hill - Pizza 0208 883 5845
290 Muswell Hill Broadway, London, N10 2QR

New Curry Garden - Indian 0208 368 8640
347 Bowes Road, Arnos Grove, London, N11 1AA

Café Rouge - French 0208 446 4777
Leisure Way, Finchley, London, N12 0QZ

3 Oceans Restaurant - International 0208 446 4444
4 Lodge Lane, North Finchley, London, N12 8JR

Aqua Restaurant - Mediterranean 0208 445 3733
337, Ballards Lane, London, N12 8LT

Meze Meze Restaurant - Mediterranean 0208 445 2230
880 High Road, North Finchley, London, N12 9RH

Aragosta - Italian 0208 886 8091
354-356 Green Lanes, Palmers Green, London, N13 5TJ

Namkeen - Indian 0208 365 7771
4 Green Lanes, Palmers Green, London, N13 6JT

Bouzoukia On The Hill - Greek 0208 808 2202 / 0770 723 4256
161 - 163 Bramley Road, Oakwood, London, N14 4XA

PizzaExpress Southgate, Pizza 0208 886 3300
94/98 Chaseside, London, N14 5PH

Café Rouge - French 020 8886 3336
45-46 Cannon Hill, Southgate, London, N14 6LH

Autograf - Modern European 0208 889 2999
488 West Green Road, London, N15 3DA

Il Bacio - Italian 0207 249 3833
61 Stoke Newington, Church Street, London, N16 0AR

Abi Ruchi - Indian 0207 923 4564
42 Stoke Newington Church Street, Stoke Newington, London, N16 0LU

El Mercado Bar & Cantina - Mexican 020 7923 0555
26-30 Stoke Newington Church Street, Hackney, N16 0LU

The Royal India - Indian 0207 249 7025
47 Stoke Newington Church Street, London, N16 0NX

El Panchos Mexican Restaurant - Mexican 0207 923 9588
176 Stoke Newington Road, London, N16 7UY

African Torch - African 0208 808 8166
135 & 137, High Cross Road, London, N17 9NU

Bengal Spice - Indian 0207 561 1106
604 Holloway Road, London, N19 3PH

PizzaExpress Whetstone - Pizza 0208 446 8800
1264 High Road, London, N20 9HH

Willow - British 0208 882 5163
235 Winchmore Hill, London, N21 1QA

The Green Dragon - Thai 0208 360 0005
889 Green Lanes, Winchmore Hill, N21 2QP

PizzaExpress Winchmore Hill - Pizza 0208 364 2992
701-703 Green Lanes, London, N21 3RS

Mosaica @ The Factory - Modern European 0208 889 2400
The Chocolate Factory, Wood Green, N22 6XJ

Nexx Level - Caribbean 0208 888 8778
274 High Road, London, N22 8JT

North West London

Andy's Taverna - Greek 0207 485 9718
81a Bayham Street, London, NW1 0AG

Sen Nin Camden - Japanese 0207 096 1276
35 Pratt St, Camden, NW1 0BG

Prince Albert - Modern European 020 7485 0270
163 Royal College Street, London, NW1 0SG

Elixir Bar, - Mediterranean 0207 383 0925
162 Eversholt Street, London, NW1 1BL

Prezzo Euston Road - Italian 020 7387 5587
161 Euston Road, London, NW1 2BD

Listings are for **ILLUSTRATIVE PURPOSES ONLY**, please visit www.tastecard.co.uk for participating restaurants and offers | 53

London

Zeen Flavour of India - Indian 0207 387 0606
130 Drummond Street, London, NW1 2PA

Massala Hut - Indian 0207 387 6699
161-163 Drummond Street, London, NW1 2PB

Fine Burger Company St Pancras International - British 020 7278 8056
The Circle St Pancras International Station Pancras Road, London, NW1 2QP

PizzaExpress Euston Road - Pizza 020 7383 7102
Clifton House, London, NW1 2RA

Davy's at Regent's Place - British 0207 387 6622
Unit 2 Euston Tower, Regent's Place, London, NW1 3DP

L'Albufera - Spanish 0207 391 3000
Melia White House, Albany Street, Regent's Park, NW1 3UP

The Place - International 0207 391 3000
Melia White House, Albany Street, London, NW1 3UP

The Queens Head and Artichoke - British 020 7916 6206
30-32, Albany Street, Regents Park, NW1 4EA

Cinnamon Spice - Indian 0207 935 0212
12/14 Glentworth Street, London, NW1 5PG

L'Ulivo Baker Street - Italian 0207 935 0194
194 Baker Street, London, NW1 5RT

Khabe Restaurant - Bangladeshi 0207 724 6565
112 Lisson Grove, London, NW1 6UL

Base Baker St - Mediterranean 0207 486 7000
195 Baker Street, London, NW1 6UY

STRADA Camden - Italian 020 7428 9653
40-42 Parkway, Camden, London, NW1 7AH

Zensai - Oriental 0207 424 9527
16 Inverness St, London, NW1 7HJ

The Blues Kitchen - American 0207 387 5277
111-113 Camden High Street, London, NW1 7JN

Caponata - Italian 0207 3875959
3-7 Delancey Street, Camden, London, NW1 7NL

Yumchaa Parkway - British 0207 209 9641
35-37 Parkway, Camden, London, NW1 7PN

Mezza Express - Lebanese 0207 26 77 111
47 Parkway, Camden Town, London, NW1 7PN

PizzaExpress Camden - Pizza 0207 267 2600
83/87 Parkway, Camden, London, NW1 7PP

Yumchaa Camden Lock - British 0207 209 9641
91-92 Camden Lock Place, Camden, London, NW1 8AF

Shaka-Zulu Restaurant - African 0203 376 9911
Stables Market, Camden, London, NW1 8AH

The Cuban Camden - Cuban 0207 424 0692
Stables Market, Chalk Farm Road, Camden, NW1 8AH

Coco Bamboo - Brazilian 0207 267 6613
48 Chalk Farm Road, London, NW1 8AJ

Spiritual Caipirinha Bar - International 0207 485 6791
4 Ferdinand Street, Camden Town, London, NW1 8ER

Sardo Canale - Mediterranean 0207 722 2800
42 Gloucester Ave, Primrose Hill, London, NW1 8JD

PizzaExpress Kentish Town - Pizza 0207 257 0101
187 Kentish Town Road, London, NW1 8PD

Grand Union Bar and Grill Camden - American 020 7435 4530
102, Camden Road, Camden, London, NW1 9EA

Abbey Tavern - Caribbean 0207 267 9449
124 Kentish Town Road, London, NW1 9QB

Belushi's Camden - American 0207 388 1012
48-50 Camden High Street, London, NW1 OLT

Spice of Hampstead - Indian 0207 794 5922
448 Finchley Road, Childs Hill, London, NW2 2HY

Zeytoon Restaurant - Persian 0208 830 7434
94-96 Cricklewood, Broadway, London, NW2 3EL

Spice 6 - Indian 0208 208 2026
22 Station Parade, London, NW2 4NH

PizzaExpress Hampstead - Pizza 0207 433 1600
70 Heath Street, London, NW3 1DN

Bombay Bicycle Club Hampstead - Indian 0207 435 3544
3a Downshire Hill, Hampstead, London, NW3 1NR

Café Rouge - French 020 7435 4240
38-39 High Street, Hampstead, London, NW3 1QE

gbk Belsize Park - Antipodean 0207 443 5335
200 Havestock Hill, Belsize Park, London, NW3 2AG

PizzaExpress Belsize Park - Pizza 0207 794 6777
194a Haverstock Hill, London, NW3 2AJ

The Hill - British 0207 2670033
94 Haverstock Hill, London, NW3 2BD

The Magdala - International 020 7435 2503
2A South Hill Park, London, NW3 2SB

Brasserie Gerard Belsize Park - French 0207 431 8101
215 Haverstock Hill Belsize Park, Hampstead, London, NW3 4RB

Bombay Basement - Indian 0207 483 0223
83s ' 85a Haverstock Hill, London, NW3 4RL

PizzaExpress Swiss Cottage - Pizza 0207 794 5100
227 Finchley Road, London, NW3 6LP

Fine Burger Company 02 Centre - British 020 7433 0700
02 Centre 1st floor 02 Centre, 255 Finchley Road, London, NW3 6LU

Frascati Restaurant - Italian 0207 431 3274
33 Heath Street, Hampstead, London, NW3 6TR

The Dartmouth Arms - British 0207 485 3267
35 York Rise, Dartmouth Park, NW5 1SP

Grand Union Bar and Grill Kentish Town - American 020 7485 1837
53, Highgate Road, London, NW5 1TL

Bombay Nights Indian Cuisine - Indian 0207 435 0163
90 Fortune Green Road, West Hampstead, NW6 1DS

Walnut - Modern European 0207 794 7772
280 West End Lane, West Hampstead, London, NW6 1LJ

STRADA West Hampstead - Italian 020 7431 8678
291 West End Lane, West Hampstead, London, NW6 1RD

PizzaExpress West End Land - Pizza 0207 431 8229
319 West End Lane, London, NW6 1RN

gbk West Hampstead - Antipodean 0207 794 5455
331 West End Lane, London, NW6 1RS

Casareccia Restaurant - Italian 0207 328 0800
267 Kilburn High Road, London, NW6 7JR

PizzaExpress Mill Hill - Pizza 0208 959 3898
92/94 The Broadway, London, NW7 3TB

PizzaExpress Abbey Road - Pizza 0207 624 5577
39 Abbey Road, St Johns Wood, London, NW8 0AA

54 | Listings are for ILLUSTRATIVE PURPOSES ONLY, please visit www.tastecard.co.uk for participating restaurants and offers

The Salt House - Modern European 0207 328 6626
63 Abbey Road, London, NW8 0AE

Duke Of York - British 020 7722 1933
2 St Ann's Terrace, St John's Wood, London, NW8 6PJ

Sahara Restaurant - Lebanese 020 7722 8555
7 St. Johns Wood High Street, London, NW8 7NG

Brasserie Gerard St John's Wood - Fusion 0207 722 0400
122 St John's Wood, High Street, London, NW8 7SG

Café Rouge - French 020 7722 8366
120 High Street, St Johns Wood High St, London, NW8 7SG

Jakarta - Oriental 0208 205 3335
7 Sheavshill Parade, Sheaveshill Avenue, London, NW9 6RS

West London

San Miguels Tapas Bar & Restaurant - Spanish 0207 262 1709
256 Edgware Road, London, W2 1DS

Akash - Indian 0207 706 1788
500a Edgware Road, W2 1EJ

Phi - British 0207 706 4444
16 London Street, Paddington, London, W2 1HL

Gyngleboy - British 0207 723 3351
27 Spring Street, W2 1JA

Delima Malaysian Restaurant - Malaysian 0207 2620050
36 Southwick Street, London, W2 1JQ

Ryath Indian Tandoori - Indian 020 7723 8954
32 Norfolk Place, London, W2 1QH

Connoisseurs Indian Tandoori - Indian 0207 402 3299
8 Norfolk Place, London, W2 1QL

Island Restaurant and Bar - British 0207 551 6070
Lancaster Terrace, London, W2 2TY

Nipa - Thai 0207 551 6039
Lancaster Terrace 1st Floor Royal Lancaster Hotel, London, W2 2TY

No.35 at The Hempel - Modern European 0207 298 9000
31-35 Craven Hill Gardens, London, W2 3AE

Lagenda - Chinese 0207 7258 0269
Holiday Villa Hotel, 37 Leinster Gardens, London, W2 3AN

The Caesar - International 020 7262 0022
26-33 Queens Gardens, Hyde Park, London, W2 3BD

The Brasserie @ Thistle Kensington Gardens 08713 769 024
104 Bayswater Road, London, W2 3HL

Bel Canto - French 0207 262 1678
Corus Hotel Hyde Park, 1-7 Lancaster Gate, London, W2 3LG

Whites Restaurant @ Hyde Park Hotel - British 0871 376 9022
90 - 92 Lancaster Gate, London, W2 3NR

Taormina Restaurant - Italian 0207 262 2090
19 Craven Terrace, Bayswater, London, W2 3QH

Curry Place - Indian 0207 243 8992
36 Queensway, Bayswater, London, W2 3RX

All Star Lanes Bayswater - American 0207 313 8363
6 Porchester, Gardens, London, W2 4DB

Café Rouge - French 020 7221 1509
1509, Unit 209 Whiteleys, Queensway, London, W2 4SB

Elbow Rooms Westbourne Grove - International 020 8305 3082
103 Westbourne Grove, London, W2 4UW

Mulberry Street - Pizza 0207 313 6789
84 Westbourne Grove, London, W2 5RT

gbk Bayswater - Antipodean 0207 243 4344
50 Westbourne Grove, London, W2 5SH

cherryjam - Spanish 020 7727 9950
58, Porchester Road, London, W2 6ET

Wok Around The World - Modern European 0870 0667 123
Ramada Encore London West, 4 Portal Way, London, W3 6RT

Blue Star Chinese Restaurant - Oriental 0208 993 7977
51-53, Steyne Road, Acton, W3 9NU

PizzaExpress Chiswick - Pizza 0208 747 0193
252 High Road, Chiswick, W4 1PD

STRADA Chiswick - Italian 020 8995 0004
156 Chiswick High Road, London, W4 1PR

Caffe Piccolo Chiswick - Italian 0208 747 9989
26 Chiswick High Road, London, W4 1TE

Brasserie Gerard Chiswick - French 0208 742 1942
163-165 Chiswick High Road, London, W4 2DT

Café Rouge - French 020 8742 7447
227-229 Chiswick High Road, London, W4 2DW

gbk Chiswick - Antipodean 0208 9954 548
131 Chiswick High Road, London, W4 2ED

Rowans Cafe Bar - International 0208 742 1649
8 Stile Hall Parade, London, W4 3AG

Café Rouge - French 020 8995 6575
85 Strand on the Green, London, W4 3PU

Hole in the Wall - Modern European 020 8742 7185
12 Sutton Lane North, Chiswick, London, W4 4LD

The Bollo - International 0208 994 6037
13 Bollo Lane, Chiswick, London, W4 5LR

Napa - British 0208 996 5200
626 Chiswick High Road, London, W4 5RY

La Tasca Chiswick - Spanish 0208 9944545
404-406 Chiswick High Street, Chiswick, London, W4 5TF

gbk Ealing - Antipodean 0208 998 0392
35 Haven Green, Ealing, London, W5 2NX

La Tasca Ealing - Spanish 020 8840 2041
18-19 The Mall, Ealing, London, W5 2PJ

L'Orient Indian Cuisine - Indian 0208 991 1966
9 Hanger Green, Ealing, London, W5 3EL

Trusha Restaurant - Indian 020 8752 1424
1 Grosvenor Parade, Uxbridge Road, London, W5 3NN

Zayka - Indian 0208 566 5662
8 South Ealing Road, London, W5 4QA

Balti Naz - Indian 0208 560 5900
185 South Ealing Road, London, W5 4RH

Karaam Lebanese Restaurant - Lebanese 0208 566 4433
71 New Broadway, London, W5 5AL

Chico Mexico - Mexican 0208 840 2513
41 Bond Street, Ealing, London, W5 5AS

PizzaExpress Ealing - Pizza 0208 567 7690
23 Bond Street, Ealing, London, W5 5AS

Listings are for ILLUSTRATIVE PURPOSES ONLY, please visit www.tastecard.co.uk for participating restaurants and offers | 55

London

Café Rouge - French
17 The Green, Ealing, London, W5 5DA
020 8579 2788

Chula - Indian
116 King Street, Hammersmith, London, W6 0QP
0208 748 1826

Akash Restaurant - Indian
184 King street, Hammersmith, London, W6 0RA
0208 741 7160

Lam's - Chinese
216 King Street, Hammersmith, W6 0RA
020 8748 6982

Shilpa - Indian
206 King street, Hammersmith, W6 0RA
0208 741 3127

Indian Zing - Indian
236 King Street, London, W6 0RF
0208 748 5959

Belushi's Hammersmith - American
28 Hammersmith, Broadway, London, W6 7AB
0208 748 5285

Antonia's Restaurant - Mediterranean
21-22b Hammersmith Broadway Shopping Centre, London, W6 7AL
020 8563 1218

Shimla Mirch - Indian
158a Shepherds Bush Road, Brook Green, Hammersmith London, W6 7PB
0207 602 8899

Café Rouge - French
98-100 Shepherds Bush Rd, London, W6 7PD
020 7602 7732

The Carpenter's Arms - International
89-91 Black Lion Lane, London, W6 9BG
0208 741 8386

Jongleurs Comedy Club Hammersmith - International
Rutland Grove, Hammersmith, London, W6 9DH
0870 0111 960

PizzaExpress Fulham Palace Road - Pizza
158 Fulham Palace Road, London, W6 9ER
0208 563 2064

Ruby Grand - Modern European
227 King St, Hammersmith, London, W6 9JT
0208 748 3391

La Piccola Pizzeria - Italian
243 King Street, London, W6 9LP
0208 563 7360

Seasons Dining Room - British
323 King St, Hammersmith, London, W6 9NH
0208 7482002

Juan's El Paso Mexican - Mexican
24, Fulham Palace Road, London, W6 9PH
0208 741 9913

Urban Karahi - Indian
47 Greenford Avenue, London, W7 1LP
0203 579 4474

Café Rouge - French
2 Lancer Square, Kensington Church St, London, W8 4EH
020 7938 4200

Prezzo Kensington - Italian
35a Kensington High Street, Kensington, London, W8 5BA
020 7937 2800

STRADA High Street Kensington - Italian
29 Kensington High Street, London, W8 5NP
020 7938 4648

Wodka - Modern European
12 St Albans Grove, London, W8 5PN
0207 937 6513

L-Restaurant & Bar - Spanish
2 Abingdon Road, Kensington, London, W8 6AF
0207 795 6969

Kensington Tandoori - Indian
1 Abington Road, Kensington, London, W8 6AH
0207 937 6182

Mimino Georgian Restaurant - International
197c Kensington High Street, London, W8 6BA
020 7937 1551

PizzaExpress - Earls Court Road - Pizza
35 Earls Court Road, London, W8 6ED
0207 937 0761

La Lanterna - Italian
135 Kensington Church Street, London, W8 7IP
0207 22 217 348

Sticky Fingers - American
1a Phillimore Gardens, Kensington, London, W8 7QG
0207 938 5338

Café Rouge - French
30 Clifton Road, Maida Vale, London, W9 1ST
020 7286 2266

Idlewild - Modern European
55 Shirland Road, Maida Vale, London, W9 2JD
0207 266 9198

La Sophia - French
46 Golborne Road, Notting Hill, London, W10 5PR
0208 968 2200

supperclub - International
12 Acklam Road, Notting Hill, London, W10 5QZ
020 896 466 00

s&m Cafe Portabello - British
268 Portobello Road, London, W10 5TY
0208 968 8898

Ruby and Sequoia - Modern European
6 - 8 All Saints Road, London, W11 1HH
0207 243 6363

First Floor Restaurant - Modern European
186 Portobello Rd, London, W11 1LA
0207 243 0072

The Drawing Room - Modern European
269, Portobello Road, London, W11 1LR
020 7221 7696

The Portobello Organic Kitchen - Italian
207-209 Portobello Road, London, W11 1LU
0207 7927 999

Walmer Castle - Thai
58 Ledbury Road, Notting Hill, London, W11 2AJ
0207 229 4620

Jongleurs Comedy Club Notting Hill - International
Powis Square, Notting Hill, London, W11 2AY
0870 0111 960

gbk Notting Hill - Antipodean
160 Portobello Road, London, W11 2EB
0207 243 6597

Rossopomodoro Notting Hill - Italian
184 A Kensington Park Rd., Notting Hill, W11 2ES
0207 229 9007

Gate Restaurant - Asian
87 Notting Hill Gate, Notting Hill, London, W11 3JZ
0207 727 9007

PizzaExpress Notting Hill Gate - Pizza
137 Notting Hill Gate, London, W11 3LB
0207 229 6000

Pizza Metro Pizza Notting Hill - Italian
147-149 Notting Hill Gate, London, W11 3LF
0207 727 8877

Nottingdale - European
9 Nicholas Road Off Evesham Street, London, W11 4AJ
0207 221 2223

The Clarendon - British
123 Clarendon Road, Notting Hill/Holland Park, London, W11 4JG
0207 2291 500

Bombay Bicycle Club Holland Park - Indian
128 Holland Park Avenue, Holland Park, London, W11 4UE
0207 727 7335

Fire & Stone Westfield - Italian
Shepherds Bush, London, W12 7GB
0844 371 2551

PizzaExpress White City - Pizza
Unit 3126 Westfield London Shopping Centre, Ariel Way, London, W12 7GF
0208 749 1500

Tatra - Modern European
24 Goldhawk Road, London, W12 8DH
0208 749 8193

Grand Union Bar and Grill Ravenscourt Park - American
243, Goldhawk Road, London, W12 8EU
020 8741 2312

Nepalese Tandoori - Indian
121 Uxbridge Rd, Shepherds Bush, London, W12 8NL
0208 740 7551,

Belushi's Shepherd's Bush - American
13-15 Shepherd's Bush Green, London, W12 8PH
0208 735 0270

Flamingo Restaurant - African
31 Goldhawk Road, Shepherds Bush, London, W12 8QQ
0208 740 7865

56 | Listings are for ILLUSTRATIVE PURPOSES ONLY, please visit www.tastecard.co.uk for participating restaurants and offers

Laguna - Indian 123 Uxbridge Road, Ealing, London, W13 9BD	0208 5799992
PizzaExpress Shepards Bush - Pizza 7 Rockley Road, London, W14 0DJ	0208 749 8582
The Jam Tree - British 58, Milson Road, Kensington London, W14 0LB	0207 371 3999
PizzaExpress Olympia - Pizza The Addison Rooms Olympia Exhibition Centre, Hammersmith Road, W14 8UX	0207 6026677

South East London

Raffaello Restaurant - Italian 202-206 Union Street, Southwark, London, SE1 0LH	0207 261 0209
Belushi's London Bridge - American 161-165 Borough High Street, Southwark, London, SE1 1HR	0207 939 9700
St Christopher Inn - British 121 Borough High Street, London Bridge, London, SE1 1NP	0207 407 2392
Silka - Indian 6-8 Southwark Street, London, SE1 1TL	0207 378 6161
Southwark Rooms - International 60 Southwark Street, SE1 1UN	0207 357 9301
Tentazioni - Italian 2 Mill Street, London, SE1 2BD	0207 237 1100
Auberge London Bridge - International 35 Tooley Street, London, SE1 2QJ	020 7407 5267
Skinkers - British 42 Tooley Street, Southwark, SE1 2SZ	0207 407 7720
The Shard Indian - Indian 96 Tooley street, London, SE1 2TH	0207 407 9555
Bengal Clipper Tower Bridge - Indian Shad Thames, Butlers Wharf, London, SE1 2YR	0207 357 9001
PizzaExpress Shad Thames - Pizza The Cardamom Building, 31 Shad Thames, London, SE1 2YR	0207 403 8484
Cafe Amisha - Italian 161 Grange Road, London, SE1 3GH	0207 231 7151
Champor-Champor - Malaysian 62-64 Weston Street, London, SE1 3QJ	020 7403 4600
Bermondsey Kitchen - Modern European 194 Bermondsey Street, London, SE1 3TQ	0207 407 5719
Alfies @ Bermondsey Square Hotel - British Bermondsey Square Hotel, Tower Bridge Road, London, SE1 3UN	0207 378 2456
Pho London - Vietnamese 16 Harper Road, London, SE1 6AD	0207 771 9536
Azzurro Waterloo - International Arch 145 Sutton Walk, Waterloo, London, SE1 7ND	0207 620 1300
Zen China - Chinese County Hall Riverside Building, Westminster Bridge Road, London, SE1 7PB	0207 261 1196
Baltic - Modern European 74 Blackfriars Road, London, SE1 8HA	0207 928 1111
Livebait Waterloo - Seafood The Cut, Waterloo, London, SE1 8LF	0207 928 7211
The Thames Indian - Indian 79 Waterloo Road , London, SE1 8UD	020 7928 3856
Auberge Waterloo - International 1 Sandell Street, Waterloo, SE1 8UH	0207 633 0610
PizzaExpress The Whitehouse - Pizza The White House, Belvedere Road, London, SE1 8YP	0207 928 4091
PizzaExpress Belvedere Road - Pizza Royal Festival Hall, The White House, London, SE1 8YP	020 7928 4091
Wine Wharf - International Stoney Street , Borough Market, London, SE1 9AD	0207 940 8335
gbk Clink Street - Antipodean Soho Wharf, Clink Street, London, SE1 9DG	0207 403 2379
PizzaExpress Bankside - Pizza Benbow House, 24 New Globe Walk, London, SE1 9DS	0207 401 3977
Amano Clink Street - Italian Victor Wharf, Clink Street, London, SE1 9DW	0207 234 0000
Amano Bankside - Italian 23 Sumner Street, London, SE1 9JZ	0207 633 9574
Indigo - Indian 56 Stamford Street, London, SE1 9LX	020 7593 0009
Gourmet Pizza Gabriel's Wharf - Pizza Upper Ground, Gabriel's Wharf, London, SE1 9PP	0207 928 3188
The Wharf - Seafood Riverside Walk, Gabriel's Wharf, London, SE1 9PP	0207 401 7314
PizzaExpress London Bridge - Pizza 4 Borough High Street, London, SE1 9QQ	0207 407 2995
Borough Bar - Modern European 10-18 London Bridge Street, London, SE1 9SG	0207 407 6962
Londinium - British 8-18 London Bridge Street, London, SE1 9SG	0207 855 2200
PizzaExpress Blackheath - Pizza 64/66 Tranquil Vale, London, SE3 0BN	0208 318 2595
Café Rouge - French 16-18 Montpelier Vale, Blackheath, London, SE3 0TA	020 8297 2727
STRADA Blackheath - Italian 5 Lee Road, Blackheath, London, SE3 9RD	020 8318 6644
Pizza Lenuccia at The Union Tavern - Pizza 146 Camberwell New Road, Southwark, London, SE5 0RR	0207 0910 447
Grand Union Bar and Grill Camberwell Grove - American 26 Camberwell Grove, London, SE5 8RE	0203 2471001
PizzaExpress The O2 - Pizza Peninsula Square, London, SE10 0DX	0208 293 5071
Union Square - Modern European O2 Arena Unit 11 Peninsula Square, Greenwich, London, SE10 0DX	0208 305 4980
American Bar & Grill - American Unit 2, The O2, Greenwich London, SE10 0DY	07590 356 101
Prezzo Greenwich - Italian 35 Bugsby Way, Greenwich Peninsula, Greenwich, SE10 0QJ	0208 858 2760
Belushi's Greenwich - American 180 Greenwich High Road, Greenwich, SE10 8JA	0208 858 3591
Davy's Wine Vaults Greenwich - British 161 Greenwich High Street, Greenwich, London, SE10 8JA	0208 858 7204

Listings are for ILLUSTRATIVE PURPOSES ONLY, please visit www.tastecard.co.uk for participating restaurants and offers

London

Elements Restaurant & Bar - Modern European — 0208 312 6930
Novotel Hotel, 173-185 Greenwich High Road, London, SE10 8JA

North Pole Bar & Restaurant - Modern European — 0208 853 3020
131 Greenwich High Road, Greenwich, London, SE10 8JA

The Mitre Hotel - British — 0208 293 0037
291 Greenwich High Road, London, SE10 8NA

Rivington Grill Greenwich - British — 0208 293 9270
178 Greenwich High Road, London, SE10 8NN

The Hill - Modern European — 0208 691 3626
89 Royal Hill, Greenwich, London, SE10 8SE

PizzaExpress Greenwich - Pizza — 0208 853 2770
4-6 Church Street, Greenwich, London, SE10 9BG

gbk Greenwich - Antipodean — 0208 858 3920
45 Greenwich Church Street, Greenwich, London, SE10 9BL

Admiral Hardy - British — 0208 2937 174
7 College Approach, Greenwich, London, SE10 9HY

The Coach and Horses - British — 0208 293 0880
13 Greenwich Market, Greenwich, London, SE10 9HZ

The Spread Eagle - French — 0208 853 2333
1-2 Stockwell Street, Greenwich, London, SE10 9JN

Café Rouge - French — 020 8293 6660
Hotel Ibis Greenwich, 30 Stockwell St, London, SE10 9JN

Greenwich Park Bar & Grill - Modern European — 0208 853 7860
1 King William Walk, Greenwich, London, SE10 9JY

Trafalgar Tavern - Modern European — 0208 858 2909
Park Row, Greenwich, London, SE10 9NW

Windies Cove Caribbean Restaurant & Bar - Caribbean — 020 8305 2500
135 - 137, Trafalgar Road, Greenwich, SE10 9TX

The Tommyfield - British — 0207 735 1061
185 Kennington Lane, London, SE11 4EZ

PizzaExpress Kennington - Pizza — 0207 820 3877
316 Kennington Road, London, SE11 4LD

Toulouse Lautrec Piano and Wine Bar - French — 0207 5826800
140 Newington Butts, Kennington, London, SE11 4RN

Thai Pavilion East - Thai — 0207 582 6333
78 Kennington Road, London, SE11 6NL

Grand Union Bar and Grill Kennington - American — 0207 582 6685
111, Kennington Road, London, SE11 6SF

Himalaya Restaurant - Indian — 0203 6902863
393 Lewisham High Street, London, SE13 6NZ

La Luna Restaurant and Pizzeria - Italian — 0207 277 1991
380 Walworth Road, London, SE17 2NG

Crystal Palace Tandoori - Indian — 020 8761 1515
24 Westow Hill, Crystal Palace, London, SE19 1RX

Island Fusion - Caribbean — 0208 761 5544
57B Westow Hill, Crystal Palace, London, SE19 1TS

Yak and Yeti - Indian — 020 8771 6898
107 Church Road, London, SE19 2PR

PizzaExpress Dulwich - Pizza — 0208 693 9333
94 The Village, Dulwich, London, SE21 7AQ

Café Rouge - French — 0208 6939316
96-98 Dulwich Village, Dulwich, London, SE21 7AQ

Café Rouge - French — 020 8766 0070
84 Park Hall Road, Dulwich, London, SE21 8BW

Indigo Restaurant - Indian — 0208 670 2914
101 Rosendale Road, London, SE21 8EZ

Le Chardon Dulwich - French — 020 8299 1921
65, Lordship Lane, East Dulwich, SE22 8EP

Swadesh - Indian — 020 8613 1500
120 Lordship Lane, East Dulwich, London, SE22 8HD

gbk East Dulwich - Antipodean — 0208 693 9307
121 Lordship Lane, East Dulwich, London, SE22 8HU

Barcelona Tapas Bar & Restaurant Lordship Lane - Spanish — 0208 693 5111
481 Lordship Lane, SE22 8JY

C Authentic Chinese Cuisine - Chinese — 0208 670 9755
91 Norwood High Street, London, SE27 9JS

South West London

El Panzon @ Hootenanny - Mexican — 07968 961116
95 Effra Road, Brixton, SW2 1DF

Grand Union Bar and Grill Brixton - American — 020 7274 8794
123, Acre Lane, Brixton, SW2 5UA

Bar 191 - Spanish — 0208 944 5533
191 Worple Road, Raynes Park, London, SW20 8RE

LayaLina - Lebanese — 0207 581 4296
2 / 3 Beauchamp Place, Knightsbridge, London, SW3 1NG

Kumo - Japanese — 0207 225 0944
11 Beauchamp Place, Knightsbridge, London, SW3 1NQ

PizzaExpress Beauchamp Place - Pizza — 0207 589 2355
7 Beauchamp Place, Knightsbridge, London, SW3 1NQ

Zia Teresa - Italian — 0207 589 7634
6 Hans Road, London, SW3 1RX

The Collection - Fusion — 0207 225 1212
264 Brompton Road, Chelsea, SW3 2AS

Awana - Malaysian — 0207 584 8880
85 Sloane Avenue, London, SW3 3DX

mybar Chelsea - International — 0207 225 7535
35 Ixworth Place, London, SW3 3QX

Henry J Beans Chelsea - American — 0207 352 9255
195-197 Kings Road, Chelsea, London, SW3 5ED

Phene Arms - British — 0207 352 3294
9 Phene St, Chelsea, London, SW3 5NY

Ju Ju London - International — 0207 351 5998
316-318 King's Road, Chelsea, London, SW3 5UH

PJ's Bar & Grill - International — 0207 581 0025
52 Fulham Road, Chelsea, London, SW3 6HH

The Pavement Cafe & Bistro - British — 0207 622 4944
21, The Pavement, Clapham London, SW4 0HY

Grafton House - International — 0207 4985559
13 - 19 Clapham Old Town, London, SW4 0JT

The Stonhouse - British — 0207 819 9312
165 Stonhouse Street, London, SW4 6BJ

Listings are for ILLUSTRATIVE PURPOSES ONLY, please visit www.tastecard.co.uk for participating restaurants and offers

The White House - British 0207 498 3388
65 Clapham Park Road, Clapham, London, SW4 7EH

Alba Pizzeria - Italian 0207 733 3636
3 Bedford Road, London, SW4 7SH

Aquum - British 0207 6272726
68-70 Clapham High Street, London, SW4 7UL

gbk Clapham - Antipodean 0207 627 5367
84 Clapham High Street, London, SW4 7UL

Jackson's - Caribbean 07539 601 744
62 Clapham High Street, Clapham Common, SW4 7UL

STRADA Clapham - Italian 020 7627 4847
102-104 Clapham High Street, Clapham, London, SW4 7UL

Gigalum - International 0208 772 0303
7-8 Cavendish Parade Clapham, Common Southside, London, SW4 9DW

The Abbeville - British 0208 675 2201
67-69 Abbeville Road, London, SW4 9JW

PizzaExpress Clapham - Pizza 020 8673 8878
43 Abbeville Road, Clapham, London, SW4 9JX

Village Tandoori - Indian 0208 673 5043 / 0208 675 2077
50 Abbeville Road, London, SW4 9NF

Le Chardon - French 0208 6739 300
32 Abbeville Road, Clapham, London, SW4 9NG

Café Rouge - French 020 8673 3399
40 Abbeyville Rd, Clapham, London, SW4 9NG

Fratelli - International 0207 341 6205
London Marriott Hotel Kensington, 147 Cromwell Road, London, SW5 0TH

STRADA Earl's Court - Italian 020 7835 1180
237 Earls Court Road, London, SW5 9AH

Miss Q's - American 0207 3705358
180-184 Earl's Court Road, London, SW5 9QG

gbk Earls Court - Antipodean 0207 373 3184
163 -165 Earls Court Road, London, SW5 9RF

PizzaExpress Earls Court Exhibition centre - Pizza 0207 386 5494
Earls Court Exhibition Centre, London, SW5 9TA

gbk Fulham Broadway - Antipodean 0207 381 4242
49 Fulham Broadway, London, SW6 1AE

La Tasca Fulham - Spanish 0207 385 2216
1 - 7 Jerdan Place, Fulham Island, London, SW6 1BE

PizzaExpress Fulham Broadway - Pizza 0207 381 1700
Unit 4 Fulham Broadway Retail Centre, London, SW6 1BW

Barbarella's - Italian 0207 385 9434
428 Fulham Road, Fulham, SW6 1DU

Frankie's Sports Bar & Grill - Italian 0207 957 8298
Stamford Bridge, Fulham Road, London, SW6 1HS

MARCO - British 020 7915 2929
Stamford Bridge, Fulham, London, SW6 1HS

Restaurant 55 Chelsea Football Club - Modern European 0207 565 1400
Stamford Bridge, London, SW6 1HS

El Metro - Spanish 0207 384 1264
10-12 Effie Road, Fulham Broadway, London, SW6 1TB

Seasoning - Indian 0207 386 0303
84D - 86, Lillie Road, Fulham London, SW6 1TL

The Greedy Buddha - Asian 0207 751 3311
144 Wandsworth Bridge Road, Fulham, London, SW6 2UH

Little Bengal - Indian 020 7371 7839
45 Fulham High Street, London, SW6 3JJ

Amuse Bouche - Modern European 0207 371 8517
51 Parson's Green Lane, Fulham, SW6 4JA

Ghillies - British 0207 6109675
271 New Kings Road, Parsons Green, London, SW6 4RD

STRADA Parsons Green - Italian 020 7731 6404
175 New Kings Road, Parsons Green, London, SW6 4SW

The Thai Restaurant - Thai 020 7384 1009
177 New Kings Road, Parsons Green, London, SW6 4SW

Luna Nuova - Italian 0207 371 9774
773 Fulham Road, Fulham, London, SW6 5HA

Cafe Rialto Fulham - Italian 0207 736 9429
825 Fulham Rd, Fulham, London, SW6 5HG

PizzaExpress Fulham 895 Fulham Road - Pizza 0207 731 3117
895-896 Fulham Road, London, SW6 5HU

Belushi's Fulham - American 0207 386 7577
498-504 Fulham Road, London, SW6 5NH

Fiesta Havana - South American 0207 381 5005
490 Fulham Road, London, SW6 5NH

Mandaloun Fulham - Lebanese 0207 385 8687
496 Fulham Road, London, SW6 5NH

The Fest - German 0207 736 5293
678-680 Fulham Road, London, SW6 5SA

Shezan - Indian 0207 584 9316
16-22 Cheval Place, London, SW7 1ES

Firehouse - Modern European 0207 584 7258
3 Cromwell Road, South Kensington, London, SW7 2HR

Madsen - International 020 7225 2772
20 Old Brompton Road, London, SW7 3DL

gbk South Kensington - Antipodean 0207 581 8942
107 Old Brompton Road, London, SW7 3LE

Peridot - French 0207 244 5555
The Bentley, 27-33 Harrington Gardens, London, SW7 4JX

Ten Tables - Modern European 0207 584 8100
61, Gloucester Road, London, SW7 4PE

Pasha Lounge & Restaurant - North African 0207 589 7969
1 Gloucester Road, London, SW7 4PP

68-86 Restaurant & Bar - British 0207 761 9000
68-86 Cromwell Road, London, SW7 5BT

Aubrey Restaurant - British 0207 589 6300
109-113 Queen's Gate, South Kensington, London, SW7 5LR

Lost Society - International 0207 652 6526
697 Wandsworth Road, Clapham, London, SW8 3JF

Cafe Zia - Indian 0203 202 0077
811, Wandsworth Road, Battersea, SW8 3JH

Khan-A-Punjab - Indian 0207 6221372 / 0207 8199963
39 Queenstown Road, Battersea, London, SW8 3RE

The Three Bridges - Italian 020 77200 204
153, Battersea Park Road, Wandsworth, SW8 4BX

The Oval Tandoori - Indian 0207 582 1415
64a Brixton Road, Oval, London, SW9 6BP

Rumi Lounge - Lebanese 0207 349 0810
531 Kings Road, London, SW10 0TZ

Listings are for **ILLUSTRATIVE PURPOSES ONLY**, please visit www.tastecard.co.uk for participating restaurants and offers

London

Mokssh - Indian
222 - 224 Fulham Road, London, SW10 9NB
0207 352 6548

PizzaExpress Fulham 363 Fulham Road - Pizza
363 Fulham Road, London, SW10 9TN
0207 352 5300

Gaylord Restaurant - Indian
44 Battersea Rise, London, SW11 1EE
0207 2283981

Pizza Metro Pizza Battersea - Italian
64 Battersea Rise, London, SW11 1EQ
0207 228 3812

STRADA Battersea - Italian
11-13 Battersea Rise, London, SW11 1HG
020 7801 0794

Le Bouchon Bordelais - French
5-9 Battersea Rise, Clapham, London, SW11 1HG
0207 738 0307

PizzaExpress Lavender Hill - Pizza
230-236 Lavender Hill, London, SW11 1LE
0207 223 5677

Marzano - Pizza
53 Northcote Road, London, SW11 1NJ
0207 228 8860

gbk Battersea - Antipodean
44 Northcote Road, London, SW11 1NZ
0207 228 3309

Ace Fusion - Caribbean
110 St John's Hill, Battersea, London, SW11 1SJ
0207 228 5584

Out of the Blue Bar & Kitchen - International
140 St Johns Hill, Battersea, SW11 1SL
0207 207 8548

Curry Leaf - Indian
135A Saint Johns Hill, Clapham Junction, London, SW11 1TD
0207 585 0703

St John's House and the Secret Library - British
St John's House, 165-167 St. John's Hill, Clapham London, SW11 1TQ
0207 223 4972

PizzaExpress Battersea - Pizza
46-54 Battersea Bridge Road, London, SW11 3AG
0207 924 2774

Battersea Spice Organic Indian Cuisine - Indian
344 Battersea Park Road, Battersea, London, SW11 3BY
0207 2232169

Le QuecumBar & Brasserie - French
Battersea High Street, London, SW11 3HX
0207 787 2227

Varnasi Chefs Restaurant - Indian
142 Battersea High Street, London, SW11 3JR
0207 228 3145

Chez Manny - French
145/149, Battersea High Street, London, SW11 3JS
0207 223 4040

Mazar Restaurant - Lebanese
11-12 Battersea Square, Battersea, London, SW11 3RA
0207 978 5374

Riviera Restaurant & Cocktail Bar - Italian
31-32 Battersea Square, London, SW11 3RA
0207 978 5395

Banyan on Thames - International
Hotel Rafayel, 34 Lombard Road, London, SW11 3RF
0207 801 3600

Thai on the River - Thai
2 Lombard Road, London, SW11 3RQ
0207 924 6090

Gazette Battersea - French
79 Riverside Plaza, Chatfield Road, London, SW11 3SE
0207 223 0999

Cafe Azteca Restaurant - Mexican
50a Battersea Park Road, London, SW11 4JP
0207 978 2231

The Eagle - British
231 Battersea Park Rd, Battersea, London, SW11 4LG
0207 622 4844

Lost Angel - British
339 Battersea Park Road, London, SW11 4LS
0207 6222112

The Butcher & Grill - British
39-41 Parkgate Road, Battersea, SW11 4NP
0207 924 3999

The Drawing Room Restaurant & Sofa Bar - Modern European
103 Lavender Hill, Battersea, London, SW11 5QL
0207 350 2564

Cini Kebab - Turkish
33 Lavender Hill, London, SW11 5QW
0785 833 2354

Ukai Sushi - Japanese
39 Lavender Hill, London, SW11 5QW
0207 350 2565

Bombay Bicycle Club Balham - Indian
95 Nightingale Lane, Balham, London, SW12 8NX
0208 673 6217

Gazette Balham - French
1 Ramsden Road, Balham, London, SW12 8QX
0208 772 1232

The Avalon - International
16 Balham Hill, London, SW12 9EB
0208 675 8613

Dish Dash Restaurant - Persian
11-13 Bedford Hill, Balham, SW12 9ET
0208 673 5555

PizzaExpress Balham - Pizza
47 Bedford Hill, London, SW12 9EY
0208 772 3232

Hop and Spice - Asian
53 Bedford Hill, Balham, London, SW12 9EZ
0208 675 3121

Indian Room - Indian
59 Bedford Hill, Balham, SW12 9EZ
020 8675 8611

Aroma Asia - Indian
68 Church Road, London, SW13 0DQ
0208 748 6793

PizzaExpress Barnes - Pizza
14-15 Barnes High Street, London, SW13 9LW
0208 878 1184

STRADA Barnes - Italian
375 Lonsdale Road, Barnes, London, SW13 9PY
020 8392 9216

The Naked Turtle - International
505 Upper Richmond Road West, East Sheen, Richmond, SW14 7DE
0208 878 1995

Don't Tell Fred - British
40 Sheen Lane East, London, SW14 8LW
0208 878 8266

PizzaExpress East Sheen - Pizza
305 Upper Richmond Road West, East Sheen, London, SW14 8QS
0208 878 6833

Mango and Silk - Indian
199 Upper Richmond, Road West, East Sheen, SW14 8QT
0208 876 6220

Cochin Brasserie - Indian
193 Lower Richmond Road, London, SW15 1HJ
0208 785 6004

Thai Square Putney - Thai
2-4 Lower Richmond Road, Putney, SW15 1LB
0208 780 1811

Moomba - British
5 Lacy Road, London, SW15 1NH
0208 785 9151

Royal China - Chinese
3 Chelverton Road, Putney, London, SW15 1RN
0208 788 0907

Citizen Smith - Healthy Eating
160 Putney High Street, London, SW15 1RS
0208 780 2235

gbk Putney Bridge - Antipodean
333 Putney Bridge Road, London, SW15 2PG
0208 789 1199

PizzaExpress Putney - Pizza
144 Upper Richmond Road, Putney, London, SW15 2SW
0208 789 1948

STRADA Putney - Italian
147 Upper Richmond Road, Putney, London, SW15 2TX
020 8789 6996

Ma Goa - Indian
242-244 Upper Richmond Road, Putney, London, SW15 6TG
0208 780 1767

PizzaExpress Streatham - Pizza
34-36 Streatham High Road, London, SW16 1DB
0208 769 0202

Chilli Chutney - Indian 0208 6960123
20 The High Parade, Streatham High Road, London, SW16 1EX

Nineteen - Modern European 0208 835 8285
19 The High Parade, Streatham High Road, London, SW16 1EX

Carnevale's Restaurant - Italian 0208 944 9351
558-560 Garratt Lane, Earlsfield near Wimbledon, London, SW17 0NU

Radha Krishna Bhavan - Indian 0208 682 0969
86 Tooting High Street, London, SW17 0RN

Spice Lounge Tooting - Indian 0208 767 5012
102 Tooting High St, Tooting Broadway, SW17 0RR

The Manor Bar and Grill - International 020 8672 6351
196 Tooting High Street, Tooting, London, SW17 0SF

Onam - Indian 020 8767 7655
219 Tooting High Street, London, SW17 0SZ

The Bowler Restaurant - Modern European 020 8767 9677
20 Bellevue Road, London, SW17 7EB

Cafe du Village Wandsworth - International 0844 371 2550
11 Bellevue Road, Wandsworth Common, London, SW17 7EG

PizzaExpress Wandsworth - Pizza 0208 672 0200
198 Trinity Road, London, SW17 7HR

China Boulevard on the River - Chinese 0208 874 9878
1 Boulevard, Smugglers Way, London, SW18 1DE

The Armoury Pub - British 0208 870 6771
14 Armoury Way, Wandsworth, London, SW18 1EZ

PizzaExpress Wandsworth Town - Pizza 0208 877 9812
539-541 Old York Road, London, SW18 1TG

La Pernella - Italian 0208 9469712
470-472 Garratt Lane, Earlsfield, London, SW18 4HJ

The Grand Union Bar and Grill Wandsworth - American 0208 877 1851
96 Wandsworth High Street, London, SW18 4LB

Rodizio Brazil - Brazilian 0208 871 3875
505 Garratt Lane, London, SW18 4SW

Henry J Beans Wimbledon - American 0208 5435083
153-163 The Broadway, Wimbledon, London, SW19 1NE

Cento - Italian 0208 5429456
100 The Broadway, London, SW19 1RH

gbk Wimbledon - Antipodean 0208 540 3300
88 The Broadway, London, SW19 1RH

PizzaExpress Wimbledon Broadway - Pizza 0208 543 1010
104 The Broadway, London, SW19 1RH

Reds Bar & Grill - Modern European 020 8540 8308
86 The Broadway, Wimbledon, London, SW19 1RQ

Lambourne Bar & Grill - British 0208 545 8661
247 The Broadway, Wimbledon, London, SW19 1SD

The Butcher & Grill Wimbledon - British 020 8944 8269
33 High Street, Wimbledon Village, London, SW19 5BY

Café Rouge - French 020 8944 5131
26 High Street, Wimbledon, London, SW19 5BY

Common Room - British 0208 944 1909
18 High Street, Wimbledon Village, SW19 5DX

STRADA Wimbledon - Italian 020 8946 4363
91 High Street, Wimbledon, London, SW19 5EG

PizzaExpress Wimbledon Village - Pizza 0208 946 6027
84 High Street, London, SW19 5EG

Tu Chicas Khaya - Mexican 0208 946 4300
12-14 Leopold Road, Wimbledon, London, SW19 7BD

Piaf On the Hill - Mediterranean 0208 946 3823
40 Wimbledon Hill Road, Wimbledon, SW19 7PA

Dalchini Hakka - Chinese 0208 9475966
147 Arthur Road, Wimbledon Park, London, SW19 8AB

Ocaso Tapas Bar - Tapas 020 8543 3111
292 Haydons Road, London, SW19 8JZ

Listings are for **ILLUSTRATIVE PURPOSES ONLY**, please visit www.tastecard.co.uk for participating restaurants and offers

South East

Villa Romana
Italian — **01923 779 492**

92 High St, Rickmansworth, Hertfordshire, WD3 1AQ

With the well known high quality of food and service, Villa Romana always has a great reputation for good food. A family owned and operated establishment, Villa Romana boasts fine dining in a relaxed atmosphere. Classical Italian dishes and highly acclaimed specialities are included in their menu.

Baumann's Brasserie
British — 01376 561453

4-6 Stoneham Street, Coggeshall, Essex, CO6 1TT

Featured in every major food guide in Great Britain, and recently listed in The Times as a Top 10 Brasserie in the UK; located in the charming market town of Coggeshall, Baumanns Brasserie regularly attracts plaudits from its clientele and food critics alike.

The inspiration behind the Brasserie is proprietor and award-winning chef, Mark Baumann. He has created a perfect informal environment in which to meet with friends or clients and experience cooking of a very high standard, always with top-quality locally sourced ingredients. Like the food, the emphasis in the decor is an enjoyment and just the right amount of originality.

South East

South East

Gars Chinese Restaurant
Chinese — 01273 321321

19 Prince Albert St, Brighton, East Sussex, BN1 1HF

In the heart of the famous Brighton Lanes, Gars offer a creative mix of modern and authentic Chinese cuisine with a sprinkling of Japanese and Thai favourites.

As well as a fantastic menu with equally fantastic staff, they pride themselves on how their restaurant looks; from polished bamboo flooring to bespoke modern silk shades, they have strived for a dining area with a contemporary oriental atmosphere.

Bacchus
Modern European — 01702 348 088

43 Alexandra Street, Southend on Sea, Essex, SS1 1BW

Bacchus is a beautifully designed and stylish restaurant in Alexandra Street, Southend. The ambience is very tranquil with back ground music from their resident pianist.

Whether you're wanting a full three course meal or just a snack, the menu featuring both French and English cuisine caters for all and the excellent head chef is able to create a set menu for you to meet any specific requirements you might have.

They serve a fantastic selection of fresh coffees, teas and cakes which are all served on vintage cake stands, adding a touch of class as befits this typically English ritual.

Evening sees a change of tempo, chilled vibe and candle lit for the evening menu. There is also a good selection of wine, beers and spirits all served with style.

South East

South East

Le Petite Petanque
French — 01702 353 208

The Bowling Green Pavilion, Cambridge Square Gardens, Southend, SS1 1EZ

Le Petite Petanque is a beautifully designed and stylish café bar and bistro situated on the Bowling Green Pavilion, Southend. The ambience is tranquil with back ground music from their resident pianist.

Whether you are wanting a full three course meal or just a snack, the menu featuring both English and French cuisine caters for all tastes and the excellent head chef is able to create a set menu for you to meet any specific requirements you might have.

They also serve a fantastic selection of fresh coffees, teas and cakes which are all served on vintage cake stands, adding a touch of class as befits this typically English ritual.

There is also a good selection of wine, beers and spirits all served with style.

The Document House
British — 01635 582 000

7-9 Wharf Street, Newbury, RG14 5AN

The Document House is set in a historic building, dating back as early as 1901. This listed building was used as a storage house for research documents assisting with the justice in the market town of Newbury.

Today The Document House is Newbury's most stylish and relaxed lounge bar, stocking a vast range of wines, champagnes and fine spirits. The relaxed bar, with its inspiring background music and free wireless internet connection is the ideal place to entertain guests and friends while sipping on a fine wine and teasing your taste buds with the menu of amazing fresh food to share.

Document house has one of the finest selections of mouth-watering food and drink in the area. With produce sourced from local farms, a range of fantastic continental wines and some truly exciting dishes available throughout the day and evening. Document house is a fantastic venue for working lunches, evening meals or just the odd cup of coffee.

South East

South East

Al Duomo
Italian — **01273 326 741**

7 Pavilion Buildings, Brighton, East Sussex, BN1 1EE

Al Duomo always offer a warm Italian welcome to their charming and authentic restaurant in Brighton. They offer a huge selection of fantastic Italian food from antipasti and starters, salads & pasta dishes, a fantastic pizza menu alongside main course fish and meat dishes and sides, with desserts & coffee from their a la carte menu. Whether it's a candle lit dinner for two or a pizza with your buddies pre-cinema, club or just our with freinds, you'll find a meal to suit most tastes and pockets.

Al Duomo is situated over 3 floors; their decor is extremely cool and contemporary with a brown, red, and cream colour scheme, lots of exposed brickwork and sleek leather sofas. The restaurant has a large patio area to the front for Al Fresco eating for up to 60 people and is a lovely spot to enjoy a light lunch or bite to eat on an easy summers day, the ground floor and mezzanine consists of the main restaurant area and to the back of the restaurant an open pizza oven visible on the ground floor along with a mezzanine level under a glass conservatory ceiling.

Al Duomo offers a comfortable, stylish setting, a relaxed atmosphere and an extremely efficient and friendly service.

Genevieve's
International — 0871 376 9008

Brands Hatch, J3 M25, Dartford, DA3 8PE

Only 17 miles by road from the City of London, Thistle Brands Hatch is situated at the heart of the Garden of England and overlooks the world-famous Brands Hatch motorsport race circuit

Inside the hotel, the ground floor Genevieve's Restaurant, with its French doors leading to the internal courtyard is a fabulous place to dine.

The restaurant offers a choice of delicious home-cooked British and European dishes in comfortable surroundings.

Genevieve's also keeps an extensive cellar of classic and New World wines to complement the meals.

South East

South East

Le Petit Nantais
French — 0759 530 3866

41 Bridge Road, Hampton Court, Richmond, Greater London, KT8 9ER

Le Petit Nantais is exactly how it appears – a family owned and run French Bistro specialising in fresh seafood and traditional French cooking.

The Saturday morning Oyster and shellfish stall gives customers the opportunity to buy fresh wet fish – and whether it's a cosy evening supper of Scallops or Filet de Bœuf avec Frites, we guarantee that you will receive a traditional welcome from Kim and JP Gravier.

Le Petit Nantais endeavour only to use fresh and organic products wherever possible.

Riva Waterside Restaurant & Bar

Italian — **01474 364694**

Town Pier, West Street, Gravesend, DA11 0BJ

Riva are located in Gravesend and are perched directly over the River Thames on the oldest cast iron pier in the world. Offering breath taking views and a relaxing atmosphere, this is the ideal place for wining and dining!

With its stunning lit water views and stylish decor, Riva is the perfect place for a romantic candle lit dinner or during the daytime, the perfect place to bring colleagues for afternoon tea, breakfast meetings, luncheons or even celebrations!!

This menu hosts a collection of modern Italian classics ranging from authentic pizzas, risottos and wide ranges of pasta dishes to hearty plates of perfectly cooked meat, fish and poultry.

South East

St Albans

Café Rouge - French 01727 832 777
29 Holywell Hill, St Albans, Herts, AL1 1HD

PizzaExpress St Albans - Pizza 01727 853 020
11/13 Verulam Road, AL3 4DA

Blue Plate Kitchen - British 01727 864 984
6 Verulam Road, St Albans, Herts, AL3 4DD

Mokoko - Asian 01727 852 287
26 Verulam Road, St Albans, Herts, AL3 4DE

The Snug - British 01727 856 631
The Fleur de Lys, 1 French Row, St Albans, AL3 5DU

Cibo DiVino - Italian 01727 899 189
4 - 5 Waddington Road, St Albans, Hertfordshire, AL3 5EX

Le Moulin - French 0158 283 1988
3 Mill Walk, Wheathampstead, St Albans, AL4 8DT

Prezzo Harpenden - Italian 0 582 469 007
15 Leyton Road, Harpenden, Herts, AL5 2HX

PizzaExpress Harpenden - Pizza 01582 765 714
The Gate House, AL5 2TH

The Pavillion - Indian 01582 841 436
38 High Street, Markyate, AL5 4SE

PizzaExpress Welwyn Garden City - Pizza 01707 334 231
40 Howards Gate, AL8 6BJ

Bella Italia - Italian 01707 251 990
The Galleria, Unit 63, Comet Way, Hatfield, AL10 0XY

Brighton

Nooris - Indian 0127 332 9405
70/71 Ship Street, Brighton, Sussex, BN1 1AE

La Tasca Brighton - Spanish 01273 737 342
165 '169 North Street, Brighton, West Sussex, BN1 1EA

Al Duomo - Italian 01273 326 741
7 Pavilion Buildings, Brighton, East Sussex, BN1 1EE

STRADA Brighton - Italian 01273 202 070
160 - 161 North Street, Brighton, East Sussex, BN1 1EZ

PizzaExpress Brighton Jubilee Street - Pizza 01273 697 691
A3 Block Jubilee Street, BN1 1GE

Gars Chinese Restaurant - Thai 01273 321 321
19 Prince Albert St, Brighton, East Sussex, BN1 1HF

PizzaExpress Brighton Prince Albert Street - Pizza 01273 323 205
22 Prince Albert Street, BN1 1HF

Café Rouge - French 01273 774 422
24 Prince Albert St, Brighton, BN1 1HF

Bella Italia - Italian 01273 777 607
24 Market Street, Brighton, BN1 1HH

Il Bistro - Mediterranean 01273 324 584
6 - 7a Market Street, Brighton, East Sussex, BN1 1HH

Northern Lights Restaurant - Modern European 0127 374 7096
6 Little East Street, Brighton, East Sussex, BN1 1HT

Belushi's Brighton - American 0127 320 2035
10-12 Grand Junction Road, Brighton, BN1 1NG

gbk Brighton - Antipodean 01273 685 895
44-47 Gardner Street, Brighton, BN1 1UN

Due South - Modern European 01273 821 218
139 Kings Road Arches, Brighton Beach, BN1 2FN

The Promenade Restaurant @Thistle Hotel - International 0871 376 9041
King's Road, Brighton, BN1 2GS

Belushi's Bath - American 0122 548 1444
9 Green Street, Bath, BN1 2JA

The Blanch House Restaurant - International 0127 360 3504
17 Atlingworth street, Brighton, BN2 1PL

PizzaExpress Brighton Marina - Pizza 01273 689 300
4 The Waterfront, BN2 5WA

Prezzo Brighton - Italian 01273 680 582
Brighton Marina, Brighton, BN2 5WA

STRADA Brighton Marina - Italian 01273 686 821
3 The Waterfront, Brighton Marina, Brighton, BN2 5WA

The Brasserie Fish - Mediterranean 0127 369 8989
3a Waterfront, Brighton Marina, Brighton, BN2 5WA

Café Rouge - French 01273 622 423
Unit 6, The Waterfront, Brighton Marina, Brighton, BN2 5WA

PizzaExpress Hove - Pizza 01273 770 093
107 Church Road, BN3 2AF

The Slug and Lettuce Hove - International 0127 373 3359
4/5 George Street, Hove, BN3 3YA

The Three Amigos @ The Vinyard Restaurant - Mexican 01273 835 000
42 High Street, Hurspierpoint, West Sussex, BN6 9rg

Prezzo Lewes - Italian 01273 472 179
173 High Street, Lewes, East Sussex, BN7 1YE

PizzaExpress Lewes - Pizza 01273 487 524
15 High Street, BN7 2LN

The Old Ship Pub - International 0127 381 4223
Uckfield Road, Ringmer, BN8 5RP

The Hope Inn - British 01273 515 389
West Pier, Newhaven, East Sussex, BN9 9DN

Viceroy Newhaven - Bangladeshi 01273 513 308
4a Bridge Street, Newhaven, BN9 9PJ

PizzaExpress Worthing - Pizza 01903 821 133
Warwick Street, Worthing, BN11 3EZ

The Maharaj Nepalese Restaurant - Curry 0190 323 3300
67 Rowlands Road, Worthing, BN11 3JN

Madame Geisha - Asian 01273 770 847
75-79 East Street, Brighton, BN11NF

Andalucia - Spanish 01903 502 605
60 Ferring Street, Ferring, Worthing, BN12 5JP

PizzaExpress Arundel - Pizza 01903 885 467
33 High Street, BN18 9AG

The Muse - Mediterranean 0190 388 3477
2-8 Castle Mews Tarrant street, Arundel, West Sussex, BN18 9DG

Prezzo Eastbourne - Italian 01323 722 667
1 Terminus Buildings, Upperton Road, Eastbourne, BN21 1BA

Princess - Indian 01323 722 056
Lascelles Terrace, Eastbourne, BN21 4BL

PizzaExpress Eastbourne - Pizza 24 Cornfield Road, BN21 4QH	01323 649 466
The Star Inn - British Normans Bay, Pevensey, East Sussex, BN24 6QG	01323 762 648
The Star Alfriston - British High Street, Alfriston, East Sussex, BN26 5TA	0132 387 0495
Silletts Cottage Restaurant - International Church Farm Selmeston, Polegate, East Sussex, BN26 6TZ	0132 381 1343
Prezzo Halisham - Italian The Old School House, High St Hailsham, East Sx, BN27 1AR	01323 442 010
Prezzo High St Hailsham - Italian The Old School House, High St Hailsham, East Sussex, BN27 1AR	01323 442 010

Bromley

Ivory Lounge Bromley - Modern European 2-4 Ringers Road, Bromley, Kent, BR1 1HT	0208 313 0980
Café Rouge - French 12-13 Market Square, Bromley, Kent, BR1 1MA	020 8460 0470
Basil - International 18 - 20 East Street, Bromley, Kent, BR1 1QU	0208 460 0018
PizzaExpress Bromley - Pizza 15 Widmore Road, Bromley, Kent, BR1 1RL	020 8464 2708
Papadom - Indian 18 Tylney Road, Bromley, Kent, BR1 2RL	0208 464 2531
Raj Moni - Indian 10 Plaistow Lane, Bromley, BR1 3PA	0208 313 3828
Prezzo Beckenham - Italian 145-151 High Street, Beckenham, BR3 1AG	0208 658 0747
PizzaExpress Beckenham - Pizza 189 High Street, Beckenham, BR3 1AH	0208 650 0593
gbk Beckenham - Antipodean 51 High Street, Beckenham, Kent, BR3 1AW	0208 658 7512
The Amber Fort - Indian 166a Upper Elmers End Road, Beckenham, BR3 3DY	0208 658 4444 / 07930 563 782
PizzaExpress West Wickham - Pizza 3 High Street, West Wickam, BR4 0LP	0208 777 7966
PizzaExpress Orpington - Pizza 97 High Street, BR6 0LF	01689 833 811
Caffè Uno Chislehurst - Italian 95 - 97 High Street, Kent, BR7 5AG	0208 295 4565
Café Rouge - French 9 The High St, Chislehurst, Kent, BR7 5AJ	020 8295 5000
Dhaba Indian Excellence - Indian Belmont Parade, Green Lane, BR7 6AN	020 8467 6878
PizzaExpress Chislehurst - Pizza 8 Royal Parade, Chislehurst, BR7 6NR	020 8295 0965

Cambridge

Bella Italia - Italian The Picnic on the Park, 106 Grafton Centre, Cambridge, CB1 1PS	01223 462 464
Bella Italia - Italian Unit G1, Cambridge Leisure Park, Clifton Way, Cambridge, CB1 7DY	01223 247 099
gbk Cambridge - Antipodean 43-45 Regent Street, Cambridge, CB2 1AB	0122 3312 598
PizzaExpress Cambridge Regent Street - Pizza 26-28 Regent Street, CB2 1DB	01223 306 777
Shiraz Restaurant and Bar, Middle Eastern 84 Regent Street, Cambridge, Cambridgeshire, CB2 1DP	01223 307 581
STRADA Cambridge - Italian 17 Trinity Street, Cambridge, CB2 1TB	01223 352 166
La Tasca Cambridge - Spanish 14'16 Bridge Street, Cambridge, Cambridgeshire, CB2 1UF	01223 464 630
Caffè Uno Cambridge - Italian 32 Bridge Street, Cambridge, CB2 1UJ	01223 314 954
Café Rouge - French 24-26 Bridge St, Cambridge, CB2 1UJ	01223 364 961
Bella Italia - Italian The Watermill, Newnham Road, Cambridge, CB3 9EY	01223 367 507
Henry's Cafe Bar Cambridge - International Quayside, Cambridge, Cambridgeshire, CB5 8AB	01223 324 649
PizzaExpress Cambridge Jesus Lane - Pizza 7a Jesus Lane, CB5 8BA	01223 324 033
Prezzo Ely - Italian 12-14 High Street, Ely, Cambs, CB7 4JZ	01353 659 832
PizzaExpress ELY - Pizza 43 High Street Cambs, CB7 4LF	01353 665 999
Prezzo Newmarket - Italian 2 Exeter Road, Newmarket, Suffolk, CB8 8LT	01638 669 676
PizzaExpress Newmarket - Pizza 75 High Street, CB8 8NA	01638 664 646
Prezzo Haverhill - Italian Ehringshausen Way, Haverhill, Suffolk, CB9 0BB	01440 767 878
Prezzo Saffron Waldon - Italian 1 Cross Street, Saffron Waldon, Essex, CB10 1EX	01799 521 260

Chelmsford

The Contented Sole - Mediterranean 80 High Street, Burnham-on-Crouch Essex, CM0 8AA	01621 786 900
The Polash Restaurant Burnham - Indian 169 Station Road, Burnham-on-Crouch, Essex, CM0 8HJ	01621 782 233
Prezzo Chelmsford - Italian 113-115 Bond Street, Chelmsford, Essex, CM1 1GD	01245 264 335
The Golden Fleece - International Duke Street, Essex, CM1 1JP	0124 525 6752
Cosmo Flame - Mediterranean 8-10 Broomfield Road, Chelmsford, CM1 1SN	01245 493 929
Barda Restaurant & Bar - Modern European 30 Broomfield Road, Chelmsford, Essex, CM1 1SW	01245 357 799
Corner Lounge - Italian 1 Exchange Way, Chelmsford, Essex, CM1 1XB	01245 505 880
Prezzo Chelmsford - Italian 8 Baddow Road, Chelmsford, Essex, CM2 0DG	01245 358 533

Listings are for ILLUSTRATIVE PURPOSES ONLY, please visit www.tastecard.co.uk for participating restaurants and offers

South East

STRADA Chelmsford - Italian 12 Baddow Road, Chelmsford, Essex, CM2 0DG	01245 491 991
PizzaExpress Chelmsford - Pizza 219 Moulsham Street, CM2 0LR	01245 491 466
Café Rouge - French Unit 2, 219 Moulsham St, Chelmsford, Essex, CM2 0LR	01245 250 588
La Tasca Chelmsford - Spanish 13'15 Backnang Square, Chelmsford, Essex, CM2 6FD	01245 290 305
The Bar Cafe - Fusion Kings Head Walk, Chelmsford, CM2 6FH	01245 355 330
La Vista - Italian 23-25 Church Street, Great Baddow, Essex, CM2 7HX	01245 478 884
Mustard - British 37 New London Road, Essex, CM2 0ND	01245 266 612
The Star Inn - British 7 Bridge Street Bishop's, Stortford, CM23 2JU	0127 965 4211
PizzaExpress Bishops Stortford - Pizza 25 North Street, CM23 2LD	01279 757 677
Lakeside Superbowl Bishops Stortford - International 4 Anchor Street, Bishops Stortford, Hertfordshire, CM23 3BP	0127 975 5204
Square 1 - British 15 High Street, Great Dunmow, Essex, CM6 1AB	01371 859 922
Whitehall Restaurant - British Church End Broxted, Dunmow near Stansted, Essex, CM6 2BZ	01279 850 603
The Swan at Felsted - International Station Road, Felsted, Essex, CM6 3DG	01371 820 245
Thirty Four Wine Bar and Restaurant - British 34 New Street, Braintree, Essex, CM7 1ES	01376 345 615
Prezzo Braintree - Italian Freeport Village, Charter Way, Braintree, CM7 8YH	01376 569 022
The Compasses at Pattiswick - International Compasses Road, Pattiswick, Essex, CM77 8BG	01376 561 322
PizzaExpress Braintree - Pizza R1 Freeport Designer Village, CM77 8YH	01376 528 789
Prezzo Maldon - Italian 69 High Street, Maldon, Essex, CM9 5EP	01621 842 544
STRADA Billericay - Italian 63 High Street, Billericay, Essex, CM12 9AX	01277 622 300
Thai House - Thai 21B High Street (1st Floor), Billericay, Essex, CM12 9BA	0127 763 2424
Saffron Indian Cuisine - Indian 21c High Street, Billericay, Essex, CM12 9BA	0127 763 6063
Prezzo Billericay - Italian 6 High Street, Billericay, Essex, CM12 9BQ	01277 658 273
La Toscana Italian Restaurant & Bar - Italian Old Barn Court, High Street, Billericay, CM12 9BY	0127 763 0120
Café Rouge - French 84-84a High Street, Brentwood, Essex, CM14 4AP	01277 262 466
Undaal - Indian 19 South Street, Brentwood, Essex, CM14 4BJ	01277 212 740
PizzaExpress Brentwood - Pizza 5 High Street, CM14 4RG	01277 233 569
Prezzo Brentwood - Italian 129-129A High Street, Brentwood, Essex, CM14 4RZ	01277 216 641
Zafran - Indian 309-311 Roman Road, Mount Nessing, Brentwood, CM15 0UJ	01277 355 666
Prezzo Epping - Italian 236 High Street, Epping, Essex, CM16 4AP	01992 570 056
Carriages - British Coppice Row, Theydon Bois, Essex, CM16 7EU	01992 812 268
RBG Bar and Grill @ The Park Inn Harlow - International Southern Way, Harlow, Essex, CM18 7BA	01279 829 988
Bengal Lancers - Indian The White Horse, 2 High Street, Roydon Essex, CM19 5HJ	01279 793 131

Colchester

Café Rouge - French 59 High Street, Colchester, Essex, CO1 1DH	01206 541 839
The Red Lion Hotel - British High Street, Colchester, Essex, CO1 1DJ	01206 577 986
La Tasca Colchester - Spanish 14'15 North Hill, Colchester, Essex, CO1 1DZ	01206 768 060
STRADA Colchester - Italian 19-20 North Hill, Colchester, CO1 1DZ	01206 542 854
PizzaExpress Colchester - Pizza 1 St Runwald Street, CO1 1HF	01206 760 680
Prezzo Colchester - Italian 1 Culver Street East, Colchester, Essex, CO1 1LD	01206 573 388
Fai's Noodle Bar Restaurant - Chinese 26 St Botolphs Street, Colchester, CO2 7EA	01206 762 288
China Garden Bromley Road - Chinese 21 Bromley Rd, Colchester, Essex, CO4 3JF	01206 869 086
China Garden High Street - Chinese 117 ' 119 High Street, Colchester, Essex, CO5 9JD	01206 870 783
Baumanns Brasserie - British 4-6 Stoneham Street, Coggeshall, Essex, CO6 1TT	01376 561 453
Drapers Brasserie @ Drapers Hotel - International High Street, Earls Colne, Essex, CO6 2PB	0178 722 3353
The Akbar - Indian 42 High Street, Halstead, nr Braintree, CO9 2AP	01787 479 300
Prezzo Halstead - Italian 5 Market Hill, Halstead, Essex, CO9 2AR	01787 474 271
Prezzo Sudbury - Italian 54-55 Gainsborough Street, Sudbury, CO10 2ET	01787 880 852
Prezzo Clacton-on-Sea - Italian 4 Marine Parade West, Clacton-on-Sea, Essex, CO15 1QZ	01255 223 894
PizzaExpress Clacton - Pizza 2 Marine Parade West, CO15 1RH	01255 423 248

Croydon

Aqua Brasserie - Modern European 33 South End, Croydon, CR0 1BE	0208 667 0070
PizzaExpress Croydon - Pizza 3 South End, Croydon, CR0 1BE	020 8680 0123

76 | Listings are for ILLUSTRATIVE PURPOSES ONLY, please visit www.tastecard.co.uk for participating restaurants and offers

The Chilli Room - Indian 0208 680 0033
24-26 South End, Croydon, CR0 1DN

Tiger Tiger Croydon - International 0208 662 4949
16 High Street, Croydon, CR0 1GT

Auberge Croydon - International 0208 680 8337
Units 2153 ' 2156 Whitgift Centre, Croydon , CR0 1LP

Khyber Indian Restaurant - Indian 020 8681 6565
284 - 288 High Street, Croydon, CR0 1NG

Bella Italia - Italian 020 8688 5787
18 George Street, Croydon, Surrey, CR0 1PA

Wine Vaults ' Croydon - British 0208 680 2419
122 North End, Croydon, CR0 1UD

La Tasca Croydon - Spanish 0208 680 3388
38 ' 40 High Street, Croydon, Surrey, CR0 1YB

Kerala Bhavan - Indian 0208 688 6216
16 London Road, West Croydon, Surrey, CR0 2TA

Bella Italia - Italian 02086 812 144
Unit 2, Valley Leisure Park, Hesterman Way, Croydon, CR0 4YA

Chutneys - Indian 0208 655 3757
244 Wickham Street, Croydon, CR0 8BJ

Fushia - Indian 0207 998 1693
No 3 Brighton Road , South Croydon , London , CR2 6EA

Spice n Ice - Indian 0208 604 2600
South Park Hotel, 3-5 South Park Hill Road, Croydon, CR2 7DY

Planet Spice - Indian 0208 651 3300
88 Selsdon Park Road, Addington, South Croydon, CR2 8JT

PizzaExpress Caterham - Pizza 01883 342 717
10 Croydon Road, CR3 6QB

Canterbury

Prezzo Canterbury - Italian 01227 379 571
29 High Street, Canterbury, Kent, CT1 2AZ

Marlowe's Restaurant - International 01227 462 194
55 St. Peters Street, Canterbury, CT1 2BE

STRADA Canterbury - Italian 01227 472 089
10-11 Sun Street, Canterbury, Kent, CT1 2HX

PizzaExpress Canterbury - Pizza 01227 766 938
4/5a Best Lane, CT1 2JB

Café Rouge - French 01227 784 984
Unit 3 & 5, Longmarket, Canterbury, CT1 2JS

The Cuban Canterbury, Cuban 0870 850 8975
41 - 43 High Street, Canterbury, Kent, CT1 2RY

Cantina Californian Restaurant- Mexican 01227 450 288
61 Dover Street, Canterbury, Kent, CT1 3HD

The Farmhouse - British 0122 745 6118
11 Dover St, Canterbury, CT1 3HD

The Red Lion Inn - British 0122 783 2213
75 High Street, Bridge, Kent, CT4 5LB

The Duck Inn - International 01227 830 354
Pett Bottom, Canterbury Kent, CT4 5PB

Prezzo Whitstable - Italian 01227 276 508
1-3 High Street, Whitstable, Kent, CT5 1AP

The Pearson's Arms - British 0122 727 2005
Sea Wall, Whitstable, Kent, CT5 1BT

Prezzo Broadstairs - Italian 01843 871 188
16 Albion Street, Broadstairs, Kent, CT10 1LU

PizzaExpress Ramsgate - Pizza 01843 592 186
52 Harbour Parade, CT11 8LW

The St James's Restaurant - British 07511 018 764
3A Broad Street, Ramsgate, Kent , CT11 8NQ

Patogh, Persian 0184 385 2631
2 Effingham Street, Ramsgate, Kent, CT11 9AT

Dartford

Kent Curry House - Indian 01322 291 216
56 Hythe St, Dartford, Kent, DA1 1BX

Jafflong - Indian 01322 293 858
58 Spital Street, Dartford, Kent, DA1 2DT

The Hide Out - American 01322 224 691
70 Spital St, Dartford, Kent, DA1 2DT

Genevieve's Restaurant at Thistle Brands Hatch - International 0871 376 9008
Brands Hatch, J3 M25, Dartford, DA3 8PE

Racing Bar at Thistle Brands Hatch - International 0871 376 9008
Brands Hatch, J3 M25, Dartford, DA3 8PE

Saggor Tandoori - Asian 0208 303 2904
145 Blendon Rd , Bexley , Kent, DA5 1BT

Bexleys Cyprus Village - Greek 0208 301 6247
222 Broadway, Bexleyheath, Kent, DA6 7AJ

La Siesta Tapas and Cocktail Restaurant - Spanish 0208 303 9426
176 Broadway, Bexley, London, DA6 7BT

Ivory Lounge Bexleyheath - International 0208 303 9206
167 Broadway, Bexleyheath, Kent, DA6 7ES

PizzaExpress Bexleyheath - Pizza 020 8303 3040
163 Broadway, Bexleyheath, Kent, DA6 7ES

Planters Bar @ The Bexleyheath Marriott Hotel - British 0208 298 1000
1 Broadway, Bexleyheath, Kent, DA6 7JZ

The Copper Restaurant @The Bexleyheath Marriott - British 0208 298 1000
1 Broadway, Bexleyheath, Kent, DA6 7JZ

The Bank Restaurant and Bar - British 0208 303 9918
269 Broadway , Bexleyheath, DA6 8DB

Cafe du Village Bluewater - French 0844 371 2550
The Village, Bluewater, Dartford, DA9 9SE

PizzaExpress Bluewater - Pizza 01322 427 526
The Village, Greenhithe, DA9 9SE

La Tasca Bluewater - Spanish 01322 423 902
Water Circus Bluewater, Dartford, Kent, DA9 9SG

Riva Waterside Restaurant & Bar - Modern European 01474 364 694
Town Pier, West Street, Gravesend, DA11 0BJ

Mehiraaj - Indian 0147 435 1415
32 Windmill Street, Kent, DA12 1AS

PizzaExpress Sidcup - Pizza 020 8300 5522
Sidcup, Kent, DA14 6NF

Limoncello - Italian 0208 308 0333
8-9 Marechal Niel Pde, Sidcup, Kent, DA14 6QF

South East

Listings are for ILLUSTRATIVE PURPOSES ONLY, please visit www.tastecard.co.uk for participating restaurants and offers | 77

South East

Sankofa House Bar & Restaurant, African 020 8311 3518
38 Station Rd, Belvedere, Kent, DA17 6JJ

Enfield

ZAMAN indian cuisine - Indian 0208 366 3474
101 St. Marks Road, Enfield, EN1 1BJ

Outback Steakhouse, Steak 0208 367 7881
Enfield Restaurant, Southbury Road, Enfield Middlesex, EN1 1YQ

PizzaExpress Enfield - Pizza 0208 367 3311
2 Silver Street, Enfield, EN1 3ED

Prezzo Enfield - Italian 020 8366 8817
The Coachouse, 26 The Town, Enfield, EN2 6LU

Prezzo Cockfosters - Italian 0208 441 6917
127-129 Cockfosters Road, Cockfosters, Herts, EN4 0DA

Tandoori Nights - Indian 0208 441 9539
27 Station Parade, Cockfosters Road, Cockfosters, EN4 0DW

Cock & Dragon - Thai 0208 449 7160
Chalk Lane, Cockfosters, Barnet, EN4 9HU

After Office Hours - Spanish 020 8449 1142
70 High Street, Barnet, Greater London, EN5 5SJ

The Reks - Asian 0208 440 0799
Old Hadley Oak, 149 High Street, High Barnet, EN5 5SU

Tokyo Joes, Pan Asian 0208 4 400 180
192-194 High Street, Barnet, EN5 5SZ

Brasserie Gerard Barnet - French 0208 441 6112
238-240 High Street, Barnet, London, EN5 5TD

PizzaExpress Barnet - Pizza 020 8449 3706
242-248 High Street, Barnet, Hertfordshire, EN5 5TD

Mumbai Brasserie - Indian 01707 878 744
20 Station Road, Cuffley, Pottersbar, EN6 4HT

De Ja Vu - Indian 01992 636 325
19 High Street, Cheshunt, Herts, EN8 0BX

Mint Leaf Restaurant - Indian 0199 263 9988 / 0199 262 0099
284 High Street, Waltham Cross, EN8 7EA

Guildford

m.Brasserie and Bar - Modern European 01483 303 030
36 ' 40 London Road, Guildford, Surrey, GU1 2AE

PizzaExpress Guildford - Pizza 01483 300 122
237-241 High Street, GU1 3BJ

Olivetto - Italian 01483 563 277
124 High Street, Guildford, GU1 3HQ

STRADA Guildford - Italian 01483 454 455
222 High Street, Guildford, Surrey, GU1 3JD

Cambio Italian Restaurant - Italian 01483 577 702
2- 4 South Hill, Guildford, Surrey, GU1 3SY

Olivo - Italian 01483 303 535
53 Quarry Street, Guildford, GU1 3UA

Café Rouge - French 01483 451 221
8-9 Chapel St, Guildford, Surrey, GU1 3UH

The Rose Valley - Indian 0148 357 2572
50-52 Chertsey Street, Guildford, Surrey, GU1 4HD

The Son Of Sombrero Mexican - Mexican 0148 345 3434
Chertsey Street, Guildford, Surrey, GU1 4HL

The Harrow Inn - International 0148 381 0379
The St. Compton, Guildford, Surrey, GU3 1EG

PizzaExpress Cranleigh - Pizza 01483 271 119
96-102 High Street, GU6 8AJ

PizzaExpress Godalming - Pizza 01483 860 880
127-129 High Street, GU7 1AF

Prezzo Godalming - Italian 01483 428 746
8 Queen Street, Godalming, Surrey, GU7 1BD

PizzaExpress Farnham - Pizza 01252 733 220
74 Castle Street, GU9 7LS

Prezzo Farnham - Italian 01252 737 849
7 The Borough, Farnham, Surrey, GU9 7NA

Café Rouge - French 01252 733 688
Units 4&5, Town Hall Buildings, The Borough, Farnham, GU9 7ND

The Hollybush - International 01252 793 593
Shortfield Common Rd, Frensham, Surrey, GU10 3BJ

Prezzo Camberley - Italian 01276 23945
Park Street, Camberley, GU15 3GP

PizzaExpress Camberley - Pizza 01276 21846
52 Park Street, GU15 3PT

Bella Italia - Italian 01276 686 724
The Atrium, Park Street, St Mary's Road, Camberley, GU15 9PG

La Piazza Restaurant and Pizzeria - Italian 01276 64484
2 the parade, High street, Frimley, GU16 7HY

The Elegance Lounge - Indian 0127 637 848
82 London Road, Blackwater, Camberley, GU17 0AE

Auberge Woking - French 0148 376 4080
1st Floor The Peacocks Centre, Woking, GU21 6GQ

Big Apple Woking - International 0148 372 7100
Crown Square, Woking, Surrey, GU21 6HR

PizzaExpress Woking - Pizza 01483 750 310
65/67 Goldsworth Road, GU21 6LJ

Four Seasons - British 01276 857 238
14-22 High Street, Chobham Woking, Surrey, GU24 8AA

The Inn at West End - British 01276 423 913
42 Guildford Rd West End, Woking, Surrey, GU24 9PW

PizzaExpress Haslemere - Pizza 01428 642 245
1 Causeway Side, Haslemere, GU27 2JZ

The Hamilton Arms - Thai 01730 812 555
School Lane, Stedham, Nr Midhurst, GU29 0NZ

PizzaExpress Midhurst - Pizza 01730 812 214
11 North Street, GU29 9DH

Prezzo Midhurst - Italian 01730 817 040
West St, Midhurst, GU29 9NQ

PizzaExpress Petersfield - Pizza 01730 710 357
25-27 Chapel Street, GU32 3DY

The Flying Bull Inn - British 01730 892 285
London Road, Rake, GU33 7JB

PizzaExpress Alton - Pizza 01420 89839
5 Market Square, GU34 1HD

78 | Listings are for ILLUSTRATIVE PURPOSES ONLY, please visit www.tastecard.co.uk for participating restaurants and offers

Prezzo Alton - Italian 01420 85580
1-2 Market Square, Alton, Hants, GU34 1HD

Golden Triangle - Indian 01252 616 352
192 - 196 Fleet Road, Fleet, GU51 4BY

PizzaExpress Fleet - Pizza 01252 813 777
200 Fleet Road, GU51 4BY

Harrow

Kangana - Indian 0208 904 2636
763-765 Harrow Road, Wembley, HA0 2LW

PizzaExpress Harrow - Pizza 020 8427 9195
2 College Road, Harrow, HA1 1BE

Prezzo Harrow - Italian 0208 427 9588
Unit 26 St Georges Shopping Centre, St Ann's Road Harrow, Middlesex, HA1 1HS

Prezzo St Georges Shopping Centre - Italian 0208 427 9588
St Georges Shopping Centre, St Ann's Road, Harrow, HA1 1HS

Freddy's Bar and Grill - Modern European 0208 424 8300
190-194 Station Road, Harrow, HA1 2RH

Jaidurka Mahal 020 8863 3593
64 Station Rd, North Harrow, Harrow, HA2 7SL

Ram's - Indian 0208 907 2022
203 Kenton Road, Harrow, HA3 0HD

Fiddler's Restaurant - Italian 0208 863 6066
221-227 High Road, Harrow Weald, Middlesex, HA3 5EE

Claye Chef Indian - Indian 0208 861 5671
391 High Road, Harrow, HA3 6EL

The Red Turban - Indian 0208 238 9999
244 Streatfield Road, Harrow, HA3 9BX

Café Rouge - French 01895 678 572
10 High Street, Ruislip, Middlesex, HA4 7AW

PizzaExpress Ruislip - Pizza 01895 625 100
86 High Street, HA4 8LS

Hot Red Chillies - Indian 0208 868 0900
219 Field End Road, Pinner, HA5 1QZ

The Spice Room - Indian 0208 868 8835
12 Kaduna Close, Pinner, HA5 2PZ

Pinner Tandoori - Bangladeshi 020 8866 5474
141 - 143, Marsh Road, Pinner, HA5 5PB

PizzaExpress Pinner - Pizza 020 8866 9848
33-35 High Street, Pinner, Middlesex, HA5 5PJ

Café Rouge - French 020 8429 4424
13-13a High Street, Pinner, Middlesex, HA5 5PJ

Prezzo Pinner - Italian 020 8966 9916
36 High Street, Pinner, HA5 5PW

Prezzo Northwood - Italian 01923 829 941
29 Greenlane, Northwood, HA6 2PY

PizzaExpress Stanmore - Pizza 020 8420 7474
55 The Broadway, Stanmore, Middlesex, HA7 4DJ

Jonathans Stanmore - Italian 020 8416 0213
67-69 The Broadway, Stanmore, HA7 4DJ

Simply Scrumptious - British 0208 958 6886
226 Station Road, Edgware, HA8 7AU

Bombay Dreams - Indian 0208 902 3334
3 Sevenex Parade, London Road, Wembley, HA9 7HQ

Hemel Hempstead

Oojam Restaurant - British 01442 255 085
Riverside, Hemel Hempstead, HP1 1BT

PizzaExpress Hemel Hempstead - Pizza 01442 256 131
5a Riverside, HP1 1BT

Restaurant 65 - British 0144 223 9010
Old High Street, Hemel Hempstead, Hertfordshire, HP1 3AN

Café Rouge - French 01442 878 141
296-298 High Street, Berkhamstead, Herts, HP4 1AH

PizzaExpress Berkhamsted - Pizza 01442 879 966
350 High Street, HP4 1HT

Martins Pond - British 1442864318
The Green Potten End, Berkhamsted, HP4 2QQ

PizzaExpress Amersham - Pizza 01494 725 735
12 Sycamore Road, HP6 5DR

Prezzo Amersham - Italian 01494 727 228
3 Whielden Street, Amersham, Buckinghamshire, HP7 0HT

PizzaExpress Beaconsfield,- Pizza 01494 677 077
14 London End, HP9 2JH

La Tasca High Wycombe - Spanish 0845 126 2984
Eden Shopping Centre, High Wycombe, Buckinghamshire, HP11 2DB

PizzaExpress High Wycombe - Pizza 01494 558 100
40/41 Oxford Street, HP11 2DJ

The Terrace Restaurant @ Alexandra Hotel - British 0149 446 3494
Queen Alexandra Road, High Wycombe, Buckinghamshire, HP11 2JX

The Tree Hotel at Cadmore End - International 0149 488 1183
Marlow Road, Cadmore End, High Wycombe, HP14 3PF

Annie Baileys - British 01494 865 625
Chesham Road, Great Missenden, HP16 0QT

Kashmir Gardens - Indian 0129 641 5644
122 High Street, Aylesbury Buckinghamshire, HP20 1RB

La Tasca Aylesbury - Spanish 01296 424 974
Unit 2 Exchange Street, Aylesbury, Buckinghamshire, HP20 1UB

PizzaExpress Aylesbury - Pizza 01296 399 867
58 Kingsbury, Aylesbury, HP20 2JE

Desire Restaurant - Asian 0129 648 2070
40 Kingsbury, Aylesbury, Buckinghamshire, HP20 2JE

Prezzo Aylesbury - Italian 01296 339 437
39/41 Buckingham Street, Aylesbury, Bucks, HP20 2NQ

Mela - Indian 01296 630 110
103, London Road, Aylesbury, HP22 5LD

Jubraj Tandoori Restaurant - Indian 01442 825 368
53a High St, Tring, Hertfordshire, HP23 5AG

Ilford

London Darbar - Indian — 0208 518 3533
198 Cranbrook Road, Ilford, Essex, IG1 4LU

Apollonia - Greek — 0208 554 1121
376-378 Cranbrook Road, Gants Hill, London, IG2 6HW

TopGolf Chigwell - American — 020 8500 2644
Abridge Road, Chigwell, Essex, IG7 6BX

Prezzo Woodford Green - Italian — 020 8505 2400
8 Johnson Road, Woodford Green, Essex, IG8 0XA

PizzaExpress Loughton - Pizza — 020 8508 3303
281 High Road, Loughton, Essex, IG10 1AH

The Kings Oak Hotel - International — 0208 508 5000
Paul's Nursery Road, High Beach, Essex, IG10 4AE

Café Rouge - French — 020 8502 2011
179-181 High Road, Loughton, Essex, IG10 4LF

Fortune Inn - Chinese — 0208 594 3311
14 London Road, Barking, Essex, IG11 8AG

Bengal Lancer - Indian — 0208 594 9598
84 Longbridge Road, Barking and Dagenham, Greater London, IG11 8SF

Ipswich

PizzaExpress Ipswich Lloyds Avenue - Pizza — 01473 212 651
24/26 Lloyds Avenue, IP1 3HD

PizzaExpress Ipswich Regatta Quay - Pizza — 01473 288 600
The Cambria 13 Regatta, IP4 1FH

China Garden Felixstowe - Chinese — 01394 282 100
8 Hamilton Rd, Felixstowe, Suffolk, IP11 7AU

Prezzo Suffolk - Italian — 01394 610 401
1 Church Street, Woodbridge, Suffolk, IP12 1DS

Prezzo Woodbridge - Italian — 01394 610 401
1 Church Street, Woodbridge, Suffolk, IP12 1DS

Prezzo Aldeburgh - Italian — 01728 454 452
146 High Street, Aldeburgh, Suffolk, IP15 5AQ

Prezzo Ipswich - Italian — 1728454452
146 High Street, ALDEBURGH, Ipswich, IP15 5AQ

STRADA Bury St Edmunds - Italian — 01284 700 771
Cupola House, Cupola House 7 The Traverse, Bury St Edmunds, IP33 1BJ

Café Rouge - French — 01284 764 477
59 Abbeygate St, Bury St Edmunds, Suffolk, IP33 1LB

PizzaExpress Bury St Edmunds - Pizza — 01284 704 802
40 Abbeygate Street, IP33 1LW

La Tasca Bury St Edmunds - Spanish — 0128 470 1011
21 Abbeygate Street, Bury St Edmunds, Cambridgeshire, IP33 1UA

Kingston Upon Thames

Cammasan Oriental Restaurant - Chinese — 020 8549 3510
8 High Street, Kingston, Surrey, KT1 1EH

La Tasca Kingston Upon Thames - Spanish — 0208 439 1002
52a High Sreet, Kingston Upon Thames, Surrey, KT1 1EU

gbk Kingston - Antipodean — 0208 546 1649
42-46 High Street, Kingston Upon Thames, KT1 1HL

Riverside Vegetaria – Vegetarian — 0208 546 7992
64 High Street, Kingston-upon-Thames, Surrey, KT1 1HN

Ha Ha Bar & Grill Kingston - Fusion — 0208 481 0009
Charter Quay, High Street, Kingston, KT1 1HT

STRADA Kingston - Italian — 020 8974 8555
1 The Griffin Centre, Market Place, Kingston, KT1 1JT

PizzaExpress Kingston High Street - Pizza — 020 8546 1447
41 High Street, Kingston upon Thames, Surrey, KT1 1LQ

Al Forno - Italian — 0208 439 7555
1 2 3 Townsend Parade, High Street, Kingston Upon Thames, KT1 1LY

PizzaExpress Kingston Rotunda - Pizza — 020 8547 3133
5 The Rotunda, Kingston upon Thames, Surrey, KT1 1QJ

Karahi Dubba - Indian — 0208 541 3666
51 Surbiton Road, Kingston-Upon-Thames, Surrey, KT1 2HG

China Royal - Chinese — 0208 541 1988
110 Canbury Park Row, Kingston, London, KT2 6J2

Norbiton & Dragon - Thai — 0208 546 1951
16 Clifton Rd, Kingston Upon Thames, KT2 6PW

Lime Leaves - Fusion — 020 8974 6638
60-62 Coombe Road, Kingston upon Thames, Greater London, KT2 7AE

The Atrium Brasserie @ The Kingston Lodge Hotel - British — 0208 541 4481
94 Kingston Hill, Kingston Lodge Hotel, KT2 7NP

PizzaExpress Worcester Park - Pizza — 020 8337 7039
87 Central Road, Worcester Park, Surrey, KT4 8DY

The Italian Taste - Italian — 020 8241 2105
44 Victoria Road Surbiton, Kingston upon Thames, Greater London, KT6 4JL

Duke of York - International — 0208 339 9277
64-65 Victoria Road, Surbiton, KT6 4NQ

Riverview Restaurant and Bar - Fusion — 0208 786 6565
Holiday Inn London Kingston South, Kingston upon Thames, Surrey, KT6 5QQ

Broadway Bar Cafe - British — 0208 399 7698
47 Tolworth Broadway, Surbiton, KT6 7DW

Raintree - Indian — 0208 339 3737
Raintree - Restaurant & Bar, 162 Portsmouth Road, Surrey, KT7 0XR

Le Chien Qui Fume - French — 0208 979 7150
107 Walton Road, East Molesey, Greater London, KT8 0DR

Shahee Mahal - Indian — 020 8979 0011
101 Walton Road, East Molesey, London, KT8 0DR

PizzaExpress Hampton Court - Pizza — 0208 941 3347
19 Creek Road East, Molesey, Surrey, KT8 9BE

Le Petit Nantais - French — 0759 530 3866
41 Bridge Road Hampton Court, Richmond, Greater London, KT8 9ER

The Hampton's Hot Stone Restaurant & Bar - Modern European 0208 979 7676 2-6 Bridge Road, Hampton Court, East Molesey, KT8 9HA	
Caffe Piccolo - Italian 01372 465 596 10 High Street, Esher, Surrey, KT9 9RT	
Café Rouge - French 01372 465 550 Portsmouth Rd, Esher, Surrey, KT10 9AD	
Layla, Eastern European 01372 462 333 110 High Street, Esher, Greater London, KT10 9QL	
PizzaExpress ESHER - Pizza 01372 470 435 34-38 High Street Surrey, KT10 9QY	
STRADA Cobham - Italian 01932 596 967 13-15 Between Street, Cobham, Surrey, KT11 1AA	
PizzaExpress Cobham - Pizza 01932 862 588 20-22 Anyards Road, KT11 2JZ	
gbk Walton On Thames - Antipodean 01932 242 378 Unit 8A, The Heart, Walton on Thames, KT12 1GH	
Glo Walton on Thames - International 01932 222 004 6 The Heart, New Zealand Avenue, Walton-on-Thames, KT12 1GH	
PizzaExpress Walton On Thames - Pizza 01932 243 404 111-115 New Zealand Avenue, KT12 1QA	
Khyber Pass - Indian 0193 222 5670 54 Terrace Road, Walton-On-Thames, Greater London, KT12 2SA	
Bengal Clipper Weybridge - Indian 01932 844 488 7 Temple Market, Queens Road, Weybridge, KT13 2DL	
Prezzo Weybridge - Italian 01932 844 430 44 Church Street, Weybridge, Surrey, KT13 8DP	
PizzaExpress Weybridge - Pizza 01932 829 059 1 Monument Hill, KT13 8RX	
Café Rouge - French 01932 851 777 85 Queens Road, Weybridge, Surrey, KT13 9UG	
Prezzo Kingston Upon Thames - Italian 020 8549 8687 The Rotunda, Clarence Street, Kingston Upon Thames, KT14 1QS	
TopGolf Surrey - American 01932 858 551 Moated Farm Drive, Addlestone, Surrey, KT15 2DW	
The Organ & Dragon, Oriental 0208 393 2242 65 London Rd, Ewell, Epsom, KT17 2BL	
Stoneleigh Brasserie - Indian 0208 786 8262 17/19 The Broadway, Stoneleigh, Epsom Surrey, KT17 2JA	
PizzaExpress Epsom - Pizza 01372 729 618 8 South Street, KT18 7PF	
Café Rouge - French 01372 749 131 96-98 High Street, Epsom, Surrey, KT19 8BR	
Prezzo Leatherhead - Italian 01372 379 625 21-25 Church Street, Leatherhead, Surrey, KT22 8DN	
The Anchor Bookham - British 0137 245 2429 161 Lower Road, Leatherhead, Surrey, KT23 4AH	

Luton

PizzaExpress Luton - Pizza 01582 456 229 3 Church Street, LU1 3JE	
Baltistan - Indian 01582 413025 / 01582 482 091 317 Hitchin Road, Round Green, Luton, LU2 7SL	
Flava, Caribbean 01582 581 171 16 Purley Centre, Luton, Bedfordshire, LU3 3SR	
Tong Sam - Asian 01582 666 880 84 High Street North, Dunstable, Bedfordshire, LU6 1LH	

Medway

The Dragon Inn - Chinese 0163 478 9779 236-238 High Street, Rochester, ME1 1HY	
The Atrium Restaurant - British 01634 847 776 86 High Street, Rochester, Kent, ME1 1JY	
PizzaExpress Rochester - Pizza 01634 812 171 21-23 High Street, ME1 1LN	
Mamma Mia Rochester - Italian 01634 827 027 4 High St, Rochester, Kent, ME1 1PT	
The Eagle Tavern - International 0163 440 9040 124 high street, rochester, Kent, ME1 1JT	
Karma Indian Cuisine - Indian 0163 440 0450 74 High Street, Chatham, Kent, ME4 4DS	
Poco Loco, Tapas 01634 844 198 60 High Street, Chatham, Kent, ME4 4DS	
Coco Diner - Indian 01634 842 489 330 High Street, Chatham, Kent, ME4 4NR	
The Gurkha Village - Indian 0163 466 6054 Victoria Cross 614 Lords Wood Lane, Chatham, Kent, ME5 8QX	
The Star Gillingham - British 0163 485 1174 Watling Street, Gillingham, ME7 2AA	
The Spice Court - Indian 01634 850 150 56-58, Balmoral Road, Gillingham Kent, ME7 4PG	
Le Restaurant Fabrice - French 01795 521 330 London Road, Teynham, Sittingbourne, ME9 9PS	
Prezzo Maidstone - Italian 01622 677 499 45 Earl Street, Maidstone, Kent, ME14 1PD	
PizzaExpress Maidstone - Pizza 01622 683 549 32 Earl Street, ME14 1PF	
La Tasca Maidstone - Spanish 01622 669 626 58 Earl Street, Maidstone, Kent, ME14 1PS	
Mexxa Mexxa- Mexican 01622 662 020 40 Earl Street, Maidstone, Kent, ME14 1PS	
Tacos Locos Restaurant- Mexican 01622 759 555 29 Lower Stone Street, Maidstone, ME15 6LH	
The Hook and Hatchet - British 01622 880 830 Church Road, Hucking, Maidstone, ME17 1QT	
Lime Tree on the Square - Modern European 01622 859 509 8-10 The Square, Lenham, Maidstone, ME17 2PQ	

Milton Keynes

The Grange - Indian 01908 340 607 132 Dunthorne Way, Milton Keynes, MK8 0LW	
STRADA Milton Keynes - Italian 01908 238 900 500 The Hub, Midsummer Boulevard, Milton Keynes, MK9 2BE	

Listings are for **ILLUSTRATIVE PURPOSES ONLY**, please visit www.tastecard.co.uk for participating restaurants and offers

South East

Glo Reading - International
62/63 St Mary's Butts, Reading, RG1 2LG
0118 959 9025

La Tasca Reading - Spanish
59 St Mary's Butts, Reading, RG1 2LG
0118 959 5801

PizzaExpress Reading St Mary's Butts - Pizza
56 St Mary's Butts, RG1 2LG
0118 939 1920

Khukuri - Indian
82 London St, Reading, Berkshire, RG1 4SJ
01189 511 881

Madras Currys Reading - Indian
7 Queens Walk, Broadstreet Mall, Reading, RG1 7QF
0121 555 7750

Standard Nepalese Tandoori Restaurant - Asian
141-145 Caversham Road, Reading, Berkshire, RG1 8AU
0189 590 093

Bina Tandoori - Indian
21 Prospect Street, Caversham, Reading, RG4 8JB
0118 946 2116

The Fox and Hounds - British
Station Road, Theale, Reading, RG7 4BE
0118 930 2295

Blue Cobra - Fusion
20 High Street, Theale, Reading, RG7 5AN
0118 930 4040

PizzaExpress Henley - Pizza
35 Market Place, RG9 2AA
01491 411 448

Antico Restaurant - Italian
49-51 Market Place, Henley-on-Thames, Oxfordshire, RG9 2AA
01491 573 060

Café Rouge - French
37 Hart Street, Henley, Oxfordshire, RG9 2AR
01491 411 733

STRADA Henley - Italian
49 Bell Street, Henley-On-Thames, Oxfordshire, RG9 2BG
01491 571 497

PizzaExpress Newbury - Pizza
19 Market Place, RG14 5AA
01635 569 284

STRADA Newbury - Italian
21-25 Market Place, Newbury, Berkshire, RG14 5AA
01635 569 193

The Document House - British
7-9 Wharf Street, Newbury, RG14 5AN
01635 582 000

Prezzo Newbury - Italian
58 Cheap Street, Newbury, Berkshire, RG14 5DH
01635 31957

The Crown & Garter - British
Inkpen Common, Hungerford, Berkshire, RG17 9QR
01488 668 325

The Lamb Inn Indian Restaurant & Bar - Indian
Long Lane, Curridge, Newbury, RG18 9LY
0163 520 0348

Lakeside Superbowl Newbury - International
Newbury Leisure Park Lower Way, Newbury, Berkshire, RG19 3AL
01635 874 222

The Guru - Indian
The Harrow, Newbury, Headley, RG19 8LG
01635 269 999

La Tasca Basingstoke - Spanish
Festival Square, Festival Place Shopping Centre, Basingstoke, RG21 7BB
01256 477 949

gbk Basingstoke - Antipodean
Unit R8 Lower Ground, Festival Square, Basingstoke, RG21 7BE
01256 35 4864

Café Rouge - French
20A Winchester Street, Basingstoke, Hamps, RG21 7DZ
01256 334 556

PizzaExpress Basingstoke - Pizza
The Whitehouse, RG22 6HL
01256 354 439

Bartons Mill Restaurant - British
Bartons Lane, Old Basing, Basingstoke, RG24 8AE
0125 646 6332

Café Rouge - French
30 Market Place Wokingham, Rg40 1ap
01189 799 128

Prezzo Wokingham - Italian
31 Broad Street, Wokingham, RG40 1AU
0118 978 5139

Prezzo Wokingham - Italian
Montague House, 31 Broad Street, Wokingham, RG40 1AU
0118 978 5139

PizzaExpress Wokingham - Pizza
25 Broad Street, RG40 1AU
01189 770 826

Prezzo Wokingham - Italian
Denmark Street, Wokingham, Berkshire, RG40 2LD
01189 892 090

Waterloo Hotel - British
Duke's Ride, Crowthorne near Bracknell, Berkshire, RG45 6DW
0134 446 7900

Redhill

Mela Restaurant Redhill - Indian
1 Linkfield Street, Redhill Surrey, RH1 1HQ
0173 776 6154

Prezzo Redhill - Italian
33 London Road, Redhill, Surrey, RH1 1NJ
01737 779 927

Gulaab - Indian
1 Brighton Road, Redhill, Surrey, RH1 6PW
01737 769 009

Café Rouge - French
1 Church Street, Reigate, Surrey, RH2 0AA
01737 223 700

39 Prime Restaurant - British
39 Prime, 39-41 Church Street Reigate, Surrey, RH2 0AD
01737 237 977

STRADA Reigate - Italian
12 Church Street, Reigate, Surrey, RH2 0AN
01737 240 089

La Barbe - French
71 Bell Street, Reigate, Surrey, RH2 7AN
01737 241 966

La Lanterna - Italian
73 Bell Street, Reigate, Surrey, RH2 7AN
01737 245 113

PizzaExpress Reigate - Pizza
15 High Street, RH2 9AA
01737 241 969

Café Rouge - French
170-172 High Street, Dorking, Surrey, RH4 1BG
01306 743 400

PizzaExpress Dorking - Pizza
235 High Street, RH4 1RT
01306 888 236

Cafe Rialto (Dorking) - Italian
55 South Street, Dorking, Surrey, RH4 2JX
01306 742 885

Red Chilli - Indian
Horsham Road Mid-Holmwood, Dorking, Surrey, RH5 4EH
01306 644 816

Gatwick Oriental, Oriental
Sofitel Hotel, North Terminal, RH6 0PH
01293 579 400

PizzaExpress Oxted - Pizza
153-155 Station Road East, RH8 0QE
01883 723 142

Prezzo Crawley - Italian
60 High Street, Crawley, RH10 1BT
01293 512 459

PizzaExpress Crawley - Pizza
2 The Boulevard, RH10 1XX
01293 531 678

Bella Italia - Italian
Unit 8, Crawley Leisure Park, Crawley, RH10 8LR
01293 521 974

The Gatwick Manor - International
London Road, Crawley, West Sussex, RH10 9ST
0129 386 6619

Prezzo Horsham - Italian
46 Carfax, Horsham, RH12 1EQ
01403 230 245

84 | Listings are for **ILLUSTRATIVE PURPOSES ONLY**, please visit www.tastecard.co.uk for participating restaurants and offers

PizzaExpress Horsham - Pizza 19-23 East Street, RH12 1HH	01403 249 274
STRADA Horsham - Italian 5 East Street, Horsham, RH12 1HH	01403 248 887
PizzaExpress Haywards Heath - Pizza 22 The Broadway, RH16 3AL	01444 456 627
Prezzo Haywards Heath - Italian 60 The Broadway, Haywards Heath, Sussex, RH16 3AR	01444 451 001
Café Rouge - French 33 The Broadway, Haywards Heath, W Sussex, RH16 3AS	01444 440 888
The Oak Inn - British Street Lane, Ardingly, Haywards Heath, RH17 6UA	0144 489 2244
Best Western The Birch Hotel - British Lewes Road, Haywards Heath, West Sussex, RH17 7SF	01444 451 565
PizzaExpress East Grinstead - Pizza 39 High Street, RH19 3AF	01342 313 343
Prezzo East Grinstead - Italian 13 High Street, East Grinstead, West Sussex, RH19 3AF	01342 300 211

Romford

La Tasca Romford - Spanish The Brewery Shopping Centre, Romford, Essex, RM1 1AU	01708 734 662
PizzaExpress Romford - Pizza The Brewery, RM1 1AU	01708 725 690
Outback Steakhouse Essex - American The Brewery Waterloo Road, Romford, Essex, RM1 1AU	01708 737 955
Riyadz Contemporary Indian Restaurant - Indian 96 Ardleigh Green Road, Hornchurch, Essex, RM11 2LG	0170 844 9777
Prezzo Hornchurch - Italian High Street, Hornchurch, Essex, RM11 3XT	01708 455 501
The Fig Leaf Restaurant - Mediterranean 100 South Street, Romford, Essex, RM11RX	0170 875 4411
Prezzo Upminster - Italian 53 Corbets Tey Road, Upminster, Essex, RM14 2AJ	01708 642 096
PizzaExpress Upminster - Pizza 131-133 St Mary's Lane, RM14 2SH	01708 224 111
RBG Bar & Grill@ The Park Inn Thurrock - British Park Inn Thurrock, High Road, North Stifford, RM16 5UE	01708 719 988
The Red Bar @ The Park Inn Thurrock - Fusion Park Inn Thurrock, High Road, North Stifford, RM16 5UE	01708 719 988
Bella Italia - Italian Unit 1B, The Broadwalk, Lakeside Shopping Centre, Thurrock, RM20 2ZN	01708 890 776
Café Rouge - French Unit 1A, The Broadwalk, Lakeside Shopping Centre, Thurrock, RM20 2ZN	01708 890 857
La Tasca Lakeside - Spanish Unit 6 The Boardwalk, Lakeside Shopping Centre Thurrock, Essex, RM20 2ZP	01708 890 855
PizzaExpress Lakeside - Pizza Lakeside, RM20 2ZP	01708 891 080
STRADA Lakeside - Italian The Boardwalk, Lakeside Shopping Centre, Thurrock, RM20 2ZP	01708 890 038
Old Orleans Thurrock, South American Unit 900 Lakeside Shopping Centre, West Thurrock, RM20 2ZS	0170 886 8454

Stevenage

Medusa The Steakhouse Bar Restaurant & Grill, Steak 1-3 Queensway, Stevenage, Hertfordshire, SG1 1DA	01438 360 500
Prezzo Stevenage - Italian Stevenage Leisure Park, Kings Way, Stevenage, SG1 2UA	01438 355 591
Prezzo Stevenage 128 High Street - Italian 128 High Street, Stevenage, SG1 3DB	01438 361 576
PizzaExpress Stevenage - Pizza 124-126 High Street, Stevenage, SG1 3DW	01438 361 270
Turpins Restaurant @ The Roebuck Inn - International London Road, Broadwater, Stevenage Herts , SG2 8DS	01438 365 445
STRADA Hitchin - Italian 25b-26 Sun Street, Hitchin, Hertfordshire, SG5 1AH	01462 457 746
Café Rouge - French 11 High Street, Hitchin, Herts, SG5 1BH	01462 432 962
PizzaExpress Hitchin - Pizza 19 Market Place, SG5 1DT	01462 450 596
Prezzo Hitchin - Italian 15 Bancroft, Hitchin, Herts, SG5 1JQ	01462 453 366
Doughty's Brasserie - British 87 Bancroft, Hitchin, Hertfordshire, SG5 1NQ	01462 456 363
Doughty's at GL-14 The Health Club - British Fairfield Hall Hitchin Road, Stotfold, Bedfordshire, SG5 4JJ	01462 835 525
Zeus Hotel and Restaurant - British 20 High Street, Baldock, Hertfordshire, SG7 6AX	0146 289 3620
The Cabinet at Reed - International The Cabinet, High Street Reed Near Royston, Hertfordshire , SG8 8AH	01763 848 366
Le Spice Merchant - Indian Flutes House, 14 High Street, Ware Herts, SG12 9BX	01920 468 383
Masters House Hotel - British Fore Street, Hertford, SG14 1AA	0199 266 0660
PizzaExpress Hertford - Pizza 80 Fore Street, SG14 1BY	01992 509 550
Café Rouge - French 3 Parliament Square, Hertford, Herts, SG14 1EX	01992 535 363
The Crown @ Northill - International Northill, Biggleswade, Central Bedfordshire, SG18 9AA	01767 627655

Slough

PizzaExpress Slough - Pizza 80 High Street, SL1 1EL	01753 825 893
The Temple Monkey - Indian The Upton Park Hotel, 39 Upton Park, Slough, SL1 2DA	01753 578215
Peppers Indian Cuisine - Indian 69 High Street, Burnham, Berkshire, SL1 7JX	0162 860 5511
Three Tuns - British 8 Market Street, Windsor, Berkshire, SL4 1PB	01753 861 615
Garden and Grill - Thai 8 - 9 Church Street, Windsor, SL4 1PE	01753 832 757

Listings are for **ILLUSTRATIVE PURPOSES ONLY**, please visit www.tastecard.co.uk for participating restaurants and offers | 85

South East

gbk Windsor - Antipodean 0175 385 7814
Unit 60-61 Windsor Royal Shopping Centre, Windsor, SL4 1PJ

La Tasca Windsor - Spanish 01753 852 288
Unit C10, Windsor Royal Station, Berkshire, SL4 1PJ

Café Rouge - French 01753 831 100
31-32 Royal Station Parade, Thames Street, Windsor, SL4 1PJ

PizzaExpress Windsor - Pizza 01753 856 424
7/8 Thames Street, Windsor, SL4 1PL

Bella Italia - Italian 01753 864 122
30 Thames Street, Windsor, SL4 1PR

Mango Lounge Windsor - Indian 01753 855 576
9 Datchet Road, Windsor, SL4 1QB

The Union Inn - Modern European 01753 424 702
17 Crimp Hill, Windsor, SL4 2QY

The Palmer Arms - British 01628 666 612
Village Rd Dorney, Windsor, Berkshire, SL4 6QW

PizzaExpress Sunningdale - Pizza 01344 628 277
16 London Road, SL5 0DH

Berry's Restaurant - International 01628 670 056
Taplow House Hotel Berry Hill, Maidenhead, Berkshire, SL6 0DA

Oak & Saw Village Inn - British 0162 360 4074
Rectory Road , Taplow , Berkshire, SL6 0ET

Ivory Lounge Maidenhead - Modern European 01628 784 652
Unit 2 Grenfell Island, Maidenhead, Berkshire, SL6 1DY

Asian Fusion - Asian 01628 822 140
Bath Road, Littlewick Green, Maidenhead, SL6 3QR

PizzaExpress Maidenhead - Pizza 01628 676 878
2-4 Bridge Street , SL6 8BJ

Jonathans Maidenhead - Italian 01628 780 227
9-10 Bridge Street, Maidenhead, Berkshire, SL6 8BJ

Boulters Riverside Brasserie - International 01628 621 291
Boulters Lock Island, Maidenhead, SL6 8PE

Shaah's Fine Indian Dining - Indian 01628 298 525
Lower Road , Cookham, Maidenhead, SL6 9HJ

PizzaExpress Marlow - Pizza 01628 475 333
48 High Street, SL7 1AW

Adam Simmonds at Danesfield House - British 01628 891 010
Danesfield House Hotel & Spa Henley Road, Marlow-on-Thames, SL7 2EY

Orangery Brasserie - British 01628 891 010
Danesfield House Hotel & Spa, Henley Road, Marlow-on-Thames, SL7 2EY

Pachanga Mexican Restaurant - Mexican 0162 848 6000
West Street, Marlow, Bucks, SL7 2NB

Thai Thai - Thai 01628 523 331
Heart in Hand Cores End Road, Bourne End, Buckinghamshire, SL8 5HH

Café Rouge - French 01753 880 601
25 - 27 Station Road, Gerrards Cross, SL9 8ES

Greyhound Inn - British 01753 883 404
High Street, Buckinghamshire, SL9 9RA

Sutton

Ivory Lounge - British 0208 642 4930
33 - 35 High Street, Sutton, Surrey, SM1 1DJ

PizzaExpress Sutton High Street 020 8643 4725
4 High Street, Sutton, Surrey, SM1 1HN

Tandav - Indian 0208 642 1833
260 High Street, Sutton, Surrey, SM1 1PG

The Thai Jasmine - Thai 0208 642 2666
318 High Street, Sutton, Surrey, SM1 1PR

PizzaExpress CHEAM 020 8770 0082
4-6 Ewell Road , Cheam, Surrey, SM3 8BU

Prezzo Cheam - Italian 020 8643 7490
26 Station Way, Cheam, Surrey, SM3 8SQ

Princess of India - Indian 0208 646 8222
10 Morden Court Parade, Merton, London, SM4 5HJ

PizzaExpress Wallington 020 8669 7285
40 Stafford Road, Wallington, Surrey, SM6 9AA

PizzaExpress Banstead - Pizza 01737 379 476
24 High Street, SM7 2LJ

Southampton

Tariq Manzilf - Indian 0238 023 1002 / 0238 033 5560
21A Bevios Vally Road, Southampton, Hampshire, SO14 0JD

Manzil Tandoori - Indian 02380 227 423
54 Onslow Road, Southampton, Hampshire, SO14 0JN

Bella Italia - Italian 023 8033 9215
19 Hanover Buildings, Southampton, SO14 1JX

La Margherita - Italian 0238 033 3390
1 Town Quay, Southampton Hampshire, SO14 2AQ

Prezzo Southampton - Italian 02380 226 181
25 Oxford Street, Southampton, Hants, SO14 3DJ

Ras Raj - Indian 0238 023 3433
1 Oxford Street, Southampton, SO14 3DJ

PizzaExpress Southampton - Pizza 02380 499 090
31/32 Oxford Street, SO14 3DS

Tap's William Street - Mediterranean 0238 022 8621
Shamrock Quay William Street, Northam, Southampton, SO14 5QL

Bella Italia - Italian 023 8022 7664
107 Above Bar, Southampton, SO14 7FH

Buon Gusto - Italian 02380 012 915
1 Commercial Road, Hampshire, Southampton, SO15 1GF

Bengal Brasserie - Indian 0238 023 0988
7 Bedford Place, Southampton, Hampshire, SO15 2DB

Fat Fig Greek Taverna - Greek 023 8021 2111
5 Bedford Place, Southampton, Hampshire , SO15 2DB

Chowdhury's Curry Lounge - Indian 0238 033 8833
206 Shirley Rd, Southampton, Hampshire , SO15 3FL

Chilworth Manor Hotel - International 0238 076 7333
Chilworth, **Southampton, SO16 7PT**

Five Restaurant, Eastern European 0238 058 4674
104 Portswood Rd, Southampton, Hampshire, SO17 2FW

Prezzo Winchester - Italian 01962 864 256
16 Jewery Street, Winchester, Hants, SO23 8RZ

PizzaExpress Winchester - Pizza 01962 841 845
1 Bridge Street, SO23 9BH

86 | Listings are for ILLUSTRATIVE PURPOSES ONLY, please visit www.tastecard.co.uk for participating restaurants and offers

Gourmet Pizza Winchester - Pizza 01962 842 553
21 The Square, Winchester, Hampshire, SO23 9EX

The Bush Inn - International 0196 273 2764
Ovington, Alresford, Winchester, SO24 0RE

PizzaExpress Alresford - Pizza 01962 738 758
32 Broad Street, Alresford, SO24 9AQ

Prezzo Lymington - Italian 01590 677 910
55 High Street, Lymington, Hants, SO41 9AH

Prezzo Lyndhurst - Italian 02380 282 680
The Old Pump House, 20 High Street, Hants, SO43 7BD

Fra Noi - Italian 0238 178 9966
74 High Street, Lyndhurst, Hampshire, SO43 7BJ

Prezzo Eastleigh - Italian 0238 061 0772
Unit L1A Swan Leisure Centre, Eastleigh, Hants, SO50 5FX

Prezzo Romsey - Italian 01794 517 353
21 Palmerston Street, Romsey, Hants, SO51 8GF

Southend on Sea

Paris Bistro - Modern European 01702 330 004
719 London Road, Westcliff on Sea, Essex, SS0 9ST

Bacchus - Modern European 01702 348 088
43 Alexandra Street, Southend on Sea, Essex, SS1 1BW

Le Petite Petanque - French 01702 353 208
The Bowling Green Pavilion, Cambridge Square Gardens, Southend, SS1 1EZ

PizzaExpress Southend - Pizza 01702 435 585
9 London Road, SS1 1NZ

La Tasca Southend - Spanish 0845 126 2972
Units 9 - 11, London Road, Southend, SS1 1PE

Bella Italia - Italian 01702 341 353
5-6 London Road, Southend-On-Sea, SS1 1TJ

The Camelia Hotel Restaurant - International 0170 258 7917
178 Eastern Esplanade, Southend-On-Sea, Essex, SS1 3AA

The Polash Restaurant Shoeburyness - Indian 01702 294 721
84-86 West Road, Shoeburyness, Essex, SS3 9DS

Monsoon - Indian 0170 254 5352
45 North Street, Rochford, Essex, SS4 1AB

The Shepherd and Dog - British 0170 225 8279
Ballards Gore, Stambridge, Rochford, SS4 2DA

Marco's Bar - Spanish 0126 877 3311
30 Eastwood Road, Rayleigh, Essex, SS6 7JQ

Wheelers Tandoori - Indian 01268 757 868
458 London Road, Benfleet, Essex, SS7 1AW

Maharaja - Indian 0126 879 4541
358 London Road, Benfleet, Essex, SS7 1BG

Sand Bar & Seafood Company, Seafood 0170 248 0067
71 The Broadway, Leigh on Sea, Essex, SS9 1PE

Tandoorian Nights - Indian 01702 713040 / 01702 715 917
1350 London Road, Leigh on Sea, Essex, SS9 2UH

Balti Lord - Indian 01268 763 300
48 High St, Wickford, Essex, SS12 9AT

PizzaExpress Basildon - Pizza 01268 526 622
Unit 2 Festival Leisure Park, SS14 3AD

Tonbridge

STRADA Tunbridge Wells - Italian 01892 520 007
74 - 76 Mount Pleasant Road, Tunbridge Wells, Kent, TN1 1RJ

Prezzo Tunbridge Wells - Italian 01892 547 558
84 Mount Pleasant Road, Tunbridge Wells, Kent, TN1 1RT

PizzaExpress Tunbridge Wells - Pizza 01892 543 112
81 High Street, TN1 1YG

Palio Restaurant - Italian 0189 251 5558
84-86 Grosvenor Road, Tunbridge Wells, Kent, TN1 2AS

Mooli Nepalese Cuisine - International 01892 545 499
57 - 59 Calverley Road, Tunbridge Wells, Kent, TN1 2UY

Saint John's Yard Restaurant - British 01892 619 376
66 St. Johns Road, Tunbridge Wells, Kent, TN4 9PE

Mamma Mia Tonbridge - Italian 01732 353 660
163 High Street, Tonbridge, Kent, TN9 1BX

PizzaExpress Tonbridge - Pizza 01732 368 787
91 High Street, TN9 1DR

The Kentish Rifleman - International 0173 281 0727
Silver Hill Dunks Green, Shipbourne, Tonbridge Kent, TN11 9RU

Spice Cottage - Indian 0162 287 1282
2 Bullen Lane, East Peckham, Tonbridge, TN12 5LX

Thai Square Sevenoaks- Thai 01732 462 785
22 London Road, Sevenoaks, Kent, TN13 1AJ

Café Rouge - French 01732 450 395
Unit SU27, Bligh's Meadow, Pembroke Road, Sevenoaks, TN13 1AS

No.5 Bistro Rest @The Royal Oaks Sevenoaks - Modern Euro 0173 245 1109
High Street, Sevenoaks, Kent, TN13 1HY

STRADA Sevenoaks - Italian 01732 461 706
3c Dorset Street, Sevenoaks, Kent, TN13 1LL

PizzaExpress Sevenoaks - Pizza 01732 741 111
146/148 High Street, TN13 1XE

Donnington Manor Hotel - British 01732 462 681
London Road, Dunton Green Sevenoaks, Kent, TN13 2TD

PizzaExpress Uckfield - Pizza 01825 763 333
77 High Street, TN22 1AP

PizzaExpress Ashford - Pizza 01233 637 700
14 North Street, TN24 8JR

Prezzo Tenterden - Italian 01580 764 769
52 High Street, Tenterden, Kent, TN30 6AU

Café Rouge - French 01580 763 029
43 High Street, Tenterden, Kent, TN30 6BJ

The Black Pearl - International 0142 471 9919
9 George Street, Hastings, East Sussex, TN34 3EG

Harris Restaurant and Tapas Bar - Spanish 01424 437 221
58 High Street, Hastings, East Sussex, TN34 3EN

Gurkha Chef - Indian 01424 444 440
20 Grand Parade, St. Leonards-On-Sea, East Sussex, TN37 6DN

Listings are for ILLUSTRATIVE PURPOSES ONLY, please visit www.tastecard.co.uk for participating restaurants and offers

Twickenham

The Crown Bar and Kitchen - British 0208 892 5896
174 Richmond Road Twickenham, Middlesex, TW1 2NH

PizzaExpress Twickenham - Pizza 020 8891 4126
21 York Street, Twickenham, TW1 3JZ

Grand Union Bar and Grill Twickenham - American 020 8892 2925
11, London Road, Twickenham, TW1 3SX

Pallavi Restaurant - Indian 020 8892 2345
Unit 3 Cross Deep Court, Health Road, Twickenham, TW1 4OJ

Annapurna Restaurant - Indian 0208 893 9966
231 Powder Mill Lane, Whitton, Twickenham, TW2 6EH

Twentynine Bar and Restaurant - Modern European 020 8572 3131
The Continental Hotel, 29-31 Lampton Road, Hounslow Middlesex, TW3 1JA

Mantra - Indian 0203 572 6000
253 Bath Road, Hounslow, London, TW3 3DA

Cinnamon Lounge - Indian 020 8560 8995
181 Twickenham Road, Isleworth, Middlesex, TW7 6AB

The Old Fire Station - Fusion 0208 568 5999
55 High Street, Brentford, Middlesex, TW8 0AH

San Marco Authentic Italian Cuisine - Italian 0208 758 2777
5 Ferry Lane, Ferry Quays, Middlesex, TW8 0AT

The Island Restaurant and Bar High Street - International 0208 232 2000
Holiday Inn Brentford Lock , High Street, Brentford, TW8 8JZ

PizzaExpress Richmond - Pizza 020 8948 7460
Lion House, Richmond, TW9 1RE

STRADA Richmond - Italian 020 8940 3141
26 Hill Street, Richmond, TW9 1TW

Thai Square Richmond- Thai 0208 940 5253
29 Kew Road, Richmond Upon Thames, Surrey, TW9 2NQ

Cirrik Richmond - Turkish 0208 940 0033
94 Kew Road, Richmond, London, TW9 2PQ

Origin Asia - Indian 0208 948 0509
100 Kew Road Richmond, Surrey, London, TW9 2PQ

The Botanist Pub and Dining 0208 948 4838
3-5 Kew Green, Richmond, Surrey, TW9 3AA

Palmyra Lebanese Restaurant, Lebanese 0208 948 7019
277 Sandycombe Road, Richmond, TW9 3LU

PizzaExpress Kew - Pizza 020 8404 6000
10 Station Approach, Richmond upon Thames, TW9 3QB

gbk Richmond - Antipodean 0208 940 5440
15-17 Hill Rise, Richmond, Surrey, TW10 6UQ

PizzaExpress Teddington - Pizza 020 8943 3553
11 Waldegrave Road, Teddington, TW11 8LA

Peppers Finest Indian Cuisine - Curry 01784 420 131
18 Woodthorpe Road, Middlesex, TW15 2RY

Prezzo Shepperton - Italian 01932 269 006
109-113 High Street, Shepperton, TW17 9BL

PizzaExpress Staines - Pizza 01784 456 522
12 Clarence Street, Staines, Middlesex, TW18 4SP

Spice Lounge - Bangladeshi 01784 483 578
271 Staines Road, Wraysbury, Staines, TW19 5AJ

The Perseverance - British 0178 448 2375
2 High Street, Wraysbury, Staines, TW19 5DB

Red Rose - Indian 01784 434 303
87 High Street, Egham, Surrey, TW20 9HF

Southall

Henleys Bar & Restaurant - British 0208 759 6311
140 Bath Road, Hayes, Middlesex, UB3 5AW

Polo Bar 0208 759 6311
140 Bath Road, Hayes, Middlesex, UB3 5AW

Brasserie - British 0208 759 6311
140 Bath Road , Hayes, Middlesex, UB3 5AW

Sundarban Tandoori - Bangladeshi 020 8902 4706
3 Sudbury Heights Avenue, Greenford, UB6 0NA

Wings Restaurant @ Holiday Inn London Heathrow - International 0208 9904
509, Corner of Bath Road, Sipson Way, West Drayton, UB7 0DP

Best Sellers Bar @ Heathrow Thistle 0871 376 9021
Bath Road, Longford, West Drayton, UB7 0EQ

First Edition Restaurant @ Heathrow Thistle - International 0871 376 9021
Bath Road, Longford , West Drayton, UB7 0EQ

Oak & Avocado Lounge @ Heathrow Thistle - International 0871 376 9021
Bath Road, Longford, West Drayton, UB7 0EQ

Konkan - Indian 01895 420 973
107 Station Road, West Drayton, London, UB7 7LT

Auberge Uxbridge - French 0189 527 0111
223 High Street, Uxbridge, UB8 1LD

PizzaExpress Uxbridge - Pizza 01895 251 222
222 High Street, Uxbridge, UB8 1LD

Tiger Cubs - Indian 01895 239 503
74 Oxford Road, New Denham, Uxbridge, UB9 4DN

Watford

Villa Romana - Italian 01923 779 492
92 High St, Rickmansworth, Hertfordshire, WD3 1AQ

Rose and Crown - British 01923 897 680
Woodcock Hill, Harefield Road, Rickmansworth, WD3 1PP

Oscars Pizza Company - Pizza 01923 263 800
21 High Street, Kings Langley, WD4 8AB

PizzaExpress Radlett - Pizza 01923 859 111
114 Watling Street, WD7 7AB

Prezzo Radlett - Italian 01923 853 566
82 Watling Street, Radlett, Herts, WD7 7AB

Lagar - Mediterranean 01923 855 168
281 Watling Street, Radlett, Herts, WD7 7LA

Bellissimo Restaurant & Pizzeria - Italian 01923 232 223
106 The Parade, Watford High Street, WD17 1AW

La Tasca Watford - Spanish 01923 223 545
63, The Parade, Watford, WD17 1LJ

Cafe Mezza , Lebanese 01923 211 500
144 High Street, Watford, Herts, WD17 2EN

PizzaExpress Watford - Pizza
137 High Street, Watford, WD17 2ER
01923 213 991

Prince of Bengal - Bangladeshi
51 Langley Way, Watford, WD17 3EA
01923 253 538

The RBG Bar @The Park Inn Watford - International
30-40 St Albans Road, Watford, Hertfordshire, WD171RN
0192 342 9988

The RBG Bar and Grill @ The Park Inn Watford - International
30-40 St Albans Road, Watford, Hertfordshire, WD171RN
0192 342 9988

Il Carnevale Restaurant - Italian
195 St. Albans Road, Watford, Hertfordshire, WD24 5BH
01923 247 750

TopGolf Watford - American
Bushey Mill Lane, Watford, Herts, WD24 7AB
01923 222 045

South West

South West

Asia Chic
Asian — **01752 263 758**

Address: East Quay House, Sutton Harbour, Plymouth, Devon, PL4 0HX

The Asia Chic concept is exotic Asian cuisine, Chinese dim sum, wok and barbeque Japanese sushi, all tapas style to be shared and enjoyed in a stylish setting.

With a restaurant interior that features a state-of-the-art open kitchen where diners can watch their food being artfully prepared by a group of talented professional chefs, we think that it is safe to say that this restaurant truly exceeds all trendy sophistications.

The combination of superior produce, luxurious surrounding and friendly service ensures a unique experience of refined taste and unforgettable dining.

The Olive Tree Restaurant
British — 01392 272 709

The Queens Court Hotel, Bystock Terrace,
Exeter, EX4 4HY

The award winning Olive Tree Restaurant, Exeter is a highly regarded boutique restaurant. Chef Knockton and his team carefully craft British Cuisine dishes with a designer twist. This restaurant has won an AA Rosette, and if you visit you will experience a night to remember; however, the food is surprisingly affordable and the atmosphere relaxed. Chef Knockton serves affordable nosh that is very, very posh.

Chef Knockton uses electrically fragrant herbs and spices to massage locally reared meats and wild game; his fish dishes are freshly caught and perfectly cooked, tasting of another exotic underwater world; he drenches his deserts in sexy sauces and adorns them with twisted caramel sculptures. Chef Knockton is dedicated to using local ingredients from his trusted suppliers and believes in creating everything from scratch... The menu changes with the seasons and is complimented by a varied and select wine list. Be prepared for an evening of total indulgence such as a complimentary free shot of frosted chocolate vodka, served on a black slate before desert.

The decor is boutique chic – you will bathe in soft lighting from a glittering modern chandelier above, whilst drowning in flickering candles. You can marvel at genuine Venetian masks hanging on the walls, or a glowing glass menagerie of olive oil bottles in their crystal cabinet.

Chef Knockton marries British cuisine with European ingenuity resulting in a sensational partnership of flavours. Seared fillet of wild sea bass waits in its wrapping of sassy saffron potato on a bed of caviar; Mediterranean vegetables soak in vine tomato tea and perfectly compliment the roast tenderloin belly, which is under a duvet of blossom Honey; slowly braised pork cheek is kissed by Haricot bean puree, vibrant beetroot and pickled Shitake. All finished with a hug from the signature crème brulee or Pineapple tart tatin.

Colleagues, friends, and lovers flock here to be pampered by the friendly and attentive staff; if you join them you won't be disappointed.

South West

South West

Soushi
Japanese — **01285 641414**

The Old Post Office, 12 Castle Street, Cirencester, GL7 1QA

Soushi is located in the heart of Cirencester, just minutes from the historic market place, in the new Old Post Office development. Their small and intimate interior help to create a unique dining experience, with al fresco dining available during the summer months.

Opened in November 2009, Soushi has been bringing a real taste of authentic Japanese cuisine to the Cotswolds. Their small, carefully considered menu offers a variety of hot and cold Japanese cuisine to suit all tastes.

Soushi's lunch menu offers a healthy option for those looking for a quick turnaround, whilst the evening menu gives the opportunity to enjoy a more extensive menu for those with discerning tastes.

For those who find the prospect of Japanese food rather daunting, all the staff have a comprehensive knowledge of the menu to assist you with your choices.

Bath

Café Rouge - French 01225 462368,
15 Milsom Street, Bath, BA1 1DE

STRADA - Italian 01225 337 753
Beau Nash House, Sawclose, Bath, BA1 1EU

PizzaExpress - Pizza 01225 420 119
1-3 Barton Street, BA1 1HQ

The Slug and Lettuce - International 01225 789 050
5/6 Edgar Buildings, George Street, Bath, BA1 2EE

Bombay Nights Restaurant - Indian 01225 460400
Lower Bristol Road, Bath, BA2 3EB

The George Inn - British 01373 834 224
Norton St Philip, Bath, BA2 7LH

The Red Lion at Woolverton - British 0137 383 0350
Bath Road Woolverton, Nr Bath, Somerset, BA2 7QS

Prezzo Yeovil - Italian 01935 426 38
Old Sarum House, Yeovil, BA20 1EG

Bournemouth

Bella Italia - Italian 01202 296993
84 Old Christchurch Road, Bournemouth, BH1 1LR

PizzaExpress Bournemouth - Pizza 01202 316639
192 Old Christchurch Road, BH1 1PD

Prezzo Bournemouth - Italian 01202 556399
58 Westover Road, Bournemouth, Dorset, BH1 2BZ

Indian Lounge - Indian 0120 229 3355
148 Old Christchurch Road, Bournemouth, Dorset, BH1 1NL

Prezzo - Wimborne - Italian 01202 881119
5 West Borough, Wimborne, BH2 1LT

Jongleurs Comedy Club Bournemouth - International 0870 0111 960
The Waterfront Complex, Pier Approach, Bournemouth, BH2 5AA

Hardy's Restaurant @ The Hermitage Hotel - International 0120 255 7363
Exeter Road, Bournemouth, BH2 5AH

Indian Ocean - Indian 0120 231 1222
4 West Cliffe Road, Bournemouth, Dorset, BH2 5EY

La Tasca Bournemouth - Spanish 0845 126 2960
23-27 Bourne Avenue, Bournemouth, Dorset, BH2 6DT

Café Rouge - French 01202 757472
67-71a Seamoor Rd, Westbourne, Bournemouth, BH4 9AE

PizzaExpress Westbourne - Pizza 01202 761 765
109 Poole Road, Bournemouth, BH4 9BB

Retro - Lebanese 0120 231 5865
79-81 Charminster Rd, Bournemouth, BH8 8UE

Nippon Inn - Asian 0120 225 8859
124 Charminster Road, Bournemouth, Dorset, BH8 8UT

Bangkok Palace - Thai 0120 252 8882
313 Charminster Road, Bournemouth, BH8 9QP

The Slug and Lettuce Poole - International 0120 267 0520
35 - 37 High Street, Poole, BH15 1AB

PizzaExpress Poole - Pizza 01202 671923
30 High Street, BH15 1BP

Caesar's Bistro - International 01202 694 343
15 Dunyeats Road, Broadstone Poole, Dorset, BH18 8AA

Prezzo Christchurch - Italian 01202 496100
3 Bridge Street, Christchurch, Dorset, BH23 1DY

Waterford Lodge Hotel - International 0142 528 2100
87 Bure Lane, Friars Cliff, Christchurch, BH23 4DN

Cliffhanger Cafe - International 0142 527 8058
Waterford Road, Highcliffe, Christchurch, BH23 5JA

Avon Causeway Hotel - British 0120 248 2714
Hurn, Christchurch, BH23 6AS

Plummer's Bistro and Cafe - International 0142 547 4563
35 High Street, Ringwood, BH24 1AD

Prezzo Ringwood - Italian 01425 471200
27 Market Place, Ringwood, Hants, BH24 1AN

Bristol

Spice of India - International 0117 929 9222
13 Small Street, Bristol, Avon, BS1 1DE

Teppan - Oriental 0117 929 3516
13a Small St, Bristol, BS1 1DE

bSb Corn Street - British 0117 911 4950
41 Corn Street, Bristol, BS1 1HT

PizzaExpress Bristol Corn Street - Pizza 0117 9300239
35 Corn Street, BS1 1HT

Marco's Ristorante - Italian 0117 926 4869
59 Baldwin Street, Bristol, Avon, BS1 1QZ

Bella Italia - Italian 01179 293278
8-10 Baldwin Street, Bristol, BS1 1SA

Old India Avant Garde Indian Cuisine - Indian 0117 922 1136
34 Saint Nicolas Street, Bristol, BS1 1TG

Marlows Bar @ The Grand Bristol - International 0871 376 9042
Broad Street, Bristol, BS1 2EL

Tyrells Restaurant at The Grand Bristol - International 0871 376 9042
Broad Street, Bristol, BS1 2EL

The Lanes - American 0117 325 1980
22 Nelson Street, Bristol, BS1 2LE

Café Rouge - French 01179 544808
Unit SU51A, GU/MZ Block 2, Cabot Circus, Bristol, BS1 3BD

gbk Bristol - Antipodean 011 7927 9997
Unit SU71 Glass Walk, Cabot Circus Broadmead, Bristol, BS1 3BQ

Bella Italia - Italian 01179 277 230
Unit SU79, Cabot Circus, Bristol, Avon, BS1 3BX

Filini @ The Radisson Blu Bristol - Italian 0117 934 9500
Broad Quay, Bristol, Avon, BS1 4BY

Thai Edge Bristol - Thai 0117 927 6088
Unit 4 Broad Quay, South Block, Bristol, BS1 4DA

Zerodegrees Bristol - British 0117 925 2706
53 Colston Street, Bristol, BS1 5BA

Bombay Boulevard - Curry 0117 927 3544
4 Denmark Street, Bristol, BS1 5DQ

Listings are for ILLUSTRATIVE PURPOSES ONLY, please visit www.tastecard.co.uk for participating restaurants and offers

South West

Ciao - Italian 5 Denmark Street, Bristol, Avon, BS1 5DQ	0117 927 9516	
Antix - International 44 Park Street, Bristol, BS1 5JG	01173 705340	
Yum Yum Thai Restaurant Bristol - Thai 50 Park Street, Bristol, BS1 5JN	0117 929 0987	
gbk Bristol - Antipodean 74 Park Street, Bristol, BS1 5JX	011 7316 9162	
Dragon Grill Chinese Buffet - Chinese 1-2 Frogmore St, Bristol, Avon, BS1 5NA	0117 929 3288	
Café Rouge - French 85 Park Street, Bristol, BS1 5PJ	01179 292571	
PizzaExpress Bristol Harbourside - Pizza Unit 1 Building 8 Harbourside, BS1 5TY	0117 927 3622	
Zen Restaurant - Chinese Explore Lane, Bristol, BS1 5TY	0117 920 9370	
bSb The Waterside - British Canons Road, Bristol, BS1 5UH	0117 911 4950	
Tikka Flame - Indian South Building, Anchor Square, Canons Road Bristol, BS1 5UH	0117 316 9393	
City Cafe @ City Inn Bristol - Modern European Bristol Temple Way, Bristol, BS1 6BF	0117 925 1001	
Lounge Bar @ City Inn Bristol - International Temple Way, Bristol, BS1 6BF	0117 925 1001	
Elements Restaurant @ Novotel Bristol - International Victoria Street, Bristol, BS1 6HY	0117 976 9988	
The Punch Bowl - British 23 Old Market Street, Bristol, BS2 0HB	0117 930 4967	
Rustic Vine - British 157-159 ST Michaels Hill, Bristol, BS2 8DB	0117 973 5937	
Biblos - Lebanese 82 Mina Road, Bristol, BS2 9XW	0117 955 8887	
The Bay Bar & Kitchen - British 4-6 North Street Bedminster, Bristol, Avon, BS3 1HT	0117 953 1446	
Caffe Sazz - Turkish 232 North Street, Bedminster, Bristol, BS3 1JD	0117 963 3334	
Il Grano Italian Restaurant - Italian 149 East St, Bedminster, Avon, BS3 4EJ	0117 963 3544	
Ganesha Authentic Indian Cuisine - Indian 54-56 Bedminster Parade, Bristol, BS3 4HS	0117 953 3990	
Assilah Bistro - Mediterranean 194-196 Wells Road, Bristol, BS4 2AX	0781 620 2827	
Chef Chaouen - North African 2 High Street Easton, Bristol, Avon, BS5 6DL	0117 329 4226	
Kashmir Cuisine Restaurant - Indian 15 High Street, Easton, Bristol Avon, BS5 6DL	0117 952 0004	
Inner Fire - Curry 367 Fishponds Road, Eastville, Bristol, BS5 6RD	0117 965 7999	
The Burger Joint - American 32 Cotham Hill, Bristol Avon, BS6 6LA	0117 329 0887	
PizzaExpress Bristol Bekerley Square - Pizza 31 Berkeley Square, BS8 1HP	01179 260 300	
Krishna's Inn - Indian 4 Byron Place, Triangle South Clifton, Bristol, BS8 1JT	0117 927 6864	
Orchid Restaurant - Oriental 81 Whiteladies Rd, Bristol Avon, BS8 2NT	0117 973 2198	
bSb Whiteladies - British 93-95 Whiteladies Road, Bristol, BS8 2NT	0117 973 3989	
Papajis - British 109 Whiteladies Road, Bristol, BS8 2PB	0117 946 6144	
The Hop House - British 16 Kings Road Clifton, Bristol, BS8 4AB	0117 923 7390	
STRADA Bristol - Italian 34 Princess Victoria Street, Clifton, Bristol, BS8 4BZ	0117 923 7224	
PizzaExpress Bristol Regent Street - Pizza 2 Regent Street, BS8 4HG	01179 744 259	
Mumtaz Restaurant - Indian 61 High Street, West-On-Trym, Bristol, BS9 3ED	0117 950 3084	
Bella Italia - Italian Venue Leisure Complex, Cribbs Causeway, Merlins Road, Bristol, BS10 7SR	0117 9590982	
Balti Raj - Indian 98 Gloucester Road, Avonmouth, Bristol, BS11 9AQ	0117 982 9080	
Eastern Spice - Curry Two Mile Hill Road, Bristol, BS15 1AX	0117 935 2335, 269	
The Chequers Inn - British Ferry Road, Hanham Mills, Bristol, BS15 3NU	0117 967 4242	
Bollywood Spice - Indian 46 High Street, Warmley, Bristol, BS15 4NF	0117 967 9299	
Marhaba Bistro - African 611 Fishponds Road, Bristol, Avon, BS16 6AA	0117 965 0752	
The Griffin - British 107 London Road, Warmley, Bristol, BS30 5JN	0117 967 3385	
Café Rouge - French Unit R4, Upper Level, The Mall, The Avenue, BS34 5UR	1179508730	
The Badminton Arms - British Badminton Road, Coalpit Heath, Bristol, BS36 2QJ	01454 772 132	
The Waldegrave Arms - British Church Lane, East Harptree, Bristol, Avon, BS40 6BD	01761 221429	

Dorchester

Prezzo Dorchester - Italian 6 High West Street, Dorchester, Dorset, DT1 1UJ	01305 259678	
Chillies - Indian 10 Queen Street, Weymouth, Dorset, DT4 7HZ	01305 766 602	
Prezzo Weymouth - Italian 56 St Thomas Street, Weymouth, Dorset, DT4 8EQ	01305 787600	
Bella Italia - Italian 104 St Mary Street, Weymouth, DT4 8NY	01305 778424	
Prezzo Blandford - Italian 43 East Street, Blandford Forum, Dorset, DT11 7DX	01258 489625	

Exeter

PizzaExpress Exeter - Pizza 2 Broadgate, EX1 1HF	01392 495 788	

96 | Listings are for ILLUSTRATIVE PURPOSES ONLY, please visit www.tastecard.co.uk for participating restaurants and offers

Al-Farid 01392 494 444
3 Cathedral Yard, Exeter, Devon, EX1 1HJ

Café Rouge - French 01392 251042
Unit MSU5, 24 Bedford Street, Princesshay, Exeter, EX1 1LL

STRADA Exeter - Italian 01392 432 727
Princesshay Square, Bedford Street, Exeter, EX1 1NU

Oriental City - Chinese 0139 246 7000
1 Station Road, Pinhoe, Exeter, Devon, EX1 3SA

Prezzo Exeter - Italian 01392 477739
202 High Street, Exeter, Devon, EX4 3EB

Red Rose - Indian 0139 242 7670
13-14, North St, Exeter, EX4 3QS

Bella Italia - Italian 01392 211778
92 Queen Street, Exeter, Devon, EX4 3RP

The Olive Tree Restaurant - British 01392 272 709
The Queens Court Hotel, Bystock Terrace, Exeter, EX4 4HY

Thai Shanghai - Chinese 0139 243 1010
Cowley Bridge Road, Exeter, EX4 5BX

Exeter City FC 0139 241 3954
Exeter City Football Club, St. James' Park, Stadium Way, Exeter, EX4 6PX

The Anchor Inn - Seafood 01626 890 203
Cockwood, Exeter, EX6 8RA

The Witches Bowl - British 01626 863641
11 Queen St, Dawlish, Devon, EX7 9HB

Prezzo Exmouth - Italian 01395 269409
38-39 The Strand, Exmouth, Devon, EX8 1AH

The Bamboo Restaurant - Chinese 0139 526 7253,
31 The Strand, Exmouth, Devon, EX8 1AQ

La Rosetta - Italian 0139 556 8136
Newton Poppleford, Sidmouth, Devon, EX10 0DW

Popadom Indian Cuisine - Indian 01404 811 479
46 Mill Street, Ottery St Mary, Devon, EX11 1AD

Golden Lion - Chinese 01884 33685
72 Exeter Rd, Cullompton, Devon, EX15 1DZ

Blackberries - British 01398 331 842
19 Fore Street, Bampton, Tiverton, EX16 9ND

Zena's Restaurant - Caribbean 0127 137 8844
1 Market Street, Barnstaple, EX31 1BX

Prezzo Barnstaple - Italian 01271 376310
96 High Street, Barnstaple, Devon, EX31 1HS

PizzaExpress Barnstaple - Pizza 01271 378 553
80 High Street, EX31 1HX

Tyme Restaurant @ Trimstone Country Manor Hotel - British 0127 186 2841
Trimstone Near Woolacombe, North Devon, EX34 8NR

Beaver Inn - British 0123 747 4822
Irsha Street, Appledore, Devon, EX39 1RY

Gloucester

Sebz - Mediterranean 01452 310599
93 Northgate Street, Gloucester, Gloucestershire, GL1 2AA

Dino's Village Taverna - Greek 0145 222 5350
1 St. Catherine St, Gloucester, Gloucestershire, GL1 2BS

Prezzo Gloucester - Italian 01452 414022
46 Southgate Street, Gloucester, GL1 2DR

Shahi Balti - Indian 0145 238 5386
72 Westgate Street, Gloucestershire, GL1 2NZ

Connoisseur Tandoori - Indian 01452 304003
22 London Road, Cheltenham, Gloucestershire, GL1 3NR

Baburchi Cuisine - Asian 0145 230 0615
42 Bristol Road, Gloucester, GL1 5SD

Saffron Restaurant - Indian 0145 241 1102
72 Bristol Road, Gloucester, GL1 5SD

PizzaExpress Gloucester Quays - Pizza 01452 504 605
Gloucester Quays, GL1 5SH

The Fox & Elm - British 0145 241 7278
383 Stroud Road, Tuffley, GL4 0DA

Sorrento Restaurant and Pizzeria - Pizza 0145 376 6632
Russell Street, Stroud, GL5 3AJ

Alfreda's - Mediterranean 0145 383 9251
Market Street, Nailsworth, Stroud, GL6 0HL

Soushi - Japanese 01285 641414
The Old Post Office, 12 Castle Street, Cirencester, GL7 1QA

Piazza Fontana - Italian 0128 564 3133
30a Castle Street, Cirencester, Gloucestershire, GL7 1QH

PizzaExpress Cirencester - Pizza 01285 655655
28 Castle Street, GL7 1QH

The Eight Bells - British 0128 571 2369
East End, Fairford, Gloucestershire, GL7 4AP

The Bathurst Arms - International 0128 583 1281
North Cerney, Gloucestershire, GL7 7BZ

NUMBER SIXTY FIVE - British 0166 650 3346
65 Long Street, Tetbury, GL8 8AA

Snooty Fox 0166 650 2436
Market Place, Tetbury, Gloucestershire, GL8 8DD

Curry Leaf Indian Restaurant - Indian 01594 826800
37-39 High Street, Cinderford, Gloucestershire, GL14 2SL

The Angel Hotel - British 01594 833113
The Angel Hotel, Market Place, Coleford, GL16 8AE

River Spice Restaurant @ The Forge Hammer - Indian 0159 486 0310
The Forge Hammer, Forge Row, Lower Lydbrook, GL17 9NP

Owens Restaurant - British 01684 292703
73 Church Street, Tewkesbury, Gloucestershire, GL20 5RX

The Boat House - International 0168 427 5714
Mythe Road, King Johns Island, GL20 6EB

The Restoration - British 0124 252 2792
55-57 High Street, Cheltenham, GL50 1DX

Marinades Caribbean Restaurant Bar and Grill - Caribbean 0124 257 8811
56 High Street, Cheltenham, Glos, GL50 1EE

Bella Italia - Italian 01242 584 341
70-72 High Street, Cheltenham, GL50 1EG

La Tasca Cheltenham - Spanish 01242 220775
70 Regents Street, Cheltenham, Gloucestershire, GL50 1HW

Svea Café & Restaurant - Modern European 01242 238 134
24 Rodney Road, Cheltenham, GL50 1JJ

Bella Italia - Italian 01242 577417
23 The Promenade, Cheltenham, GL50 1LE

Central

Central

Fire & Ice
Modern European — 0115 981 9000

40 Bridgford Road, West Bridgford,
Nottingham, NG2 6AP

Fire&Ice is a family run establishment, open since 2006 delivering fresh local produce and perfectly served drinks seven days a week. The restaurant serves modern European cuisine with a menu to tantalise the tastebuds.

At Fire&Ice they believe in endeavouring to source their ingredients locally to ensure quality and freshness are guaranteed throughout the menu. The current menu samples a fusion of tastes, with influences stretching worldwide.

They can cater for the largest of appetites with mouth-watering steaks cooked to perfection on the grill and satisfying homely desserts, to those just wanting a small bite to eat in the shape of a selection of anti pasta, including a choice of four Italian breads that are served hot from the oven and the option of a range of fresh cheeses, cured meats or an array of baked and marinated vegetables.

The whole menu aims to give a tempting choice of the highest quality and freshness, with all food being prepared on the premises. Old favourites like lasagne remain and enticing new dishes such as confit of crispy duck with roasted pumpkin, sprouting broccoli on a plum puree and beetroot glaze.

Shimla Pinks
Indian — 0121 633 0366

Fiveways Leisure Centre, Broad Street, Birmingham, B15 1AY

With an extensive menu, warm, lively atmosphere and superb decor Shimla Pinks provides the ideal venue for a fun night out for Indian food lovers. It's easy to find a dish to suit your mood, as the venue offers a wide and varied menu featuring traditional favourites as well as lesser known specialities and North Indian Tandoori dishes.

The venue's signature dish is Koh-e-avadh, a traditional lamb dish rich in taste and very popular with Shimla Pink regulars and diners passionate about Indian food.

Central

Bangla Lounge
Indian — 0145 561 5111

91 Trinity Lane, Hinckley, Leicestershire, LE10 0BJ

The philosophy at Bangla Lounge, is to make your visit an enjoyable experience.

The design and decor have been put together by their concept creators Siraj and Salim to give a rich and warm welcome feel with eastern hospitality. Their staff are friendly, cheerful and attentive and it is their aim to ensure that your visit will make a lasting impression, ensuring that you come back for more.

The menu has been put together by their exclusive chef, Abdul Haque, a renowned culinary specialist in the Midlands. He has extensive culinary knowledge in different cuisines ranging from Indian, Oriental, Thai, Arabian, Singaporian, Pakistani and Bangladeshi.

Bangla Lounge have modernised Indian cuisine. They have taken it to the next level whilst keeping its authentic flavours, approaching them in a contemporary fusion manner, and using different ideas from around the world and adding them to their incredible curry dishes.

Bangla Lounge provides a unique and enjoyable experience with distinction, home style cooking with a grand approach.

Sage Restaurant at Donington Manor Hotel

International — 0133 281 0253

High Street, Castle Donington, nr Derby, DE74 2PP

Donington Manor Hotel in Castle Donington may date from the 18th century, but behind the impressive frontage to the building you will find a very chic and modern attitude towards comfort, relaxation and personalised service.

Sage restaurant, Leicestershire is an AA Rosette awarded restaurant at Donington Manor Hotel.

This beautiful restaurant retains many of the original features characteristic of a Grade II listed building, such as dramatic curved sash windows, ornate cornicing and stunning chandeliers.

These combine perfectly with a backdrop of opulent decor to create an elegant and stylish dining room, while staff offer the warmest welcome for miles around.

Sage Head Chef, Jeff Cadden, and his team love to work with fresh, seasonal ingredients wherever possible and Jeff comes up with some great taste combinations and varied menus.

Dishes are stunningly presented and are complemented by a fine selection of wines to enhance the dining experience.

All menus vary daily to make the most of seasonal produce and meals are both wholesome and refined.

The Mill Restaurant, Mediterranean — 0178 581 8456
Mill Street, Stone, Staffordshire, ST15 8BA

Malabar Stafford - Indian — 01785 227 500 / 01785 227 600
1 -2 Water Street, Stafford, ST16 2AG

Odysseus Greek Restaurant - Greek — 0178 521 3358
1 Doxey Rd, Stafford, ST16 2EW

Bella Italia - Italian — 01785 211 968
20 Greengate Street, Stafford, ST16 2HS

PizzaExpress Stafford - Pizza — 01785 256276
3 Market Square, ST16 2JH

Karma II - Indian — 0178 560 3222
14 Bailey Street, Stafford, ST17 4BG

Bistro Le Coq - French — 0188 922 3255
Station Road, Stowe By Chartley, Stafford, ST18 0LF

Spice Bazaar - Indian — 0178 528 2280
Seighford, Stafford, ST18 9PQ

The Mess Restaurant - Modern European — 01902 851 694
3 Market Place, Stafford, ST19 9BS

Daruchini - Bangladeshi — 01785 851978
1 Stafford St, Eccleshall, Stafford, ST21 6BL

The George Inn - British — 01785 850 300
Castle Street, Eccleshall, Stafford, ST21 6DF

Worcester

Bombay Palace - Indian — 0190 561 3969
38 The Tything, Worcester, Herefordshire, WR1 1JL

PizzaExpress Worcester - Pizza — 01905 726 565
1/3 College Street Cathedral Plaza, WR1 2LU

Café Rouge - French — 01905 613055
5 Friar Street, Worcester, WR1 2LZ

Farthings Restaurant @ The Bank House Hotel - British — 01886 833551
Bank House Hotel, Bransford near Worcester, Worcestershire, WR6 5JD

Rilys Evesham - Indian — 01386 42589
2/3 Waterside Evesham, Worcestershire, WR11 1BS

Brasserie @ The Childswickham Inn - International — 0138 685 2461
Broadway Road, Childswickham, Worcestershire, WR12 7HP

Wolverhampton

The Standard - Indian — 0871 717 9132
27 Cleveland Street, Wolverhampton, West Midlands, WV1 3HT

Spiceland - Indian — 01902 425 444
58 Tettenhall Road, Wolverhampton, WV1 4SL

Cafe Rickshaw - Indian — 01902 425353
20 Chapel Ash, Wolverhampton, WV3 0TN

Regency Restaurant at The Ely House Hotel - British — 0190 231 1311
The Ely House Hotel, Wolverhampton, West Midlands, WV3 9NB

Malabar - Wolverhampton - Indian — 0190 233 2080
315, Penn Rd, Wolverhampton, WV4 5QF

The Cowshed Restaurant - International — 0190 270 1888
Clive Farm, Pattngham, Wolverhampton, WV6 7EN

Alex's Restaurant, Mediterranean — 0190 275 9274
5A Bridgnorth Road, Compton, Wolverhampton, WV6 8AB

The Rajput Bar and Restaurant Wolverhampton - Indian — 01902 844 642
The Square, Codsall, WV8 1PT

"Nick Hard Design have been producing our directory for 5 years now, bringing an innovative and fresh design which combines well with our strong branding"

Matt Turner - tastecard Director

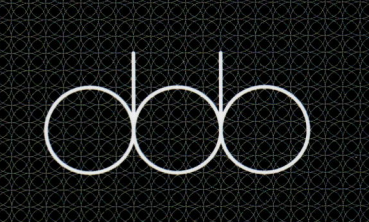

Wales

Traeth
Seafood — 0154 556 1844

South John Street, New Quay, Dyfed, SA45 9NP

Traeth Bar & Grill in New Quay, West Wales is now open daily for breakfast through dinner and everything in between.

The relaxed atmosphere welcomes you for casual all day dining and drinking, either inside or out on their balcony overlooking the harbour. The staff would love you to drop by with friends, family or alone on a whim to enjoy their company and the spectacular view of Cardigan Bay.

On offer at Traeth is hearty or light breakfasts, brunch and bistro style lunches. In the evening things move up a notch with a daily changing dinner menu featuring wonderfully cooked, amazingly fresh and locally sourced honest food.

The bar area is the perfect place to unwind with a coffee and homemade cake, browse the papers, enjoy a glass of wine from our extensive list, or make use of the free wifi.

The approach they take is upbeat yet stylish in its simplicity, combine that with an excellent can do service and we think you'll like it.

Cardamom Indian Rest
Indian — 02920 233506

442c Cowbridge Road East, Victoria Park,
Cardiff, CF5 1JN

The Cardamom was established in July 2003. Since it's opening, the restaurant has become very popular. The Cardamom went on to win the South Wales Echo; Indian restaurant of the year Award, shortly followed by The British Curry Awards Top 100: Best Indian Restaurant in the U.K. It also featured in The Top 10 Welsh Curry Houses of The Year Awards and has previously been recommended by The Guardian Newspaper.

The restaurant's success lies in the strength of the food and service. A very talented young chef, Askir Miah works at the helm of The Cardomom. The knowledge that Askir brings from his experience with some of the top Indian chef's in and around the London, helps him to create a delicious and inventive menu.

The Restaurant Manager, Alais Miah, has been passionate about food since leaving school and is experienced and committed to working, managing and running Indian restaurants.

The menu at The Cardamom consists of a mixture of traditional and fusion dishes, but a lot of their success is down to their popular speciality fish dishes.

Wales

North West

Kitchen @ the Circle
British — 0161 817 4921

13 Barton Arcade, Manchester, M3 2BB

Join them at their stunning new restaurant within the historic Victorian atrium of the Barton Arcade. The theme is rough-luxe combining traditional understated British style with modern luxurious touches. Features include a sweeping staircase, zinc bar, leather chesterfields and porter chairs.

Their new Head Chef, Emma Saville, has created a very attractive menu based on traditional rustic dishes with contemporary edges. You can join them early for freshly cooked breakfasts, light bites at lunches and in the evening for threecourse meals including fresh fish and steaks.

Sunday lunch will never be the same again, with diners able to choose from whole roasts and poultry with all the trimmings to share among groups of four to five people.

Swadesh
Indian

Various Locations – see listings for details

The teams that have been brought to Swadesh have worked in some of the finest establishments in the world. The seasonal menus features a vibrant mix of dishes from culinary areas across India and only the finest and freshest ingredients are used with many of the recipes having been handed down across generations. The beauty and the charm, diversity and depth, simplicity and complexity of Indian cuisine are all behind the showcase restaurants. Swadesh however, it is not just the welcoming ambience of the restaurant and the stunning choice of dishes, but also the personal service that they combine with it and the incredible attention to detail.

Leonis Restaurante
Italian — **0161 835 1254**

55 Cross Street, Bow Lane, Manchester, M2 4FW

Whilst keeping their passion for cooking, Leoni´s Restaurante have introduced the influence of Latin American and Spanish recipes and selected fine wines from the new world to compliment these.

Leoni's aim is to offer their guests a different spectrum of Latin American cuisine alongside all their old Italian favourites.

Most importantly they hope you have a pleasant time and enjoy the unique ambience of Leoni's that keeps people returning again and again, whether you would just like a drink in their bar or you are dining on their exquisite exotic flavours.

Leoni´s Latin Cellar is still family run and has been established for over 30 years, blending new Latin American flavours with traditional Italian dishes.

Where possible their ingredients are imported directly from the country of origin and their pizza dough is made fresh on the premises daily.

Leoni's hope you enjoy their friendly service, delicious food and unique ambience.

Livebait

Seafood — 0161 817 4110

22 Lloyd Street, Manchester, M2 5WA

At Livebait they only serve fish that is ethically sourced is served and they are proud to support sustainable fishing policies in line with the Marine Conservation Society, bringing you the freshest seafood with minimal impact on the environment.

With the most impressive restaurant entrance in Manchester, once through the doors you won't be disappointed.

Housed in a Grade II listed building this fabulous location provides a bustling yet convivial atmosphere, making it the perfect host from business lunches to that special evening meal.

With a large oyster bar area as well as some more private areas, Livebait Manchester can cater for any type of occasion, with excellent service to boot!

Burlington's Restaurant
British — **01539 442 137**

Beech Hill Hotel, Windermere, LA23 3LR

Burlington's Restaurant is set within the Beech Hill Hotel and is located in the heart of England's beautiful Lake District National Park. Set into the hillside on the eastern bank of Lake Windermere, Britain's largest lake, you will find unrivalled panoramic views across the Lake to the Cumbrian Fells beyond. Whatever the season, the vista surrounding the hotel is always beautiful to look at and the glorious countryside a joy to roam in.

This beautiful hotel Windermere, with its cosy lounge and log fire, fine restaurant, leisure facilities, landscaped gardens and Lake view rooms is the perfect place to relax, unwind and be spoiled.

The rich farmlands of Cumbria provide abundant produce of which The Burlington Hill's kitchen makes full use. The hotel is actively involved with the annual Taste of Cumbria Food and Drink Festival - an entertaining showcase for the gourmet delights available from the county. Dinner in the Burlington's Restaurant, with its award winning food, service and Lake views from almost every window, is the highlight of any stay at The Beech Hill. Saturday evenings are particularly enjoyable as guests are entertained by a jazz quartet or pianist.

The hotel has held 2 AA Rosettes for a number of years and its consistency in producing cuisine of a high standard is ably demonstrated by their mouth-watering menus.

Dinner is served daily between 6:45 pm to 8.45 pm . Dress code smart/casual, preferably no denim.

Their menu offers a mouth-watering fusion of French and English cuisine using the finest local produce and top quality ingredients.

This is a truly stunning venue serving only the finest cuisine - one surely not to be missed!

Please note the Burlington do not offer an a la carte menu, however, they are happy to offer discount to Tastecard members across their 5 course gourmet select menu.

Hastings Lytham
British — 01253 732 400

26 Hastings Place, Lytham, St. Annes, FY8 5LZ

At the Hastings, the Fylde Coasts No. 1 Eating and Drinking House, there is something for everyone and every occasion. Whichever dining opportunity you choose, you can be rest assured that your food will have been prepared by one of the North-West's top award-winning chefs – Warrick Dodd's and his team, who have recently won, for the Hastings, accreditation in the 2010 Michelin Guide.

Is it any wonder that many diners now consider the Hastings the Fylde's No. 1 Eating and Drinking establishment?

In the Hastings' main, two floor restaurant the locally sourced and often artisan supplied ingredients perfectly reflect the excellence of produce that is available on and around the Fylde coast. The stylish and relaxed environment boasts contemporary artwork of the area and makes for a fantastically informal ambiance in which to enjoy the area's finest food.

North West

The Norfolk Arms
British — **01457 851940**

Norfolk Square, Glossop, SK13 8BP

The Norfolk Arms is part of the Joseph Holt pub chain which has houses 127 pubs within a 25 mile radius of Greater Manchester.

This large pub sits in the centre of Glossop, Derbyshire and is named after the Duke of Norfolk.

The building gives the impression of a traditional old pub from the outside, but when you step inside it's very modern. The interiors are very clean and well lit with plenty of light!

For sport lover's there are several big screen TVs screening all of the major football games.

The menu offers hearty plates of British food using locally sourced produce whenever possible!

The London Carriage Works
International — 0151 705 2222

Hope Street, Liverpool, L1 9DA

The London Carriage Works is a multi award winning restaurant serving modern international dishes complemented by the use of local, fresh and seasonal produce.

The London Carriage Works acquired its name when during external renovation works the original company name became apparent in the stonework. The company was a coach and carriage builders and built around 1866 in a pervading fashion of the day, the Venetian palazzo.

The restaurant is sister to Hope Street Hotel and is open to the public seven days a week, from breakfast to nightcaps, with lunch, afternoon tea, supper, dinner and cocktails in-between. In house they also cater for many varied events from wedding suppers to meetings and corporate dining.

The Black Dog
British — **01204 811 218**

Church Street, Belmont, Bolton, BL7 8AB

The Black Dog is situated in the middle of Belmont, Bolton. Set in a quaint old pub full of character, it is in the idyllic location just metres away from the rolling hills of the moorlands.

The interior hosts a number of nooks and crannies as well as a big airy dining room, giving it that traditional feel, perfect for family pub lunches and Sunday dinners!

The menu offers hearty plates of British food using locally sourced produce whenever possible!

Blackburn

The Spice Lounge - Indian 0125 424 7583
Wilpshire Road, Rishton, Blackburn, BB1 4AD

Mai'da Indian Eatery - Curry 0125 467 6797
16 Eanam, Blackburn, BB1 5BY

Bay Horse Inn - British 01254 812 303
Longsight Road, Osbaldeston, Lancashire, BB2 7HX

The Godfather - Italian 01254 701133
189-191 Duckworth Street, Darwen, Lancashire, BB3 1AU

Mangiamo 0125 476 0770
108 Bolton Road, Darwen, BB3 1BZ

Ridings Restaurant - British 01706 831 163
Sykeside Country House Hotel, Haslingden, Rossenale Lancashire, BB4 6QE

Traders Brasserie - British 01254 602022
The Globe Centre, St. James Square Accrington, Lancashire, BB5 0RE

Over Coffee - International 0125 439 1191
70-72 Blackburn Road, Accrington, Lancashire, BB5 1LE

Spice Room - Indian 0170 621 5891
600 Blackburn Road, Rising Bridge, Accrington, BB5 2SB

Moutai Bar & Oriental Restaurant - Oriental 0125 423 8333
8 Whalley Road, Clayton le Moors, Accrington, BB5 5DT

The Assheton Arms - International 01200 441 227
Downham, Clitheroe, Lancashire, BB7 4BJ

The Woodman Inn 01282 422 715
129 Todmorden Road, Burnley, Lancashire, BB11 3EX

Pendle Inn - British 01282 614 808
Barley, Burnley, BB12 9JX

Bolton

La Tasca Bolton - Spanish 01204 402300
55 Bradshawgate, Bolton, Lancashire, BL1 1DR

PizzaExpress Bolton - Pizza 01204 528 776
8-12 Wood Street, BL1 1DY

Prosecco Pizzeria Restaurant - Italian 0120 436 3636
63 Bradshawgate, Bolton Lancashire, BL1 1QD

The Chinese Buffet - Chinese 0120 438 8222
32 Bridge Street, Bolton, BL1 2EH

Lal Qila - Indian 01204 844 466
166-168 Chorley Old Road, Bolton, BL1 3BA

The Retreat Restaurant - International 01204 849313
319-321 Chorley New Road, Bolton, BL1 5BP

Dhanak Deira - Chinese 0120 460 9085
486 Blackburn Road, Bolton, Lancashire, BL1 8PE

Latino Lounge - Italian 0120 459 1122
122 Bradshaw Brow, Bolton, BL2 3DD

Ashoka Crofters - Indian 0120 459 4386
Bradshaw Road, Bolton, BL2 3EW

The Red Bridge Tavern - International 0120 452 1969
2 Bury Old Road, Ainsworth, Bolton, BL2 5PJ

The Sunar Gaw - Curry 0120 436 4915
310 Manchester Road, Bolton, BL3 2QS

Royal Balti House - Indian 0120 457 3515
78 Lower Market St, Farnworth, Bolton Lancashire, BL4 7NY

Sottovento Restaurant - Italian 0120 486 2952
69 Worsley Rd, Farnworth, Bolton, BL4 9LU

Viva Espana - Spanish 01204 438235
12 Winter Hey Lane, Bolton, Lancashire, BL6 7AA

The Courtyard Restaurant and Courtyard Bar - International 0120 487 3500
Hospital Road, Bromley Cross, Bolton, BL7 7AE

The Black Dog - British 01204 811 218
Church Street, Belmont, Bolton, BL7 8AB

The Spread Eagle - British 01204 400999
126 Hough Lane, Bromley Cross, Bolton, BL7 9DE

Green Bengal 0120 430 4777
158 Darwen Road, Bromley Cross, Bolton, BL7 9JJ

Madisons Restaurant - Italian 0120 430 2491
Unit 1a Dunscar Business Park, Egerton, Bolton, BL7 9PQ

Baroccos - Italian 01204 303 484
501 Blackburn Road, Egerton Bolton, BL7 9PR

Victoria Hotel - British 0161 764 7427
12-14 Hall St, Walshaw, Bury, BL8 3BD

Man Yuen, Asian 0120 488 0886
17 Market Street Tottington, Bury, Lancashire, BL8 4AA

Verona Restaurant - Italian 0161 761 7993
19, Silver Street, Bury, BL9 0DH

Red Hall Hotel - British 01706 822 476
Manchester Road, Walmersley Bury, Lancashire, BL9 5NA

The Waggon at Birtle - Modern European 01706 622955
131 Bury & Rochdale Old Road, Bury, Lancashire, BL9 6UE

Asia Lounge - Indian 0161 764 7755
136 Rochdale Road, Bury, Lancashire, BL9 7BD

Flavours Restaurant - Indian 0161 766 8040
703 Manchester Rd, Bury, BL9 9SS

Metro Fish Bar - Seafood 0161 796 0134
825 Manchester Road, Bury, BL9 9TP

Carlisle

Langdales Restaurant @ Carlisle Swallow - British 0122 852 9255
London Road, Carlisle, Cumbria, CA1 2NS

PizzaExpress Carlisle - Pizza 01228 599 638
21 Lowther Street, CA3 8ES

Lovelady Country House Hotel - British 0143 438 1203
Nenthead Road, Alston, Cumbria, CA9 3LF

Cross Keys Inn - British 0153 962 4240
Main Street Tebay, Penrith, Cumbria, CA10 3UY

Glenridding Hotel - British 01768 482289
Glenridding Hotel, Ullswater, Penrith, CA11 0PB

Listings are for ILLUSTRATIVE PURPOSES ONLY, please visit www.tastecard.co.uk for participating restaurants and offers | 131

Chester

PizzaExpress Chester - Pizza — 01244 323 265
Unit 1, Chester, CH1 1DA

Bella Italia - Italian — 01244 325420
29 Eastgate Street, Chester, CH1 1LG

Café Rouge - French — 1244 315 626
29 Bridge Street, Chester, CH1 1NG

The Pelican - International — 0124 431 3258
10 Commonhall Street, Chester, CH1 2BJ

La Tasca Chester - Spanish — 01244 400887
6'12 Cuppin Street, Chester, Cheshire, CH1 2BN

Taconita - Mexican — 0124 431 2191
4 Rufus Court, Chester, Cheshire, CH1 2JW

MD's Restaurant - International — 01244 400 322
38 Watergate Street, Chester, Cheshire, CH1 2LA

Fiesta Havana - Tapas — 0124 434 7878
39-41, Watergate Street, Cheshire, CH1 2LB

Amber Lounge Bar and Restaurant - Fusion — 01244 316477
8 Watergate Row North, Chester, CH1 2LD

Moules A Go-Go - Seafood — 01244 348 818
39 - 41 Watergate Row, Chester, CH1 2LE

Bombay Palace - Indian — 01244 371194
11 Upper Northgate St, Chester, Cheshire, CH1 4EE

The Conservatory Restat The Crabwall Manor Hotel - British — 0124 485 1666
Crabwall Manor Hotel, Parkgate Road, Mollington, CH1 6NE

The Garden Room Rest @ Mollington Banstre Hotel - British — 0124 485 1471
Mollington Banastre Hotel, Parkgate Road, Mollington, Cheshire, CH1 6NN

The Lounge Bar @ Mollington Banstre Hotel - British — 0124 485 1471
Mollington Banastre Hotel, Parkgate Road, Mollington, Cheshire, CH1 6NN

The Faulkner Bar and Kitchen - International — 01244 328 195
48 Faulkner Street Hoole, Chester, Cheshire, CH2 3BE

Ring O' Bells - British — 01244 335 422
Village Rd, Christleton, Chester, CH3 7AS

Stuarts Table at the Farmers Arms - British — 01829 781342
Farmers Arms, Huxley Lane, Chester, CH3 9BG

The Calveley Arms - British — 0182 977 0619
Handley, Chester, CH3 9DT

Frogg Manor - British — 0182 978 2629
Nantwich Road, Broxton, Chester, CH3 9JH

The Olive Grove - British — 0182 978 2199
Nantwich Road, Broxton, Chester, CH3 9JH

Mitchells Wine Bar and Brasserie - Mediterranean — 0182 977 1477
Mitchells Lynedale House, High Street, Tattenhall, CH3 9PX

The Millstone Inn - British — 01244 548824
Hawarden Road, Penyffordd, Chester, CH4 0JE

Handbridge - British — 0124 467 6194
66 Handbridge, Chester, CH4 7JF

107 Dining Room - British — 0151 342 3420
107 Telegraph Road, Wirral, CH60 0AF

Britannia Spice, Bangladeshi — 0131 336 1774
18-19 The Parade, Parkgate, Neston, CH64 6SA

Agra Fort - Indian — 0151 355 8886
3-7 Cambridge Road, Ellesmere Port, CH65 4AE

Prezzo Cheshire Oaks - Italian — 0151 3571394
Unit 2 Coliseum Way, Cheshire Oaks Outlet Village, Cheshire, CH65 9HD

Bella Italia - Italian — 0151 3573251
5 Coliseum Way, Ellesmere Port, Cheshire Oaks, CH65 9HD

PizzaExpress CHESHIRE OAKS - Pizza — 0151 355 6434
57 McArthur Glen Outlet Centre, CH65 9JJ

The Red House Brasserie Cheshire Oaks - British — 0151 356 4575
Oaks Designer Outlet Kinsey Road, Ellesmere Port, South Wirral, CH65 9JJ

Café Rouge - French — 01513 571201
Unit 22a & 22b Cheshire Oaks Designer Outlet, Ellesmere Port, CH65 9JJ

Crewe

The Fox Inn - British — 0127 021 3456
58 Crewe Rd, Haslington, Crewe, CW1 5QZ

Cheshire Cheese Fusion Pub - Indian — 0127 025 8050
332 Crewe Road, Shavington, Cheshire, CW2 5AF

Cranage Hall Tempus Restaurant - British — 01477 536 666
Byley Lane, Cranage, Holmes Chapel, CW4 8EW

The Star Inn - International — 0127 062 5067
Chester Road, Acton, Nantwich, CW5 8LD

The Davenport Arms - International — 0182 926 2684
Nantwich Road, Tarporley, Calverley, CW6 9JM

The Big Lock - British — 01606 833489
Webbs Lane, Middlewich, Cheshire, CW10 9DN

Symphony Restaurant Sandbach - Modern European — 01270 763 664
48 Congleton Road, Sandbach, Cheshire, CW11 1HG

Chimney House Hotel - British — 0127 076 4141
Congleton Road, Sandbach, CW11 4SP

Blackpool

Bella Italia - Italian — 01253 751529
23/25 Church Street, Blackpool, FY1 1HJ

Palm Court at The Imperial Hotel - International — 01253 754 607
Imperial Hotel Promenade, Blackpool, FY1 2HB

Akash Tandoori Restaurant - Indian — 01253 626 677
76 Topping Street, Blackpool, FY1 3AD

Bella Italia - Italian — 01253 623952
72 Victoria Street, Blackpool, FY1 4RJ

Seafarers - British — 0125 372 2272
341-343 Clifton Drive South, Lytham St Annes, Lancashire, FY8 1LP

PizzaExpress Lytham - Pizza — 01253 738 542
82 Clifton Street, Lytham, FY8 5EN

Hastings Lytham - British — 01253 732 400
26 Hastings Place, Lytham, St. Annes, FY8 5LZ

132 | Listings are for ILLUSTRATIVE PURPOSES ONLY, please visit www.tastecard.co.uk for participating restaurants and offers

Liverpool

Bella Italia - Italian — 0151 707 2121
39 Ranelagh Street, Liverpool, L1 1JP

Blundell Street - International — 0151 709 5779
63-65 Blundell Street, Liverpool, L1 0AJ

Ephesus - Turkish — 0151 559 4325
57 Blundell St, Liverpool, Merseyside, L1 0AJ

Dando's Cafe Bar - International — 0779 271 7363
45 Ranelagh Street, Liverpool, L1 1JR

Signals Brasserie @ The Holiday Inn - International — 0151 709 7090
Lime Street, Liverpool, L1 1NQ

La Tasca Liverpool - Spanish — 0151 709 7999
4 Queens Square, Merseyside, Liverpool, L1 1RH

Leftbank Liverpool - Mediterranean — 0151 709 0922
2 Queen Square, Liverpool, Merseyside, L1 1RH

The Live Lounge - International — 0151 708 4008
13-15 Renshaw Street, Liverpool, L1 2SA

Indian Delight - Indian — 0151 709 1722
83 Renshaw Street, Liverpool, L1 2SJ

Tapas Tapas - Spanish — 0151 709 0999
14 Back Colquitt Street, Arthouse Square, Liverpool, L1 4DE

Christakis Greek Taverna - Greek — 0151 708 7377
7 York Street, Liverpool England, L1 5BN

Café Rouge - French — 01512 581 879
Unit 37, Upper Floor Level, The Met Quarter, Liverpool, L1 6AU

The Mandarin - Chinese — 0151 227 9011
73-79 Victoria Street, Liverpool, Merseyside, L1 6DE

Sofrito L1 - Mediterranean — 0151 236 0411
51/53 White Chapel, Liverpool, L1 6DT

gbk - Liverpool, Antipodean — 015 1709 3609
14 Paradise Street, Liverpool, L1 8JF

Café Rouge - French — 01517 098657
Unit P3/4, 14 Paradise Street, Liverpool, L1 8JF

The London Carriage Works - International — 0151 705 2222
Hope Street, Liverpool, L1 9DA

The Burning Kitchen - British — 0151 236 0859
133 Dale Street, Liverpool, Merseyside, L2 2JH

Andersons Bar - British — 0151 243 1330
26 Exchange Street East, Liverpool, L2 3PH

PizzaExpress Liverpool - Victoria Street - Pizza — 0151 236 4987
11/13 Victoria Street, L2 5QQ

Merchants Bar and Restaurant - International — 0151 702 7897,
62 Castle Street, Liverpool, L2 7LQ

PizzaExpress Liverpool Monarch Quay - Pizza — 0151 707 1566
16 Monarch Quay, L3 4BX

Elude Bar & Restaurant - Modern European — 0151 227 3882
15 Porter Street, Docklands, Liverpool, L3 7BL

Filini @ The Radisson Blu Hotel - Italian — 0151 966 1500
Radisson Blu Hotel Liverpool, 107 Old Hall Street, Liverpool, L3 9BD

The White Bar @ The Radisson Blu Hotel - British — 0151 966 1500
Radisson Blu Hotel Liverpool, 107 Old Hall Street, Liverpool, L3 9BD

Da Capo - Mediterranean — 0151 236 1881
Lombard Chambers, Bixteth Street, Liverpool, L3 9NG

Vista Restaurant @ Atlantic Tower - International — 0871 376 9025
Atlantic Tower, Chapel Street, Liverpool, L3 9RE

Almond - British — 0151 226 0021
16 Mill Lane, West Derby, Liverpool, L12 7JB

The Lady Jade - Chinese — 0151 228 6888
19 St Oswalds Street, Old Swan, Liverpool, L13 5SA

Romios Greek Restaurant - Greek — 0151 727 7252
20 Lark Lane, Liverpool, L17 8US

Pistachio Restaurant - International — 0151 726 0160
88-90 Lark Lane, Aigburth, Liverpool, L17 8UU

The Stables - British — 0151 427 6026
1-3 St. Marys Road, Garston, Liverpool, L19 2NJ

The Golden Castle Restaurant - Chinese — 0151 933 2499
316 Stanley Road, Bootle, L20 3ET

Chinese Delight Restaurant - Chinese — 0151 920 8887
98 South Road, Liverpool, L22 0LY

Pietra - Italian — 0151 949 0886
15/19 South Road, Waterloo, Liverpool, L22 5PE

Tapas Tapas - Tapas — 0151 949 1151
23 South Road, Waterloo, Liverpool, L22 5PE

The Ship Inn - British — 01704 840 077
6 Rosemary Lane, Haskayne, W.Lancs, L39 7JP

Lancaster

Bella Italia - Italian — 01524 36340
26/28 Church St, Lancaster, LA1 1LH

The Austwick Traddock - International — 0152 425 1224
The Austwick Traddock, Austwick Settle, North Yorkshire, LA2 8BY

The Kings Arms - British — 0152 441 0006
248 & 250 Marine Road Central, Morecambe, LA4 4BJ

McThai - Thai — 01524 409 704
271 Marine Road Central, Morecambe, Lancashire, LA4 5BX

The Longlands Inn and Restaurant - British — 01524 781 256
Tewitfield, Carnforth, Lancashire, LA6 1JH

Plato's - Modern European — 01524 274 180
2 Mill Brow, Kirkby Lonsdale, Carnforth, LA6 2AT

The Barbon Inn and Restaurant - British — 0152 427 6233
Barbon Nr Kirkby Lonsdale, Cumbria, LA6 2LJ

PizzaExpress Kendal - Pizza — 01539 728 598
6 Wainwright's Yard, Kendal, LA9 4DP

New Inn - British — 01539 735 748
98 Highgate, Kendal, Cumbria, LA9 4HE

Globe Inn - British — 01539 733589
Market Place, Kendal, LA9 4TN

The Lancastrian Hotel - British — 0122 958 3719
Mountbarrow Road, Ulverston, Cumbria, LA12 9NR

Beresford's Restaurant & Pub — 01539 488 488
Bowness-on-Windermere, Cumbria, LA23 2JG

Burlington's Restaurant - British — 01539 442 137
Beech Hill Hotel, Windermere, LA23 3LR

Listings are for ILLUSTRATIVE PURPOSES ONLY, please visit www.tastecard.co.uk for participating restaurants and offers | 133

Manchester

The Eatery - International 0161 236 0088
1-3 Stevenson Square, Manchester, M1 1DN

Bella Italia - Italian 0161 236 2342
11-13 Piccadilly, Manchester, M1 1LY

PizzaExpress Manchester Piccadilly - Pizza 0161 237 1811
1 Piccadilly Gardens, Manchester, M1 1RG

The B Lounge at Piccadilly - British 0161 236 4161
97 Piccadilly, Manchester, M1 2DB

Blue Parrot Bar and Grille - British 0161 236 8359
11 Westminster House, Portland Street, Manchester, M1 3D

Habefha Restaurant & Bar, African 0161 228 7396
29-31 Sackville Street, Manchester, M1 3LZ

St Peterburg - Modern European 0161 236 6333
68 Sackville Street, Manchester, M1 3NJ

Royal Orchid Thai Restaurant - Thai 0161 669 6033
36 Charlotte Street, Manchester, M1 4FD

Swadesh - Manchester - Indian 0161 236 1313 / 0161 236 1999
98 Portland Street, Manchester, M1 4GX

Phetpailin Thai Restaurant - Thai 0161 228 6500
46, George Street, Chinatown Manchester, M1 4HF

The New Emperor - Chinese 0161 228 2883
52-56 George Street, Manchester, M1 4HF

Siam Orchid - Thai 0161 236 1388
54 Portland Street, Manchester, M1 4QU

Pure Space Café Bar - International 0161 236 4899
11 New Wakefield Street, Manchester, M1 5NP

Cocotoo - Italian 0161 2375458
57 Whitworth Street West, Manchester, M1 5WW

101 Bar and Brasserie - British 0161 236 5122
101 Portland St, Manchester, M1 6DF

Efes restaurant, Turkish 0161 236 18 24
46 Princess Street, Manchester, M1 6HR

PizzaExpress Manchester Peter Street - Pizza 0161 839 9300
56 Peter Street, M2 3NQ

Barbirolli - International 0161 236 3060
Barbirolli Square, 31 Lower Mosley Street, Manchester, M2 3WS

Leonis Restaurante - Italian 0161 835 1254
55 Cross Street, Bow Lane, Manchester, M2 4FW

Lounge 10 - International 0161 834 1331
10 Tib Lane, Manchester, M2 4JB

Opus One Bar & Restaurant - British 0161 835 9929
Radisson Edwardian Manchester, Free Trade Hall, Peter Street, M2 5GP

Livebait - Manchester - Seafood 0161 817 4110
22 Lloyd Street, Manchester, M2 5WA

Beluga - International 0161 833 3339
2 Mount Street, Manchester, M2 5WQ

PizzaExpress Manchester Old Colony House - Pizza 0161 834 0145
Old Colony House, Manchester, M2 6DQ

Bella Italia - Italian 0161 832 4332
92/96 Deansgate, Manchester, M3 2QG

Al Bilal - Indian 0161 257 0006
87 - 91 Wilmslow Road, Manchester, M3 2BB

Kitchen @ the Circle - British 0161 817 4921
13 Barton Arcade, Manchester, M3 2BB

Café Rouge - French 0161 839 0414
82-84 Deansgate, Manchester, M3 2ER

La Tasca - Manchester - Spanish 0161 834 8234
76 Deansgate, Manchester, M3 2FW

Sawyers Arms - British 0161 834 2133
138 Deansgate, Manchester, M3 2RP

STRADA Manchester - Italian 0161 819 5691
4A Leftbank, Irwell Square, Manchester, M3 3AN

Café Rouge - French 01618 390456
Unit B3/4 Left Bank, Spinningfields, Manchester, M3 3AN

The B Lounge at the Bridge - British 0161 834 0242
58 Bridge Street, Manchester, M3 3BW

gbk Manchester - Antipodean 0161 832 2719
Unit B6 Leftbank Spinningfields, Bridge St., Manchester, M3 3ER

Evuna - Spanish 0161 819 2752
277 Deansgate, Manchester, Lancashire, M3 4EW

English Lounge - British 0161 832 4824
64-66 High St, Manchester, M4 1EA

The Market Restaurant - British 0161 834 3743
104 High Street, Manchester, M4 1HQ

Simple Bar - International 0161 832 8764
44 Tib Street, Manchester, M4 1LA

Matt & Phreds - International 0161 831 7002
64 Tib Street, Manchester, M4 1LW

Private Dining - International 0161 834 2417
The Printworks Withy Grove, Manchester, M4 2BS

The O Bar - International 0161 834 2417
The Printworks Withy Grove, Manchester, M4 2BS

Waxy O'Connor's - International 0161 835 1210
Unit 3 The Printworks, 27 Withy Grove, Manchester Lancashire, M4 2BS

Café Rouge - French 0161 832 7749
Unit 1, The Printworks, Manchester, M4 2BS

Tiger Tiger - Manchester - International 0161 385 8080
The Printworks, Withy Grove, Manchester, M4 2BS

Bella Italia - Italian 01618 342677
Unit R8, Arndale Shopping Centre, Manchester, M4 3AQ

PizzaExpress Manchester The Triangle - Pizza 0161 834 6130
The Triangle, Manchester, M4 3TR

Kuchnia - Eastern European 0161 720 7683
3 Union Terrace, Salford, M7 4ZH

Tandoori Nights Manchester - Indian 0161 740 3100
252 Middleton Road, Manchester, M8 4WA

Manzil Banqueting Hall & Restaurant - Indian 0161 820 8555
Manchester, M8 8EQ

The Greenhouse, Vegetarian 0161 224 0730
331 Great Western Street, Manchester, M14 4AN

Lal Haweli Restaurant - Indian 0161 248 9700
68-72 Wilmslow Road, Manchester, M14 5AL

Rampant Lion - International 0161 225 9925
17 Anson Road, Victoria Park, Manchester, M14 5BZ

Mughli Manchester - Indian 0161 248 0900
28-32 Wilmslow Road, Rusholme, Manchester, M14 5TQ

Thai Banana - Thai 0161 248 7752
262 Wilmslow Road, Manchester, Lancashire, M14 6JR

Chilli Grill Bar, Halal 0161 249 3999
Unit 4 - 5, Wilbraham Road, Manchester, M14 6JS

Flamez - Indian 0161 225 2000,
220-222 Wilmslow Road, Manchester, M14 6LF

Banyan Tree - International 0161 835 9906
Unit 3 Moho Building, Ellesmere Street, Manchester, M15 4JY

Lava Cafe Bar - International 0161 833 2444
Middle Warehouse, Castlequay, Manchester, M15 4NT

YABA African And Caribbean Restaurant - Caribbean 0161 226 6998
110 Hulme High St, Manchester, Lancashire, M15 5JP

M & M Caribbean Spice, Caribbean 0161 226 6067
127 Stamford St, Old Trafford, Manchester Lancashire, M16 9LT

La Tasca - Trafford Centre - Spanish 0161 749 9966
Unit R7A, Trafford Centre, Manchester, M17 8EG

PizzaExpress Manchester Trafford - Pizza 0161 747 2121
Manchester, M17 8EQ

Café Rouge - French 01617 471927
137 The Orient, The Trafford Centre, Manchester, M17 8EQ

Boston Carib - Caribbean 0161 637 2285
995 Stockport Rd, Manchester, M19 2SY

Al-Waali's - Indian 0161 249 3665
Farmside Place, Manchester, M19 3BF

New Himalayas Restaurant, Asian 0161 248 8882
945 Stockport Rd, Manchester, M19 3NP

Gurkha Grill - Indian 0161 445 3461
194-198 Burton Road, Manchester, M20 1LH

Love 2 Eat - International 0161 434 7077
190a Burton Road, Didsbury, M20 1LH

Sangam ' Didsbury - Indian 0161 446 1155
762 Wilmslow Road, Didsbury, Manchester, M20 2DR

The Famous Crown - British 0161 434 7085
770 Wilmslow Road, Didsbury, Manchester, M20 2DR

Green Tea - Chinese 0161 445 5395
222 Burton Road, West Didsbury, M20 2LW

Crazy Wendy's - Thai 0161 445 5200
210 Burton Road, West Didsbury, Manchester, M20 2LW

Khandoker Restaurant - Indian 0161 434 3596
812 Kingsway, East Didsbury, Manchester, M20 5WY

The Parrswood Hotel - British 0161 445 1783
Parrs Wood Road, East Didsbury, Manchester, M20 6JD

gbk - Didsbury, Antipodean 016 1448 7167
651 Wilmslow rd, Didsbury Manchester, M20 6QZ

Café Rouge - French 0161 438 0444
Unit D, 651-653 Wilmslow Rd, Manchester, M20 6QZ

Jade Garden - Chinese 0161 445 6979
743 Wilmslow Rd Didsbury, Manchester, Lancashire, M20 6RN

Swadesh Didsbury - Indian 0161 445 3993 / 0161 445 8668
810 Wilmslow Road, Didsbury, Manchester, M20 6UH

PizzaExpress Didsbury - Pizza 0161 438 0838
95 Lapwing Lane, M20 6UR

La Tasca - Didsbury - Spanish 0161 4380044
10 ' 12 Warburton Street, Didsbury, Manchester, M20 6WA

The Dining Rooms at The Horse & Jockey - International 0161 860 7794
9 Chorlton Green, Manchester, Lancashire, M21 9HS

Bella Zaika - Indian 0161 499 7944
14B Rowlandsway, Wythenshawe, Manchester, M22 5RF

Moss Nook Restaurant - British 0161 437 4778
Ringway Rd Moss Nook, Manchester, M22 5WD

Andaz - Indian 0161 643 6106
23-25 Market Place, Manchester, Lancashire, M24 6AE

PizzaExpress Presetwich - Pizza 0161 7984 794
130 Bury New Road, M25 0AA

The Woodthorpe Hotel - British 0161 7950032
Bury Old Road, Prestwich, Manchester, M25 0EG

Bombay Cuisine - Indian 0161 773 6311
401 Bury New Road, Prestwich, Manchester, M25 1AA

Thai Orchid - Thai 0161 798 8897
458 Bury New Road, Prestwich, Manchester, M25 1AX

The Shahbaaz - Curry 0161 725 9076
Old Barn Radcliffe Moor Rd, Radcliffe, Manchester, M26 3WL

Il Faro - Italian 0161 870 5380
21 Stand Lane, Radcliffe, Manchester, M26 1NW

Spice Cottage - Curry 0161 280 8090
156 Stopes Rd, Radcliffe, Manchester, M26 3TW

Far Pavilion Tandoori - Curry 0161 794 0373
249-251 Manchester Rd, Swinton, Manchester, M27 4TT

Rahina - Indian 0161 728 3093
Swinton, Manchester, Lancashire, M27 5AF

The Basin - International 0161 790 1427
9a-14a Standfield Centre Worsley, Manchester, Lancashire, M28 1FB

La Perla - Italian 0161 799 2266
4 Garrett Hall Road, Worsley, Manchester, M28 1AW

The Dining Rooms at the Marriott Hotel - International 0161 975 2000
Worsley Park, Manchester, M28 2QT

Cottage Tandoori - Indian 0161 790 3255
Manchester Rd, Worsley, Manchester, M28 3JX

Spring Deer Chinese Restaurant - Chinese 0194 289 5244
176-178 Elliott Street, Tyldesley, Manchester, M29 8DS

Mario's Pizzeria Ristorante - Italian 01942 891376
190 Elliott St Tyldesley, Manchester, Lancashire, M29 8DS

Pacifica Cantonese - Chinese 0161 707 8828
5-7 Church Road, Eccles, Manchester, M30 0DL

Passage to India - Indian 0161 787 7546
168 Monton Rd, Eccles, Manchester, M30 9GA

Leo's Restaurant - Italian 0161 789 7897
198 Monton Rd, Eccles Manchester, Lancashire, M30 9LJ

Forts of Bengal Restaurant - Indian 0161 973 1919
29 Northenden Road, Sale, Cheshire, M33 2DH

The Indian Curry Cottage - Indian 0161 973 8199
394 Washway Road, Sale, Cheshire, M33 4JH

Oca Restaurant - Modern European 0161 962 6666
Waterside Plaza, Sale, Greater Manchester, M33 7BS

Roma Italian Restaurant - Italian 0161 962 3363
123 Cross Street, Sale, Cheshire, M33 7JN

Listings are for **ILLUSTRATIVE PURPOSES ONLY**, please visit www.tastecard.co.uk for participating restaurants and offers

North West

Fletcher's Arms
445 Stockport Road, Denton, Manchester, M34 6EG
0161 336 5555

Old Rectory Hotel - British
Meadow Lane, Haughton Green, Manchester, M34 7GD
0161 336 7516

Mangos Cafe Bar, Caribbean
642 Oldham Road, Failsworth, M35 9DU
0161 684 9958

Mumbai Spice - Indian
327 Hollinwood Avenue, New Moston Manchester, Lancashire, M40 0JA
0161 683 4157

Bay Horse - British
65 Berry Brow Clayton Bridge, Manchester, Greater Manchester, M40 1GR
0161 371 1904

The Spices, North African
254 Moston Lane, Manchester, M40 9WF
0161 203 6402

Standard Balti Restaurant - Indian
12 Victoria Parade Urmston, Manchester, Lancashire, M41 9BP
0161 748 2806

The Roebuck Hotel - British
2 Church Road, Flixton, Manchester, M41 6HD
0161 7484046

Cafe Mef - Italian
Chill Factore, Trafford Way Urmston, Manchester, M41 7JA
0161 748 2255

Kulshi Restaurant - Indian
1 Stretford Road Urmston, Manchester, Lancashire, M41 9JY
0161 747 1777

Sundorbon Tandoori - Indian
40 Liverpool Road, Cadishead, Manchester, M44 5AF
0161 775 2812

PizzaExpress Salford Quays - Pizza
The Lowry Designer Outlet, Stanley Street, Broughton, Salford, M50 3AZ
0161 877 3585

Bella Italia - Italian
Unit G40a Lowry Centre, Manchester, Salford Quays, M50 3AZ
01618 728729

Café Rouge - French
Unit G40B, The Lowry Outlet Mall, Salford Quays, Manchester, M50 3AZ
0161 877 3971

Tempus Bar and Restaurant - International
The Palace Hotel, Oxford Road, Manchester, M60 7HA
0161 233 5176

Oldham

Casa La Tapas - Tapas
20 Retiro Street, Oldham, OL1 1SA
0161 627 1521

Blue Tiffin - Indian
Laurel Trading Estate, Higginshaw Lane Royton, OL2 6LH
0161 628 2005

Yen House - Chinese
41 Market St, Shaw, Oldham, OL2 8NR
0170 688 1416

Chefology @ The Golden Fleece - International
41 Oldham Road, Denshaw, Oldham, OL3 5SS
0145 787 4910

New Sagor Indian Restaurant - Indian
274 Lees Road, Oldham, OL4 1PA
0161 624 9268

Roebuck Inn - International
Brighton Road Strinesdale, Oldham, Lancashire, OL4 3RB
0161 624 7819

Hei Hei - Chinese
Boodle Street, Ashton-under-Lyne, OL6 8NF
0161 339 8888

Brasserie One - International
Hotel Smokies Park, Ashton Road, Oldham, OL8 3HX
0161 785 5000

Voujon - Indian
688 - 692 Manchester Road, Oldham, Lancashire, OL9 7JT
0161 682 4600

The Bower Hotel - British
Hollinwood Avenue, Chadderton, Greater Manchester, OL9 8DE
0161 682 7254

Santorini - Greek
Moss Hall Road, Heywood, OL10 2RF
0161 425 7876

Veenas Restaurant Club - Indian
41 York Street, Heywood, Lancashire, OL10 4NW
0170 636 6822

L'Italiano Restaurant - Italian
370 Oldham Road, Rochdale, OL11 2AL
0170 634 6523

Zeera Indian Cuisine - Indian
853 Manchester Road, Rochdale, Lancashire, OL11 2UY
01706 653111

Star of Bengal - Curry
171 Yorkshire St, Rochdale, OL12 0DR
0170 664 9901

Suhag Spice Lounge - Indian
185 Yorkshire Street, Rochdale, OL12 0DR
0170 664 3187

Ruchi Indian Restaurant
69-71 Whitworth Road, Rochdale, Lancashire, OL12 0RD
0170 652 1101

Raj Restaurant - Indian
444-446 Edenfield Road, Rochdale, OL12 7PD
0170 671 3713

Owd Betts Country Inn - British
Edenfield Rd, Norden, Rochdale, OL12 7TY
0170 664 9904

Emni Restaurant - Indian
Edenfield Road, Norden, Rochdale, OL12 7TY
0179 234 0696

Mirco's Ristorante Italiano - Italian
Whitworth, Rochdale, Lancashire, OL12 8SZ
0170 635 1632

Hanuman Restaurant - Thai
15 Water St, Todmorden, OL14 5AB
01706 817010

The Tapas Bar - Spanish
54 Burnley Road, Todmorden, West Yorkshire, OL14 5EY
01706 819499

The Vedas, Bangladeshi
26-32, Rochdale Road, Todmorden, OL14 7LD
0170 681 4009

The Waterside Bar & Restaurant - British
1 Inghams Lane, Littleborough, OL15 0AY
0170 637 6250

The Cedar Tree - British
14 Huddersfield Rd, Newhey, Rochdale, OL16 3QF
0170 684 2626

Miah's - Indian
127 Yorkshire Street, Rochdale, OL16 1DS
0170 671 3350

Fusion Lounge - Indian
4-6 St. Marys Gate, Rochdale, OL16 1DZ
0170 634 5888

Bar 5 - International
5 South Parade, Rochdale, England, OL16 1LR
0170 635 9800

China City Restaurant - Chinese
6 Nelson St, Rochdale, OL16 1NL
0170 663 8797

The Top Tier Grill - British
Soccer Village, Wild House Lane, Milnrow, OL16 3TW
01706 644513

Preston

Slice of Sicily - Italian
7 Priory Lane, Preston, PR1 0AR
01772 750040

PizzaExpress Preston - Pizza
14-17 Winckley Street, PR1 2AA
01772 201 580

Fusion Room - British
80 Friargate, Preston, PR1 2ED
0177 288 0180

King Karai - Indian
28-30 Watery Lane, Ashton-on-Ribble, Preston, PR2 2NN
0177 273 6838

136 | Listings are for **ILLUSTRATIVE PURPOSES ONLY**, please visit www.tastecard.co.uk for participating restaurants and offers

Wheatsheaf - British　01995 603 398
Park Hill Road, Garstang, Preston, PR3 1EL

Salvatore's - Garstang - Italian　0199 560 1725
18 Church Street, Garstang, Lancashire, PR3 1PA

The White Bull - British　0125 487 8303
Church Street, Ribchester, PR3 3XP

Burlington's - British　0177 286 3424
502 Garstang Road, Broughton, Preston, PR3 5HE

Springfield Restaurant @ Springfield House - British　0125 379 0301
Wheel Lane, Pilling, Preston, PR3 6HL

Bangla Fusion - Indian　0177 261 0800
Liverpool Old Road, Much Hoole, Preston, PR4 5JQ

Porcini's - Asian　01772 619 555
84 Liverpool Road, Longton, Preston, PR4 5NB

Preston Swallow - International　0177 287 7351
Preston New Road, Preston, PR5 0UL

Vardon's Restaurant - British　0125 726 9221
Shaw Hill Hotel Golf and Country Club, Chorley, Lancashire, PR6 7PP

Bay Leaves - Indian　0125 726 0331
54 Park Road, Chorley, PR7 1QU

The Railway - International　01257 275005
35 Wigan Road Euxton, Chorley, Lancashire, PR7 6LA

Cinnamon Bar Lounge - International　0170 453 6926
13-17 Scarsbrick Avenue, Southport, PR8 1NN

The Wine Cellar - Mediterranean　0170 453 0002
Eastbank Square, Lord Street, Southport, PR8 1NY

Bella Italia - Italian　01704 514571
Unit. 4, Ocean plaza, Marine parade, Southport, PR8 1SB

The Richmond - British　01704 545782
Scarisbrick New Road, Southport, PR8 5HL

PizzaExpress Southport - Pizza　01704 501 636
671 Lord Street, PR9 0AW

Auberge Brasserie - Modern European　0170 453 0671
1B Seabank Road, Southport, PR9 0EW

Cambridge House Hotel - International　0170 453 8372
4 Cambridge Road, Southport, PR9 9NG

Isolabella - Italian　0177 245 9393
81 Hough Lane, Leyland, PR25 2YD

Viceroy - Indian　0177 262 1031
3 Golden Hill Lane, Leyland, PR25 3NP

Stockport

Harappa Urban Indian Cuisine - Indian　0161 477 6757
106 Higher Hillgate, Stockport, SK1 3QH

Saffron - Curry　0161 487 3511
5- 6 The Precinct, Amlwch Avenue, Stockport, SK2 5RR

The Puss in Boots　0161 456 5200
147 Nangreave Road Offerton, Stockport, Cheshire, SK2 6DG

Mister Ali's Tandoori & Balti Cuisine - Indian　0161 480 6361
13-15 Buxton Road, Stockport, SK2 6LS

Kantipur Nepalese Restaurant - Curry　0161 476 2688
238 Wellington Road, Stockport, SK2 6NW

Jamuna - Indian　0161 4835379
405-407 Buxton Road, Stockport, SK2 7EY

Last Monsoon - Bangladeshi　0161 476 4266
54 King Street West, Stockport, Cheshire, SK3 0DT

East India - Indian　0161 491 1359
223a Stockport Rd, Stockport, SK3 0RH

Chilli Chilli - Indian　0161 476 0786
20 Wellington Rd South, Stockport, SK4 1AA

Kushoom Koly Indian Restaurant - Indian　0161 432 9841
6-8 Shaw Rd, Stockport, Cheshire, SK4 4AE

Savoy Spice - Indian　0161 406 9000
148 Stockport Rd Romiley, Stockport, Cheshire, SK6 3AN

Peruga At Woodheys - British　0161 241 0412
Glossop Road, Marple Bridge, Cheshire, SK6 5RX

The Romper - Mediterranean　0161 427 1354
Ridge End, Marple, Stockport, SK6 7ET

The Marple Tavern - British　0161 449 8279
14 Cross Lane, Marple, Stockport, SK6 7PZ

Olivers Restaurant - British　0161 440 8715
547 Chester Road, Woodford Stockport, Greater Manchester, SK7 1PR

Khandoker - Bramhall - Indian　0161 439 1050
10 Fir Road, Bramhall, Cheshire, SK7 2NP

Alfresco Restaurant - Italian　0161 483 5511
162 London Road, Hazel Grov, Stockport, SK7 4DJ

Huffys Cafe Bar - International　0161 419 9110
251, London Road, Hazel Grove Bramhall, SK7 4PS

Three Bears　0161 439 0611
Jacksons Lane, Hazel Grove, Stockport, SK7 5JH

PizzaExpress Cheadle - Pizza　0161 491 1442
83-85 High Street, SK8 1AA

The Griffin Hotel - British　0161 437 2459
124 Wilmslow Road, Heald Green, Cheadle, SK8 3BE

Sangam - Heald Green - Indian　0161 436 8809
202 Wilmslow Road, Heald Green, Cheadle, SK8 3BH

Cinnamon Tree Restaurant - Indian　0161 437 5701
224 Finney Lane, Heald Green, Cheadle, SK8 3QA

Mousam Indian Restaurant - Indian　0161 428 8833
2 Old Hall Rd, Gatley, Cheadle, SK8 4BE

Mhariam Indian Restaurant - Indian　0161 485 4387
124 Turves Rd, Cheadle Hulme, Cheadle, SK8 6AW

The Hesketh Tavern - British　0161 485 3216
63 Hulme Hall Road, Cheadle Hulme, Cheadle, SK8 6JZ

gbk - Wilmslow - Antipodean　016 2552 4238
9/11 Rex Buildings, Alderly Rd. Wilmslow, Manchester, SK9 1HY

PizzaExpress Wilmslow - Pizza　01625 540 055
26-28 Alderley Road, SK9 1PL

Wilmslow Tavern - British　0162 553 9588
Ringstead, Deive, Wilmslow, SK9 2HA

Chilli Wok - Chinese　0162 553 7086
Summerfield Village Centre, Dean Row Road, Wilmslow, SK9 2TA

STRADA Wilmslow - Italian　01625 418 698
22 - 24 Water Lane, Wilmslow, Cheshire, SK9 5AA

The Seed House - British　01625 522 128
Ned Yates Garden Centre Moor Lane, Wilmslow, Cheshire, SK9 6DN

Listings are for **ILLUSTRATIVE PURPOSES ONLY**, please visit www.tastecard.co.uk for participating restaurants and offers

Alderley Rose - Chinese
34 London Rd, Alderley Edge, Cheshire, SK9 7DZ
01625 585557

The Drum & Monkey - British
Moss Rose, Alderley Edge, Cheshire, SK9 7LD
0162 558 4975

PizzaExpress Macclesfield - Pizza
4 Market Place, SK10 1EX
01625 425 175

The Wizard Inn - British
Macclesfield Road Nether Alderley, Macclesfield, Cheshire, SK10 4UB
01625 584000

Briscola - Italian
88-90 Palmerston Street, Macclesfield, Cheshire, SK10 5PW
01625 573898

Viceroy Indian Cusine - Indian
22 Ingersley Road, Bollington, SK10 5RF
0162 557 3006

The Fools Nook - British
Leek Road, Sutton, Macclesfield, SK11 0JF
0126 025 3662

El Rio, Mexican
5 Black Wallgate Street, Macclesfield, SK11 6LQ
0162 543 1355

Sylk Restaurant - British
3-7 Samuel Street, Macclesfield, SK11 6UW
0162 542 0333

Balti Kitchen - Indian
22 Park Green, Macclesfield, SK11 7NA
0162 550 3070

The Egerton Arms - British
Knutsford Road, Chelford, Cheshire, SK11 9BB
01625 861 366

The Black Swan - International
Trap Street, Lower Withington, Macclesfield, SK11 9EQ
0147 757 1602

Deeba Restaurant - Indian
1 Fountain Place, Poynton, Stockport, SK12 1QX
01625 879885

Il Pomodoro - Italian
62-66 Park Lane, Poynton, Stockport Cheshire, SK12 1RE
0162 587 8989

The Norfolk Arms - British
Norfolk Square, Glossop, SK13 8BP
01457 851940

Garlic Indian Cuisine - Indian
10 The Square, Hyde, Cheshire, SK14 2QR
0161 368 4040

Stables Restaurant - British
276 Stockport Rd, Hyde, SK14 5RF
0161 366 0300

The Gun Inn - British
2 Market St, Hollingworth, Hyde, SK14 8LN
0145 776 2388

Spice Room - Curry
677 Huddersfield Rd, Carrbrook, Stalybridge, SK15 3LE
0145 783 9113

Flamin Nosh - Mediterranean
Dog & Pheasant, 97 Stamford Street, Stalybridge, SK15 1LH
0161 338 5555

Curry Lounge - Indian
150 High Street, Stalybridge, Cheshire, SK15 1TN
0161 304 8027

Zurri Indos Tapas Bar & Restaurant - Indian
84 Market Street, Stalybridge, Cheshire, SK15 2AB
0161 338 3211

Grand Surruchi - Indian
1 Trinity Street, Stalybridge, Cheshire, SK15 2PW
0161 338 8426

Astley Arms - British
1 Chapel Hill, Dunkinfield, Cheshire, SK16 4BT
0161 330 3565

Curry Cottage Restaurant & Takeaway - Indian
1 Concord Way, Dukinfield, Cheshire, SK16 4DB
0161 343 1271

Herb and Spice - Indian
99 Foundry Street, Dukinfield, Cheshire, SK16 5PN
0161 343 5961

PizzaExpress Buxton - Pizza
14 Cavendish Arcade, SK17 6BQ
01298 24922

Warrington

Mojo Bar & Tapas - International
15 Cairo Street, Warrington, Cheshire, WA1 1EE
0192 557 6576

Duckegg Bluu - International
453 Warrington Rd, Culcheth, Warrington Cheshire, WA3 5SJ
0192 576 7555

The Poacher Public House - British
40 Gorse Covert Rd Birchwood, Warrington, Cheshire, WA3 6UG
01925 831015

Spirit - British
Victoria Park Knutsford Road, Warrington, WA4 1DQ
0192 523 2527

PizzaExpress Stockton Heath - Pizza
3 Victoria Buildings, Stockton Heath, Cheshire, WA4 2AG
01925 860 865

Capri Rest @Best Western Fir Grove Hotel - Modern European
Knutsford Old Road, Warrington, WA4 2LD
0192 526 7471

Cardamon Cuisine - Indian
109A London Road, Warrington, Cheshire, WA4 6LG
01925 212552

Hilltops Restaurant @ Forest Hills Hotel - International
Overton Hill, Frodsham, Cheshire, WA6 6HH
0192 873 5255

Helter Skelter - International
Church Street, Frodsham, WA6 6PN
0192 873 3361

Efe's - Mediterranean
138-142 Widnes Road, Widnes, WA8 6AX
0151 257 9722

The Hillcrest Hotel - International
Cronton Lane, Widnes, WA8 9AR
0151 424 1616

Le Frog Bistro - French
2 Haydock Street, St Helens, WA10 1DA
0174 473 0060

Lounge Bar @ the Thistle Haydock - British
Penny Lane, Haydock, Merseyside, WA11 9SG
0871 376 9044

Beechers Restaurant @ Thistle Haydock - British
Penny Lane, Haydock, Merseyside, WA11 9SG
0871 376 9044

Sahib Indian Restaurant - Indian
4-6 The Cross, Lymm, Cheshire, WA13 0HP
01925 757576

Trattoria Baci - Italian
18 The Cross, Lymm, WA13 0HU
0192 575 6067

Dilli - Indian
60 Stamford New Road, Cheshire, WA14 1EE
0161 929 7484

The Grapes Bar & Restaurant - British
15 Regent Road, Altrincham, Cheshire, WA14 1RY
0161 928 8714

The Bowden Hotel - British
Langham Road, Bowdon, Cheshire, WA14 2HT
0161 928 7121

Ishta - Indian
23 The Downs, Altrincham, Cheshire, WA14 2QD
0161 233 0303

Swadesh ' Bowdon - Indian
3 Richmond Road, Bowdon, WA14 2TT
0161 941 5311

The Hale Kitchen and Bar - International
149 Ashley Road, Hale, Cheshire, WA14 2UE
0161 926 4670

Essence Tandoori Restaurant - Indian
83 Manchester Rd, Altrincham, WA14 4RJ
0161 928 1504

La Famiglia - Italian
18 The Square, Hale Barns, Altrincham, WA15 8ST
0161 980 0009

PizzaExpress Hale - Pizza
142/144 Ashley Road, WA15 9SA
0161 928 6644

Mughli - Knutsford - Indian
44-46 King Street, Knutsford, WA16 6DT
01565 631 010

Mae Gaew - Thai
48 King St, Knutsford, Cheshire, WA16 6DT
01565 631621

PizzaExpress Knutsford - Pizza
117a King Street, WA16 6EH
01565 651 898

The Cottage Restaurant & Lodge - British
London Road, Allostock, Knutsford Cheshire, WA16 9LU
0156 572 2470

Wigan

Mortimer's - British
34-35 King Street, Wigan, WN1 1BT
0194 282 4180

The Spice Lounge - Indian
Flax Mill, Brethertons Row, Wigan, WN1 1LL
0194 249 4909

The Chinese Buffet - Chinese
63 Standishgate, Wigan, WN1 1UP
0194 282 0277

Sofrito - Mediterranean
13 Upper Dicconson Street, Wigan, WN1 2AD
0194 224 2000

Park Hotel - International
625 Wigan Rd, Ashton-in-Makerfield, Wigan, WN4 0BY
0194 227 1298

Jamal - Indian
3 Anjou Boulevard, Robin Park, Wigan, WN5 0UJ
0194 221 2228

Winstons - Italian
190 Upholland Road, Billinge, Wigan, WN5 7DJ
0169 562 7692

Taste of Bengal - Indian
11 High St Standish, Wigan, Lancashire, WN6 0HA
01257 473119

Cinnamon Indian Restaurant - Indian
487 Preston Road Standish, Wigan, Lancashire, WN6 0QD
01257 426661

The Olive Garden - Italian
489 Preston Road, Wigan, Lancashire, WN6 0QD
0125 742 1144

RBG Bar and Grill @ The Park Inn Leigh - British
Leigh Sports Village, Sale Way, Leigh, WN7 4JY
0194 236 6334

The Beacon at **Dalton** - British
Beacon Lane, Dalton, Wigan, WN8 7RR
0169 562 2771

North East & Yorkshire

Live Bait
Seafood — 0113 2444 144

11-15 Wharf Street, Shears Yard, The Calls, LS2 7EH

Visit one of the four fabulous restaurants at Waterloo, Covent Garden, Leeds or in Manchester to experience the beauty and simplicity of fresh fish, cooked to perfection. Try Livebait's famous fish and chips – choose either Icelandic line-caught cod or haddock, served with chunky chips and tartare sauce, or try a 'market fish of the day', cooked just as you like it to order.

At Livebait they only serve fish that is ethically sourced and they are proud to support sustainable fishing policies in line with the Marine Conservation Society, bringing you the freshest seafood with minimal impact on the environment.

Tucked away in Shears Yard, just off The Calls, Livebait Leeds provides an intimate setting for sampling the best fish and seafood in Leeds.

Just a stone's throw away from Leeds city centre, a cosy, retro interior and a large patio for al fresco dining means Livebait Leeds can spectacularly cater to any occasion.

City 3

International — 0113 244 2000

Neville Street, Leeds, LS1 4BX

The City 3 Restaurant, Brasserie and Bar within the Hilton hotel on Neville street in the heart of Leeds, has a relaxed atmosphere serving modern cuisine with an eclectic twist.

This contemporary restaurant has wooden brasserie-style tables and seating, and a relaxed ambience, for informal business meetings or a celebration. Locals and guests at the Hilton Leeds City hotel enjoy fantastic dishes such as home-made fish pie or a fillet steak, all complimented by an extensive wine selection.

Thai Edge
Thai — 0113 243 6333

New Portland Place, 7 Calverley Street,
Leeds, LS1 3DA

Thai Edge is an award winning Thai restaurant offering inspirational dishes in a unique oriental contemporary setting together with impeccable service. Ideally positioned over-looking Millennium Square in Leeds, Thai Edge has created the most exciting and memorable dining experience outside of Asia.

Thai Edge provide the very best in Thai cuisine. The combination of classical and authentic seasonings together with only the freshest ingredients and choice seafood and meats creates an extraordinary array of distinctive dishes to satisfy the most discerning palette.

Thai Edge is really a departure from the norm. Gone are the heavily themed, crimson shades and cluttered environments that are typical of oriental eateries. These are replaced by an approach that gives great emphasis to clean crisp lines, balance and intelligent use of space.

Thai cuisine is popular for its subtle blending of flavours, utilising herbs and roots such as lemongrass, basil, coriander, galangal, krachai, ginger, garlic and chillies.

The Thai Edge menu offers an extensive choice of a hundred and forty five dishes for a complete Thai culinary experience.

Their internationally renowned head chief brings with him the culinary heritage of Thailand with recipes and techniques he has perfected through years of experience. Drawing on centuries old oriental and European influences he prepares mouth watering dishes using only the freshest ingredients that give Thai Edge its authentic taste of Thailand.

Casa Mia
Italian — 0845 688 3030

33 - 37 Harrogate Road, Leeds, LS7 3PD
Great George Street, Leeds, LS2 3AD

There are 2 Casa Mias in Leeds, Grande and Millenium.

For a sophisticated dining experience, relax and enjoy a wonderful meal at the award-winning Casa Mia Grande. Experience the feeling of a bustling Italian atmosphere, where you can sit back and enjoy its truly Mediterranean cuisine.

Casa Mia Grande's speciality is fish and every day you can select from an array of fresh fish cooked and prepared before your very eyes and traditional meat dishes freshly cooked to your liking with a wonderful choice of classic Italian wines to complement every course. Fresh homemade pasta is also a favourite from a traditional 'Bolognese' to their unique, award-winning dish "Leccabaffi" with scampi and mango which are just superb.

Casa Mia Millennium is located off Great George Street in the exclusive Millennium Square, situated in Leeds; it opened its doors in July 2004. The restaurant has a coffee bar with an amazing array of hot beverages to choose from, a deli counter, a licensed bar and a fantastic spacious restaurant set over two floors including extensive al fresco dining.

You can enjoy the hustle and bustle of the City Centre while feasting on a tasty brioche, mouth – watering pasta dish or a freshly cooked pizza. Customers can also pop in for a coffee and snack on their way into work or even pick up something for dinner on their way home!

With tremendous views across Millennium Square, Casa Mia Millennium is undoubtedly the place to see and be seen in Leeds!

North East & Yorkshire

North East & Yorkshire

Olive Tree Restaurant
Greek

Located at Chapel Allerton, Headingley and Rodley (all Leeds) for details see individual listings

Established in 1982, The Olive Tree group of family owned restaurants has grown over the years and there are now three in Leeds.

The restaurants are run by the husband and wife team George and Vasoulla and son Solos. Since opening they have received many culinary awards and were selected as 'Restaurant of the Year' by the Yorkshire Evening Post in 1986 and 2006.

George has a philosophy of 'real ingredients cooked by real people' and believes we should go back to the way our grandmothers cooked, using only the best ingredients cooked in an honest wholesome manner.

As You Like It
International — 0871 911 6537

Block A Scottish Life House, Archbold Terrace,
Newcastle Upon Tyne, NE2 1DB

As You Like It is set over three sprawling floors, featuring four stunning bars, an elegant garden terrace, Jesmond's most beautiful restaurant, the city's best bar menu, "The Supper Club" and "Frangipani", their extraordinary chintz free function room.

All they want to do is serve great quality food – simply done and simply served. It's honest home style cooking at its best & you can choose to sample it either in the bar or their award winning restaurant, recently voted "7th sexiest restaurant in the world" Observer 08.

North East & Yorkshire

William & Victoria
British — 01423 521510

6, Cold Bath Road, Harrogate, HG2 0NA

William & Victoria is a family run restaurant and wine bar serving traditional British food in the heart of Harrogate. Owned and run by the Straker family for over 20 years, you are assured a warm welcome from David and his team whenever you visit.

With chandeliers hanging from high ceilings and opulently dressed windows William & Victoria aim to re-create the classic dining experience in a relaxing and welcoming way, embracing a passion for tradition and excellence.

The menu reflects the beautiful surrounding with its fine tuned dishes that include William & Victoria's drunken bullock and roast loin of Yorkshire lamb.

The Churhill Hotel
British — **01904 644456**

65 Bootham, York, YO30 7DQ

The Churchill Hotel is a luxury hotel situated in York city centre. The building is a superb example of a late Georgian mansion built around 1827. Set in its own grounds, the Churchill is one of best situated hotels in York, just a short walk from the York Minster and all of York's major attractions.

The fine dining restaurant's décor is inspirational, the original magnificent architecture enhanced by the discerningly modern interior. Comfy chairs, candlelight, the soft chords of the baby grand piano being played and above all attentive service combine to provide the perfect setting to savour the exquisite fine dining cuisine provided by their talented team of chefs.

The chefs take a modern stylish approach to their cuisine at the Churchill Hotel, York. Fresh, seasonal produce from local York suppliers is used whenever possible to create dishes with imaginative twists, made using cutting edge techniques and through exciting presentation. Their talents have been acknowledged with the initial awarding of an AA Rosette for their fine dining in 2008 and towards the end of 2009 were delighted to be awarded a second Rosette signifying The Piano Restaurant to be one of the very best in York.

The Management and team would like to extend a warm welcome to taste members.

North East & Yorkshire

Winteringham Fields
Modern European — 0172 473 3096

1 Silver St, Winteringham, Scunthorpe, DN15 9ND

Winteringham Fields is a justifiably world-renowned restaurant with rooms in Scunthorpe.

Upon each visit to this venue, customers will always enjoy discreet and understated service from attentive, knowledgeable staff and a range of superb dishes to satisfy the most discerning palate.

Local produce is featured very strongly in the restaurant's menus. Fresh fish is delivered daily from Grimsby, game in season from local shoots, and vegetables and herbs grown in Winteringham Fields' own gardens, plus an abundance of fresh fruit from around the world.

It is the restaurant's aim to offer a place where discerning patrons know that they will always find the best of everything, presented with that extra touch of thoughtfulness and flair, by staff able to anticipate each guest's unspoken wish.

The Outside In
International — 0113 258 1410

6 Town Street, Horsforth, Leeds,
West Yorkshire , LS18 4RJ

At the Outside-In you can dine al fresco style without having to worry too much about the vagaries of the British weather, under the beautifully decorated ceiling, yet surrounded by greenery as if you were dining outside.

This long-established Horsforth eatery, as the name suggests, brings the outside inside with stone floors, twinkling ceiling lights and vines help create a romantic feel.

The extensive menu ranges from pasta, pizzas and burgers to a selection of steak, chicken and fish mains.

North East & Yorkshire

Bradford

Tulsi Restaurant - Vegetarian 0127 472 7247
9 Aldermanbury, Bradford, BD1 1SD

Balanga Bar & Restaurant - Eastern European 01274 739112
6 Godwin Street, Bradford, West Yorkshire, BD1 3PT

The Russian Restaurant - Eastern European 0127 473 3121
15 Manor Row, Bradford, BD1 4PB

Nawaab - Bradford - Asian 01274 720 371
32 Manor Row, Bradford, West Yorkshire, BD1 4QE

Red Chilli 3 - Bangladeshi 01274 667427
1422-1424 Leeds Road, Bradford, BD3 7AE

Charco's Bradford - Mediterranean 01274 743742
375-377 Leeds Road, BD3 9LY

Cue Gardens - British 01274 607990
Stadium Mills, Pearson Road, Bradford, BD6 1BJ

Omars Balti House - Indian 0127 441 4188
46 Great Horton Road, Bradford, BD7 1AL

Royal Balti Restaurant - Indian 0127 473 0433
44 Great Horton Road, Bradford, West Yorkshire, BD7 1AL

Kebabeesh - Indian 0127 461 7188
165 New Line, Bradford, BD10 0BN

Best Western Guide Post Hotel - International 0845 409 1431
Common Road, Low Moor, Bradford, BD12 0ST

Prune Park Bar and Brasserie - British 0127 448 3516
Prune Park Lane, Allerton, Bradford, BD15 9BJ

The Old Tramshed - British 0127 458 2111
199 Bingley Road, Saltaire, West Yorkshire, BD18 4DH

The Whitcliffe Hotel - International 01274 873 022
Prospect Road, Cleckheaton Bradford, West Yorkshire, BD19 3HD

Lazeez - Indian 0153 560 0096
1 Russell Street, Keighley, BD21 2JU

Skipton Balti - Indian 01756 793960
1B Court Lane, Skipton, North Yorkshire, BD23 1DD

Napiers Restaurant - British 01756 799 688
Chapel Hill, Skipton, BD23 1NL

Nosh Brasserie @ 25 - International 0175 670 0060
25 Newmarket Street, Skipton, North Yorkshire, BD23 2JE

Rendezvous Hotel - British 0175 670 0100
Keighley Road, Skipton, North Yorkshire, BD23 2TA

The Devonshire Fell Hotel - International 01756 729000
Burnsall Village, Skipton North Yorkshire, BD23 6BT

Old Hall Inn - International 0175 675 2441
Main St, Threshfield, BD23 6LD

Durham

Oldfields - British 0191 370 9595
18 Claypath, Durham, County Durham, DH1 1RH

The Brown's Restaurant @ Three Tuns Hotel - International 0191 386 4326
New Elvet, Durham, County Durham, DH1 3AQ

El Coto - Durham - Spanish 0191 384 4007
17 Hallgarth Street, Durham, DH1 3AT

La Tasca Durham - Spanish 0845 1262958
58 Saddler Street, Durham, DH1 3NU

PizzaExpress Durham - Pizza 0191 383 2661
64 Sadler Street, DH1 3PG

Bella Italia - Italian 0191 386 1060
20-22 Silver Street, Durham, DH1 3RB

Café Rouge, French 01913 843429
21 Silver Street, Durham, DH1 3RB

Darlington

Foffano's - Italian 0132 524 2086
3-5 Bakehouse Hill, Darlington, DL1 5QA

PizzaExpress Darlington - Pizza 01325 488 771
1 Skinnergate, DL3 7NB

Aroma - Indian 01609 774239
Zetland Street, Northallerton, North Yorkshire, DL6 1NB

Allerton Court Hotel - International 0160 978 0525
Darlington Road, Northallerton, North Yorkshire, DL6 2XF

PizzaExpress Northhallerton - Pizza 01609 772 443
141 High Street, DL7 8PE

Simonstone Hall Country House Hotel - British 0196 966 7255
Hawes, North Yorkshire, DL8 3LY

Doncaster

Curry Mahal Doncaster - Indian 01302 310928
205 Balby Road, Balby, Doncaster, DN4 0NE

The Cafe Bar @ The Park Inn Doncaster - British 01302 760710
Decoy Bank South, White Rose Way, Doncaster, DN4 5PD

Stallingborough Grange Hotel - British 0146 956 1302
Riby Road, Stallingborough, North East Lincolnshire, DN41 8BU

The White Bear - British 0142 787 2544
Belton Road, Epworth, Doncaster, DN9 1JL

The White Horse Inn - British 0130 271 0211
High Street, Misson, Doncaster, DN10 6ED

Simply Indian Restaurant - Indian 01405 869 618
Main Street, Pollington, DN14 0DN

Pearl City Cantonese Restaurant - Chinese 0172 485 5755
Jubilee Hall 2a, Laneham St, Scunthorpe, DN15 6LJ

Salt & Pepper Village Restaurant - Indian 01724 851442
51-53 Doncaster Rd, Doncaster, South Humberside, DN15 7RG

Winteringham Fields - Modern European 0172 473 3096
1 Silver St, Winteringham, Scunthorpe, DN15 9ND

Prezzo Gainsborough - Italian 01427 611934
Unit 26 Marshalls Yard, Beaumont Street, Gainsborough, DN21 2NA

The Drawing Room - International 0177 786 0077
22 The Square, Retford, Nottinghamshire, DN22 6DQ

Caspers - Italian 0147 224 2422
102 Victoria Street, Grimsby, DN31 1BA

152 | Listings are for ILLUSTRATIVE PURPOSES ONLY, please visit www.tastecard.co.uk for participating restaurants and offers

Royal Bengal Tandoori - Indian 01472 356 650
152 Victoria Street, Grimsby, DN31 1NX

China Delight - Chinese 01472 242 668
102-104 Cleethorpe Road, Grimsby, DN31 3HW

Grill @ Millfields Hotel - International 0147 235 6068
53 Bargate, Grimsby, Lincolnshire, DN34 5AD

Fizz Champagne Bar & Restaurant - British 0147 269 1111
1 St Peter's Avenue, Cleethorpes, Lincolnshire, DN35 8HQ

Dovedale Hotel and Restaurant - International 0147 269 2988
Albert Road, Cleethorpes, DN35 8IX

Rajdhani - Indian 01472 290 881
31 Market St, Cleethorpes, DN35 8LY

Huddersfield

The Keys - British 01484 516 677
The Crypt of St Peters, The Parish Church Byram Street, HD11BU

The George Hotel Restaurant - British 01484 515444
The George Hotel St George's Square, Huddersfield, HD1 1JA

Shabab - Indian 0148 454 9514
37 New Street, Huddersfield, HD1 2BQ

Gurkha Thali Nepalese Restaurant - Asian 0148 451 7457
Halfmoon Street, 1 Cherry tree Centre, Huddersfield, HD1 2JD

Oriental Kitchen - Thai 0148 453 1999
32 King Street, Huddersfield, HD1 2QT

Chutney Mahal - Indian 01484 532 244
Folly Hall, Chapel Hill, Huddersfield, HD1 3PA

Balooshai - Indian 01484 559 055
3 Viaduct St, Huddersfield, HD1 5AW

Thai Sakon - Thai 01484 450 159
5 St John's Road, Huddersfield, HD1 5AY

Gringo's Mexican Rest & Buddha Bar - Mexican 0148 442 2411 / 0148 476 8986
8 Railway Arches, Viaduct Street, Huddersfield, HD1 5DL

Leena's Restaurant - Indian 0148 464 6466
17-19 Lidget Street, Lindley, Huddersfield, HD3 1JB

The Lockwood - International 0148 442 8804
1 Woodhead Road, Lockwood, Huddersfield, HD4 6ER

The Rose and Crown - International 01484 660790
The Village, Thurstonland, Huddersfield, HD4 6XU

nosh Restaurant - British 01484 430004
93-97 Northgate Almondbury, Huddersfield, HD5 8UU

Asha Restaurant - Asian 01484 847524
1024 Manchester Road Linthwaite, Huddersfield, Yorkshire, HD7 5QQ

Volare - Mediterranean 0148 486 0262
9 Commercial Road Skelmanthorpe, Huddersfield, West Yorkshire, HD8 9DA

La Dolce Vita - Italian 01484 861 199
145 Wakefield Road, Scissett, Huddersfield, HD8 9HR

No 21 - International 0148 486 6060
21-23 High Street, Clayton West, Huddersfield, HD8 9PD

The Balcony - Asian 01484 683 007
10-12 Dunford Road, Holmfirth, West Yorkshire, HD9 2DP

Massala Lounge - Indian 01484 680742
57 Huddersfield Road, Holmfirth, West Yorkshire, HD9 3JH

Harrogate

Muckles Pub - International 0142 385 8153
11 West Park, Harrogate, HG1 1BL

PizzaExpress Harrogate - Pizza 01423 531 041
2 Albert Street, HG1 1JG

Prezzo Harrogate - Italian 01423 520447
2-4 Albert Street, Harrogate, North Yorkshire, HG1 1JG

La Tasca Harrogate - Spanish 01423 566333
1 John Street, Harrogate, North Yorkshire, HG1 1JZ

Café Rouge - French 01423 500043
21-29 Beulah Street, Harrogate, N Yorks, HG1 1QH

Le Jardin & Petit Bistro - International 01423 507323
7 Montpellier Parade, Harrogate, Yorkshire, HG1 2TJ

Cedar Court Hotel - British 01423 858585
Park Parade off Knaresborough Road, Harrogate, North Yorkshire, HG1 5AH

B.e.d - British 01423 568 600
24 Kings Road, Harrogate, HG1 5JW

The West Park Hotel - International 0142 352 4471
19 West Park, Harrogate, HG1 1BJ

Caramba - Fusion 1423505300
34a Oxford Street, Harrogate, HG1 1PP

William and Victoria - International 01423 521510
6, Cold Bath Road, Harrogate, HG2 0NA

The Travellers Rest - British 0142 388 3960
Crimple Lane, Crimple, Harrogate, HG3 1DF

The Black Swan - British 01423 871 031
Burn Bridge Road, Harrogate, HG3 1PB

The Buck Inn - International 0167 742 2461
The Village Green, Thornton Watlass, Ripon, HG4 4AH

Samuels Restaurant @ Swinton Park Hotel - British 0176 568 0900
Swinton Park, Masham, Ripon, HG4 4JH

The George at Wath - British 0176 564 1324
Main Street, Wath, Ripon, HG4 5EN

The Bruce Arms - British 01677 470325
West Tanfield, North Yorkshire, HG4 5JJ

The Bull Inn - British 0167 747 0678
Church Street, Ripon, HG4 5JQ

So Bar and Eats - International 01423 863202
1 Silver Street, North Yorkshire, North Yorkshire, HG5 8AJ

Hull

The Heart of Hull at The White Hart - British 0148 222 813
Alfred Gelder Street, Hull, HU1 1EP

The Railway Inn - British 0196 456 3770
New Ellerby, Hull, HU1 1EP

Ye Olde White Harte - British 01482 326363
25 Silver Street, Hull, North Humberside, HU1 1JG

Leonardo's at Quayside - International 0148 222 8475
Princes Dock Street, Hull, HU1 2JX

North East & Yorkshire

Listings are for ILLUSTRATIVE PURPOSES ONLY, please visit www.tastecard.co.uk for participating restaurants and offers | 153

North East & Yorkshire

The Whittington and Cat - British 0148 232 7786
Commercial Road, Hull, HU1 2SA

Tangerine Cafe Bar - Italian 01482 334 455
56-57 Carr Lane, Hull, North Humberside, HU1 3RF

Prezzo Hull - Italian 01482 223277
Unit 41, St Stephens Ferensway, Kingston Upon Hull, HU2 8LN

Raj Pavilion - Indian 0148 258 1939
56a/58, Beverley Road, Kingston Upon Hull, HU3 1YE

Barinda Bar & Grill - Indian 0148 250 0800
61 Boothferry Road, Kingston upon Hull, HU3 6UA

Verve Grill Restaurant at The Village Hotel Hull - International 0148 264 2422
Henry Boot Way, Priory Way, Hull, HU4 7DY

Kuchnia - Eastern European 01482 446 495
226 Beverley Road, Hull, HU5 1AH

Lattitude Cafe Bar, Fusion 0148 247 1390
177 Newland Avenue, Hull, North Humberside, HU5 2EP

Koo Bar - International 01482 440 00
206 Newland Avenue, Hull, HU5 2ND

La Perla Italian Restaurant - Italian 0148 244 6261
26 Newland Avenue, Kingston-Upon-Hull, HU5 3AF

The Boars Nest - British 01482 445 577
22-24, Princes Avenue, Hull, HU5 3QA

Fudge Cafe Restaurant - International 0148 244 1019
93 Princes Avenue, Hull, HU5 3QP

Taman Ria Tropicana, Malaysian 0148 234 5640
45-47 Princes Avenue, Hull, HU5 3RX

Masti Indian Restaurant & Lounge Bar - Indian 0148 249 2563
36 Cottingham Rd, Hull, North Humberside, HU6 7RA

bailey's Bistro - British 0148 266 2359
1-3 Skillings Lane, Brough, North Humberside, HU15 1BA

The Black Horse - British 01430 423270
Church Lane Ellerker, Brough, North Humberside, HU15 2DN

Alishaan - Indian 0148 284 7255, 205
Hallgate, Hull, East Yorkshire, HU16 4BB

Dine on the Rowe - British 01482 502269
12-14 Butcher Row, Beverley, North Humberside, HU17 0AB

Khan's Restaurant - Indian 01482 868 300
Wylies Road, Beverley, East Yorkshire, HU17 7AA

PizzaExpress Beverley - Pizza 01482 679 105
37 North Bar Within, HU17 8B

Beverley Arms Hotel - International 01482 869 241
North Bar Within Beverley, East Beverley, HU17 8DD

Halifax

Ricci & Capone - American 0142 230 0553
20 Powell St, Halifax, West Yorkshire, HX1 1LN

Kamran Balti House - Curry 0142 234 5678
27 Union Street, Halifax, HX1 1PR

Franganos - International 01422 365 566
10 & 12 Crown Street, Halifax West Yorkshire, HX1 1TT

The Crown Tandoori - Indian 0142 234 9270
31 Crown Street, Halifax, West Yorkshire, HX1 1TT

Othello - Greek 0142 235 5353
91 Northgate, Halifax, HX1 1XF

Il Gusto - Italian 01422 344 775
8 Bull Green, Halifax, HX1 5AB

The Causeway Foot Inn - British 01422 240273
13 Causeway Foot, Ogden, Halifax, HX2 8XX

Ashiana - Indian 01422 377 325
Town Hall Buliding, Southgate, Elland, HX5 0EU

Leeds

Baby Jupiter - International 0113 242 1202
11 York Place, Leeds, LS1 2DS

Ego - Mediterranean 0113 244 9014
Atlas House 31 King Street, Leeds, West Yorkshire, LS1 2HL

PizzaExpress Leeds Park House - Pizza 0113 244 5858
Park House, LS1 2PS

The Tiled Hall - British 0113 263 7915
Calverley Street, Leeds, West Yorkshire, LS1 3AB

Thai Edge - Thai 0113 243 6333
New Portland Place, 7 Calverley Street, Leeds, LS1 3DA

Bianco - Italian 0113 246 5225
40 Great George Street, Leeds, LS1 3DL

The Cosmopolitan Bar and Restaurant - International 0113 243 6454
Cosmopolitan Hotel, Lower Briggate, Leeds, LS1 4AE

The Roast - British 0113 244 9080
1 Whitehall Riverside, Leeds, LS1 4BN

City 3 Restaurant - International 0113 244 2000
Neville Street, Leeds, LS1 4BX

Crowne Plaza Hotel Boccagrande Restaurant - International 0871 942 9170
Wellington Street, Leeds, LS1 4DL

Crowne Plaza Hotel 'Leeds' Roundhay Bar - International 0871 942 9170
Wellington Street, Leeds, LS1 4DL

Elements Restaurant @the Leeds Novotel Hotel - International 0113 242 6446
Novotel Hotel, 4 Whitehall Quay, Leeds, LS1 4HR

Lazy Lounge - International 0113 244 6055
Westpoint (opposite Novotel), Leeds, LS1 4JY

The Northern Monkey - International 0113 242 6630
115 The Headrow, Leeds, LS1 5JW

gbk - Leeds, Antipodean 011 3243 5866
Minerva House 29 East Parade, Leeds, LS1 5PS

La Tasca Leeds - Spanish 0113 2442205
4 Russells Street, Leeds, Yorkshire, LS1 5PT

The Park Row Bar and Brasserie - British 01132 432300
123 The Headrow, Leeds, LS1 5RD

Mr Foley's - British 0113 242 9674
159 The Headrow, Leeds, LS1 5RG

Henry's Cafe Bar - Leeds - International 0113 245 9424
10 Greek Street, Leeds, West Yorkshire, LS1 5RU

STRADA Leeds - Italian 01132 471883
6 Greek Street, Leeds, LS1 5RW

Quid Pro Quo - British 0113 247 1759
26 East Parade, Leeds, LS1 5SH

154 | Listings are for ILLUSTRATIVE PURPOSES ONLY, please visit www.tastecard.co.uk for participating restaurants and offers

Prohibition Leeds - International Yorkshire House, Greek Street, Leeds, LS1 5SH	0113 224 0005
The Pack Horse - British Pack Horse Yard, Briggate, Leeds, LS1 6AT	0113 242 4810
Bella Italia - Italian 145 Briggate, Leeds, LS1 6BR	0113 2454630
Milo Bar - Pizza 10-12 Call Lane, Leeds, LS1 6DN	0113 245 7101
Distrikt - International 7 Duncan street, Leeds, LS1 6DQ	0113 243 3674
The New Conservatory - International Albion Place, Leeds, West Yorkshire, LS1 6JL	0113 246 1853
The Ship - International 71a Briggate, Leeds, West Yorkshire, LS1 6LH	0113 246 8031
Bar Fibre - International 168 Lower Briggate, Leeds, LS1 6LY	0870 120 0888
Roots and Fruits - Vegetarian 10 - 11 Grand Arcade, Leeds, West Yorkshire, LS1 6PG	0113 242 8313
Ho's Bar & Restaurant - Chinese 115, Vicar Lane, Leeds, LS1 6PJ	0113 242 8828
Chini Indian Restaurant - Bangladeshi 20 Merrion Street, Leeds City Centre, LS1 6PQ	0113 245 2025
Café Rouge - French Unit 2, The Light, 64 The Headrow, Leeds, LS1 8EH	0113 246 1620
Casa Mia Millennium - Italian Great George Street, Leeds, LS2 3AD	0845 688 3030
Spice Quarter - Indian Electric Press Building, Great George Street, Leeds, LS2 3ADS	0113 246 9241
PizzaExpress Leeds White Cloth Hall - Pizza 25 Crown Street, Leeds, LS2 7DA	0113 246 5207
Livebait Leeds - Seafood 11 - 15 Wharf Street, Shears Yard, The Calls, LS2 7EH	0113 2444 144
Calls Landing - International 36 The Calls, Leeds, West Yorkshire, LS2 7EW	0113 242 5299
River Plate Argentinean Steakhouse - Argentinean 36-38 The Calls, Leeds, LS2 7EW	0113 391 2792
Hansa's Vegetarian Restaurant - Curry 72 /74 North Street, Leeds, LS2 7PN	0113 244 4408
Tiger Tiger Leeds - International The Light, 117 Albion Street, Leeds Yorkshire, LS2 8DY	0113 236 6999
Bar Risa Leeds - British Units 1-4 The Cube Albion Steet, Leeds, LS2 8ER	0113 247 1759
Halikarnas - Turkish 57 -59, New Briggate, Leeds, LS2 8JD	0113 245 6655
Starlets Bar and Restaurant @The Merrion Hotel - International The Merrion Centre, Wade Lane, Leeds, LS2 8NH	0113 243 9191
Charco's Leeds - Mediterranean 162 Woodhouse Lane, LS2 9HB	0113 217 0809
Café Rouge - French Waterloo House, Assembly St, Leeds, LS3 7DA	0113 245 1551
Shanti Louisiana - American Unit 11 Cardigan Fields, Leeds, LS4 2DG	0113 203 8458
Hasan's Restaurant - Indian 352-354 Kirkstall Road, Leeds, LS4 2HQ	0113 278 8990

7 Spices - Indian 203-205 Woodhouse Street, Leeds, LS6 2NY	0113 243 5758
Citrus Restaurant Bar & Lounge - International 11-13 North Lane, Headingley, Leeds West Yorkshire, LS6 3HG	0113 274 9002
Thai Sabai - Thai 2 The Parade North Lane, Leeds, LS6 3HP	0113 275 8613
Giorgios Ristorante Italiano - Italian 70-72 Otley Road, Leeds, LS6 4BA	0113 278 2030
Olive Tree Greek Restaurant Headingley - Greek 74-76 Otley Road, Headingley Leeds, Yorkshire, LS6 4BA	0113 274 8282
Sala Thai - Thai 13-17 Shaw Lane, Leeds, LS6 4DH	0113 278 8400
Casa Mia - Grande - Italian 33 - 37 Harrogate Road, Leeds, LS7 3PD	0845 688 3030
Angel's Share - American Stainbeck Corner, Harrogate Rd, Chapel Allerton, LS7 3PG	0113 307 0111
Olive Tree Greek Restaurant Chapel Allerton - Greek 188-190 Harrogate Road, Chapel Allerton, Leeds, LS7 4NZ	0113 269 8488
PizzaExpress Leeds Street Lane - Pizza 96-98 Street Lane, Leeds, LS8 2AL	0113 268 4509
The Flying Pizza - Italian 60 Street Lane, Leeds, LS8 2DQ	0113 266 6501
The Thai Erawan - Thai 629 Roundhay Road, Oakwood, Leeds, LS8 4AR	0113 240 1010
The Saffron Restaurant - Indian 331 Roundhay Rd, Leeds, West Yorkshire, LS8 4HT	0113 248 5555
Charco's Roundhay Road - Mediterranean 228-230 Roundhay Road, LS8 5AA	0113 240 4060
Maureens West Indian - Caribbean 105 Roundhay Rd, Roundhay, LS8 5AJ	0113 240 6006
Red Sea Restaurant, African 159 Roundhay Road, Leeds, LS8 5AJ	0113 240 0349
Kalabash - Caribbean 258 Harehills Lane, Leeds, West Yorkshire, LS8 5DH	0113 249 2324
Tasty's Karahi Restaurant - Indian 138 Roundhay Rd, Leeds, West Yorkshire, LS8 5NA	0113 240 7050
Raies Restaurant - Indian 162 Roundhay Road, Leeds, LS8 5PL	0113 249 2493
PizzaExpress Leeds Clarence Dock - Pizza Clarence Dock, LS10 1LU	0113 245 4445
Cafe Guru - Indian 6 Brewery Place, Leeds, LS10 1NE	0113 244 2255
Nazma - Indian 11 Ring Road, Beeston Park, Leeds, LS11 5LG	0113 276 1954
Olive Tree Greek Restaurant - Rodley - Greek 55 Rodley Lane, Rodley Leeds, Yorkshire, LS13 1NG	0113 256 9283
The Beehive Restaurant - International Main Street, Thorner, Leeds, LS14 3DE	0113 201 7171
Moreno's - Mediterranean 54/56 Templenewsam road, Halton, Leeds, LS15 0DR	0113 260 4844
Gascoigne Arms - International 2 Main Street, Leeds, LS15 4JQ	0113 281 2265
Spice House - Indian 249 Selby Road, Halton, Cross Gates, LS15 7JR	0113 260 5098

Listings are for ILLUSTRATIVE PURPOSES ONLY, please visit www.tastecard.co.uk for participating restaurants and offers

East India Restaurant - Indian 0113 260 2530
Crossgates Shopping Centre Unit 8, 1st Floor, Leeds, LS15 8ET

La Cantina 44 - Mediterranean 0113 368 0066
1a Austhorpe Road, Cross Gates, Leeds, LS15 8QR

Dough Bistro - British 0113 278 7255
293 Spen Lane, Leeds, LS16 5BD

Verve Grill @ Village Hotel North Leeds - International 0844 980 8031
Village Leisure Hotel 186, Otley Road, Leeds, LS16 5PR

Stables Pub - British 0113 230 6000
Otley Road, Leeds, Yorkshire, LS16 5PS

El Bareto - Spanish 0113 266 6946
120 Gledhow Valley Road, Leeds, LS17 6LX

Thai Lotus - Thai 0113 294 7000
300 Harrogate Road, Leeds, West Yorkshire, LS17 6LY

Leeds Seventeen - British 0113 2662594
Nursery Lane, Leeds, LS17 7HW

Enigma - International 0113 239 0110
145 New Road Side, Leeds, West Yorkshire, LS18 4QD

The Last Viceroy - Indian 0113 258 0293
141-145 New Road Side, Horsforth, Leeds, LS18 4QD

The Outside-In - International 0113 258 1410
6 Town Street, Horsforth Leeds, West Yorkshire, LS18 4RJ

Prachee Indian Restaurant - Indian 01943 872531
6 Bradford Rd, Guiseley, Leeds, LS20 8NH

The Drop Inn - British 01943 874967
29 Town St, Guiseley, Leeds, LS20 9DT

The Royalty - International 0194 346 1156
Yorkgate, Otley, Leeds, LS21 3DG

Sunrise - Asian 0193 758 3675
Westgate House, Market Place, Wetherby West Yorkshire, LS22 6LQ

The Bridge Wetherby - British 0193 758 0115
Walshford, Wetherby, Leeds, LS22 5HS

The Fox And The Hounds Walton - British 01937 842 192
Hall Park Road, Walton, West Yorkshire, LS23 7DQ

Sunar Bangla - Bangladeshi 0193 755 7738
The Railway Station Station Rd, Church Fenton, Tadcaster, LS24 9RA

Sonali Restaurant - Indian 0193 753 0607
20 Bridge St, Tadcaster, North Yorkshire, LS24 9AL

Aiolis Restaurant @ The Holiday Inn Leeds - International 0113 286 6556
Holiday Inn Leeds, Wakefield Road, LS25 1LH

China Palace - Chinese 01977 684789
Scireburn House London Rd, South Milford, Leeds, LS25 5DP

The Claret Jug at Oulton Hall - British 0113 282 1000
Oulton Hall Rothwell Lane, Rothwell, Leeds, LS26 8HN

The Needless Inn - International 0192 447 2986
Scotchman Lane, Morley, Leeds, LS27 0NZ

East Bar & Grill - International 0113 257 9991
Richardshaw Lane, Pudsey, Leeds, LS28 6BN

Abids Restaurant and Bar - Indian 0113 255 266
116 Town Street, Stanningley, Pudsey, LS28 6EZ

Viet Thai Cuisine - Thai 0113 257 0893
134 Bradford Road Stanningley, Pudsey, Leeds, West Yorkshire, LS28 6UR

the stroom restaurant and function rooms - British 0113 257 0140
9 Chapeltown, Pudsey, West Yorkshire, LS28 7RZ

La Rosa Restaurant and Bar - Italian 0127 466 5506
483 Bradford Rd, Pudsey, LS28 8ED

Palok, Bangladeshi 0194 386 3948
78 Main Street, Burley, West Yorkshire, LS29 7BT

PizzaExpress Ilkley - Pizza 01943 817776
9B Station Plaza, LS29 8HF

Brasserie 1 at the Craiglands Hotel - British 0194 343 0001
Craiglands Hotel, Cow Pasture Road, Ilkley, LS29 8RQ

Newcastle

Noosh Restaurant - International 0191 232 4663
Amen Corner, The Side, Newcastle Upon Tyne, NE1 1PE

PizzaExpress Newcastle - Pizza 0191 221 0120
10 Dean Street, NE1 1PG

La Tasca Newcastle Quayside - Spanish 0191 230 4006
106, The Quayside, Tyne and Wear, NE1 3DX

Oliviana's - Italian 0191 232 5537
5-7 Side, Newcastle-Upon-Tyne, NE1 3JE

Da Mimmo's - Italian 0191 222 0659
6-10 Leazes Park Road, Newcastle upon Tyne, NE1 4PF

Shearers - American 0191 201 8688
St James' Park, Strawberry Place, Newcastle-Upon-Tyne, NE14ST

Thai Siam Restaurant - Thai 0191 232 0261
16 Stowell Street, Newcastle-Upon-Tyne, NE1 4XQ

Rendez Vous Rest @The County Hotel Newcastle - British 0871 376 9029
Neville Street, Newcastle, NE1 5DF

Tiger Tiger - Newcastle - International 0191 235 7065
The Gate, Newgate St, Newcastle, NE1 5RE

Freyas Restaurant at Aspers - British 0191 255 0400
The Gate Complex, Newgate Street, Newcastle-Upon-Tyne, NE1 5TG

La Tasca Newcastle Grey Street - Spanish 0191 260 3533
42 - 50, Grey Street, Newcastle Upon Tyne, NE1 6AE

Living Room Newcastle - International 0191 255 4450
12 Grey Street, Newcastle, NE1 6AE

Starters & Puds Restaurant - International 0871 911 6539
2-6 Shakespeare Street, Newcastle, NE1 6AQ

The Godfather - Italian 0191 232 6171
3 Market Street, Newcastle-Upon-Tyne, Tyne and Wear, NE1 6JE

STRADA Newcastle - Italian 0191 261 6070
Old Eldon Square, Blackett Street, Newcastle, NE1 7JG

Brasserie Black Door - International 0191 260 5411
16 Stoddart Street, Newcastle upon Tyne, NE2 1AN

As You Like It - International 08719116537
Block A Scottish Life House, Archbold Terrace, NE21DB

Whites Hotel - American 0191 281 5126
38 - 42 Osbourne Road, Jesmond, Newcastle Upon Tyne, NE2 2AL

PizzaExpress Jesmond - Pizza 0191 281 4767
92 Osborne Road, NE2 2TD

PizzaExpress Gosforth - Pizza 0191 285 9799
125 High Street, NE3 1NA

General Havelock Inn - Modern European 0143 468 4376
9 Ratcliffe Rd, Haydon Bridge, Hexham, NE47 6ER

The Gateshead Swallow - British 0191 477 1105
High West Street, Gateshead, NE8 1PE

Windows Tyne Bar & Lounge @Hilton Newcastle - International 0191 490 9700
Bottle Bank, Gateshead, NE8 2AR

Windows Tyne Restaurant @Hilton Newcastle - International 0191 490 9700
Bottle Bank, Gateshead, NE8 2AR

The Red House Brasserie Metro Centre - British 0191 460 9942
Upper Yellow Mall, Metrocentre, Gateshead, NE11 9XF

Café Rouge - French 01914 605502
Catering Unit 1, Redmall, MetroCentre, Gateshead, NE11 9XR

PizzaExpress Gateshaed - Pizza 0191 460 6130
Unit 122 Yellow Quadrant, NE11 9XZ

Greens Brasserie, Healthy Eating 0191 213 0070
Gosforth Parkway, Newcastle-Upon-Tyne, NE12 8ET

Sheffield

Picasso Rest & Bar @The Park Inn Sheffield - International 0114 220 4000
Blonk Street Sheffield, South Yorkshire, S1 2AU

Tulip Lounge - British 0114 276 5870
21-23 North Church St, Sheffield, South Yorkshire, S1 2DH

STRADA Sheffield - Italian 0114 279 5948
6 Leopold Square, Leopold Street, Sheffield, S1 2JG

Café Rouge - French 0114 275 3815
Unit 1, Sheffield Centre, St Paul's Place, Sheffield, S1 2JL

Silversmiths - International 0114 270 6160
111 Arundel Street, Sheffield, S1 2NT

The Cutler's Hotel - British 0114 273 9939
George Street, Heart of the City, Sheffield, S1 2PF

Elements Restaurant Novotel - International 0871 310 4954
50 Arundel Gate, Sheffield Centre, Sheffield, S1 2PR

Olive Bar and Restaurant - British 0114 221 4004
73-75 Division Street, Sheffield, South Yorkshire, S1 4GE

Antibo Sheffield - Italian 0114 272 7222
Unit 10 The Plaza, Fitzwilliam Street, Sheffield, S1 4JB

23 Bar And Restaurant - International 0114 272 23 23
West One Plaza, 8 Fitzwilliam Street, Sheffield, S1 4JB

Zing Vaa - Chinese 0114 275 6633
55 The Moor, Sheffield, S1 4PF

PizzaExpress Sheffield Devonshire Street - Pizza 0114 275 2755
124 Devonshire Street, S3 7SF

7 Spices Balti - Indian 0114 275 7695
120 Mayfair Court, City Centre, Sheffield, S3 8PP

Bangla Cottage - Curry 0114 285 343
481 Langsett Rd, Sheffield, S6 2LN

Vito's Italian Restaurant - Italian 0114 233 3574
284 South Road, Sheffield, S6 3TE

Bella Roma - Italian 0114 231 6880
92 Middlewood Rd, Sheffield, South Yorkshire, S6 4HA

Shimul Restaurant - Curry 0114 235 9911
329 Meadowhead, Sheffield, S8 7UP

Café Rouge, French 011 4256 8867
Unit OR4A (54A The Oasis), Meadowhall Centre, Sheffield, S9 1EE

La Tasca - Meadowhall - Spanish 0114 256 9986
3a The Oasis, Meadowhall, Sheffield, S9 1EP

PizzaExpress Sheffield The Oasis - Pizza 0114 256 9623
The Oasis, S9 1EP

Prezzo Sheffield - Italian 0114 2447477
Unit 4 Valley Centertainment, Broughton Lane, Sheffield, S9 2EP

Bella Italia - Italian 0114 243 1923
Unit 3, Valley Centertainment, Sheffield, S9 2EP

Maharaj Restaurant - Indian 0114 266 4193
22 - 24 Commonside, Sheffield, S10 1GB

Saffron Club - Indian 0871 310 4981 / 0114 276 6150
Old Baths, 223 Glossop Road, Sheffield, S10 2GW

Pizza Volante - Italian 0114 2739056
255-257 Glossop Road, Sheffield, S10 2GZ

Balti King - Indian 0114 266 6655
216 Fulwood Road, Sheffield, S10 3BB

UK Mama, Caribbean 0114 268 7807
257 Fulwood Road, Sheffield, S10 3BD

Clay Oven - Indian 0114 230 8312
139-141 Oakbrook Road, Sheffield, S11 7EB

Champs Sports Bar & Restaurant - American 0114 266 6333
315-319 Ecclesall Road, Sheffield, S11 8NX

Uncle Sam's Chuck Wagon - American 0114 266 8588
298 Ecclesall Road, Sheffield, South Yorkshire, S11 8PE

Café Rouge - French 0114 268 2232
383-385 Ecclesall Rd, Sheffield, S11 8PG

La Tasca Sheffield - Spanish 0114 266 6242
509 Ecclesall Road, Sheffield, S11 8PR

Caffé Uno Sheffield - Italian 0114 267 0565
631 - 633 Ecclesall Road, Sheffield, S11 8PT

Viva Tequila - Spanish 0114 265 4414
960 Gleadless Road, Sheffield, S12 2LL

Darcy's Brasserie at Mosborough Hall - British 0871 674 4006
High Street, Mosborough, Sheffield, S20 5EA

Gemelli's - Italian 01246 433395
1 Barbers Row, Renishaw, Sheffield, S21 3UA

The Yellow Lion - British 0871 207 8530
Worksop Road, Aston, Sheffield, S26 2EB

Bayleaves Restaurant - Indian 0114 240 1919
129 High Street, Ecclesfield, Sheffield, S35 9UA

Cerrone - Italian 0114 246 1666
62 High Steet Ecclesfield, Sheffield, South Yorkshire, S35 9XD

Buckingham's Hotel - British 0124 620 1041
85 Newbold Road, Chesterfield, Derbyshire, S41 7PU

The Old Post Restaurant 01246 279 479
43 Holywell Street, Chesterfield, Derbyshire, S41 7SH

Il Bacio - Italian 0170 983 7373
53 Sheffield Road, Rotherham, South Yorkshire, S60 1DA

Sanam Restaurant - Indian 01709 720 720 / 01709 83 87 87
14/16 Domine Lane, Rotherham, S60 1QA

The RBG Bar and Grill @ The Park Inn Rotherham - British 0170 976 0666
Manvers Way, Wath-upon-Dearne, Rotherham, S63 7EQ

Latinos Restaurant - Mediterranean 01226 283 263
Hanson Street, Barnsley, S70 2HZ

Listings are for **ILLUSTRATIVE PURPOSES ONLY**, please visit www.tastecard.co.uk for participating restaurants and offers | 157

Best Western Ardsley House Hotel & Health Club - British — 0122 630 9955
Doncaster Road, Ardsley, Barnsley, S71 5EH

Al Naz Restaurant - Indian — 0122 673 4142
335 Pontefract Road, Lundwood, Barnsley, S71 5HS

Thaal Ltd - Indian — 0122 675 5464
18 Doncaster Rd, Darfield, Barnsley, S73 9HH

Dil Raj Tandoori Restaurant - Indian — 01226 202606
8-12 High Street, Dodworth, Barnsley, S75 3RE

Curry Mahal - Curry — 0122 620 1188
28 Barnsley Road, Dodworth, Barnsley, S75 3RN

The Chilli Lodge - Curry — 0122 679 2300
Westfield Park Equestrian Centre Knabbs Lane, Barnley, S75 4RD

The Normanton - International — 0162 383 5333
Clumber Park Hotel And Spa, Clumber Park, Near Worksop, S80 3PA

The Moorhen Restaurant at The Charnwood Hotel - British — 0190 959 1610
The Charnwood Hotel, Sheffield Road, Worksop, S81 8HF

Sunderland

Tavistock Grangetown - Italian — 0191 510 1100
Queen Alexandra Road, Grange Town, Sunderland, SR2 9PF

Tavistock Italia at Best Western Hotel Roker - Italian — 0191 567 1786
Roker Terrace, Sunderland, SR6 9NB

Tavistock Thai China at Best Western Hotel Roker - Thai — 0191 567 1786
Roker Terrace, Sunderland, SR6 9NB

Cleveland

Restaurant @ Thistle Middlesbrough - International — 0871 376 9028
Fry Street, Middlesbrough, TS1 1JH

Eliano's Brasserie - Italian — 01642 868566
20-22 Fairbridge Street, Off Grange Road, Cleveland, TS1 5DJ

Tavistock Italia at Best Western Hotel Middlesbrough - Italian — 0164 281 7638
Marton Road, Middlesbrough, TS4 2PA

The Brasserie - British — 0164 289 0020
16 High Street, Yarm, Stockton--On-Tees, TS15 9AE

The Sportsman's Hotel - British — 0164 278 0223
Station Road, Eaglescliffe Stockton on Tees, County Durham, TS16 0BU

Parkmore Hotel & Leisure Club - International — 0164 278 6815
636 Yarm Road Eaglescliffe, Stockton-on-Tees, Tees Valley, TS16 0DH

PizzaExpress Stockton on Tees - Pizza — 01642 612693
6 The Teesside Retail Park, Stockton on Tees, Cleveland, TS17 7BW

Cafe Sapore - Italian — 0164 258 5141
4 Harper Parade, Hartburn, Stockton--On-Tees, TS18 5EQ

Tavistock Italia at Best Western Grand Hotel - Italian — 0142 926 6345
Swainson Street, Hartlepool, TS24 8AA

Raudin's at The York Hotel - International — 01429 867 373
185 York Road, Hartlepool, Cleveland, TS26 9EE

Wakefield

Jongleurs Comedy Club Wakefield - International — 0192 438 2569
84-86 Westgate, Wakefield, WF1 1JZ

Hing Lung - Chinese — 0192 436 6603
George Street, Wakefield, WF1 1NE

The Othello Cafe - British — 01924 371 355
86 Kirkgate, Wakefield, West Yorkshire, WF1 1TB

The New Union - British — 01924 378215
2 Almsgate, Wakefield, WF1 1UZ

The Plough Inn - British — 0192 489 2007
45 Warmfield Lane, Warmfield, Wakefield, WF1 5TL

The Park - British — 01924 248666
Waterton Park The Balk, Walton, Wakefield, WF2 6QL

The Lupset - International — 0192 437 3382
328 Horbury Rd, Wakefield, WF2 8JF

Unicorn Inn - International — 0113 282 2366
Main Street, Carlton, Wakefield, WF3 3RW

Cedar Court Hotel La Brasserie - British — 01924 276 310
Denby Dale Rd, Calder Grove, Wakefield, WF4 3QZ

Orlando's - Italian — 01924 840762
5 Wakefield Road, Grange Moor, Wakefield, WF4 4DS

The Sun - British — 0192 484 8603
62 Barnsley Road, Flockton, Wakefield, WF4 4DW

Bistro 42 - International — 01924 278 123
Horbury, Wakefield, West Yorkshire, WF4 5LE

Arooje - Indian — 0192 422 0075
16 Market Street, Normanton, WF6 2AR

Al Jamil Balti Restaurant - Indian — 0197 779 7002
3-5 Front Street, Town Centre, Pontefract, WF8 1DA

The Fox & Hounds Inn - British — 01977 620 082
Pontefract Rd, Thorpe Audlin Pontefract, West Yorkshire, WF8 3EL

Vissett Cottage Hotel and Cantonese Restaurant — 01977 610 765
Barnsley Road, Hemsworth, Pontefract, WF9 4PQ

PizzaExpress Caslteford - Pizza — 01977 556 800
Unit 11 Xscape, WF10 4TA

Bella Italia - Italian — 01977 514 200
Unit 7, Xscape, Colorado Way, Castleford, WF10 4TA

Palm Court Pizzeria - Italian — 0197 755 4766
Whitwood Common Lane, Castleford, West Yorkshire, WF10 5PT

The Rising Sun - British — 0197 755 4766
Whitwood Common Lane, Castleford, West Yorkshire, WF10 5PT

Raaz Restaurant - Indian — 0192 446 2266
49c Bath Street, Dewsbury, WF13 2JR

Gray Ox Inn - British — 0127 487 2845
15 Hartshead Lane, Liversedge, WF15 8AL

Don Luigis - Italian — 0127 4 873636
399A Halifax Road, Bradford, West Yorkshire, WF15 8DU

Parmars Indian Restaurant and Bar - Indian 0127 487 3566
471 Halifax Road, Hightown, Liversedge, WF15 8HU

The New Charnwood - British 0192 440 6512
4 Westgate, Heckmondwike, WF16 0EH

Bella Italia - Italian 01924 422374
Centre 27 Retail Park, Birstall, Wakefield, WF17

York

Bella Italia - Italian 01904 611221
89 Low Petergate, York, YO1 2HY

The RBG Bar & Grill @ The Park Inn York - International 01904 459988
Park Inn York, North Street, York, YO1 6JF

The RBG Lounge @ The Park Inn York - International 0190 445 9988
Park Inn York, North Street, York, YO1 6JF

PizzaExpress York River House - Pizza 01904 672 904
River House, 17 Museum Street, York, YO1 7DJ

STRADA York - Italian 01904 672 999
75 Low Petergate, York, YO1 7HY

Café Rouge - French 01904 673293
The Adams House, 52 Lower Petergate, York, YO1 7HZ

La Tasca York - Spanish 01904 521100
21, Back Swinegate, York, YO1 8AD

gbk York - Antipodean 019 0463 9537
7 Lendal, York, YO1 8AQ

Kennedys Bar and Restaurant - International 0190 462 0222
1 Little Stonegate, York, YO1 8AX

Stonegate Yard - International 0190 462 5870
8-10 Little Stonegate, York, YO1 8AX

PizzaExpress York Saint Sampson's Square - Pizza 01904 630 930
10 Saint Sampson's Square, York, YO1 8RN

Fiesta Mehicana - Mexican 0190 461 0243
14 Clifford Street, York, YO1 9RD

Caesars at Silvanos - Italian 0190 462 5036
2 Cumberland Street, York, YO1 9SW

Langtons Brasserie @ The York Pavilion Hotel - British 01904 622099
45 Main Street, Fulford, York, YO10 4PJ

Elements Restaurant at York Novotel Hotel - International 0190 461 1660
Fishergate, York, YO10 4FD

Bombay Spice - Indian 01723 354324
9 - 10 Queen Street, Scarborough, North Yorkshire, YO11 1HA

The Sea View Lounge & Bar @ The Royal Hotel - British 0172 336 433
The Royal Hotel, St. Nicholas Street, Scarborough, YO11 2HE

The Sea View Restaurant @ The Royal Hotel - British 0172 336 4333
The Royal Hotel, St. Nicholas Street, Scarborough, YO11 2HE

The Theatre Bar @ The Royal Hotel - British 0172 336 4333
The Royal Hotel, St. Nicholas Street, Scarborough, YO11 2HE

The Copper Horse Restaurant - British 01723 862 029
15 Main Street, Seamer, Scarborough, YO12 4RF

The Derwent Restaurant @ Hackness Grange Hotel - British 0172 388 2345
Hackness Grange Country House Hotel Nr. Scarborough, YO13 0JW

The Lakeside Lounge & Bar @Hackness Grange Hotel - British 0172 388 2345
Hackness Grange Country House Hotel, Nr. Scarborough, YO13 0JW

The Ellis Cocktail Lounge & Bar @The Wrea Head Hotel - British 0172 337 8211
Wrea Head Country House Hotel, Barmoor Lane, Scalby YO13 0PB

The Four Seasons Restaurant @The Wrea Head Hotel - British 01723 378 211
Wrea Head Country House Hotel, Barmoor Lane, Scalby YO13 0PB

Old Lodge Hotel - International 0165 369 0570
Old Maltongate, Malton, YO17 7EG

The Thai House at Malton - Thai 0165 369 6117
47 Wheelgate Malton, North Yorkshire, YO17 7HT

The Drovers Rest @ The Fleece - British 0194 475 8464
9-11 Westgate, Rillington, Malton, YO17 8LN

The Blackboard @ The Beansheaf Hotel - British 01653 668614
Malton Road, Pickering, YO176UE

Castlegate Taberna - Spanish 0175 147 6481
1 Castlegate, Pickering, YO18 7AX

PizzaExpress York Saint Nicholas Avenue - Pizza 01904 678 683
St Nicholas Avenue, York, YO19 4TA

The Tempus Restaurant at The Royal York Hotel - International 0190 465 3681
Station Parade, York, North Yorkshire, YO24 1AA

The Chequers Inn - British 0142 335 9637
Church Lane, Bilton In Ainsty, YO26 7NN

The Sidings Hotel and Restaurant - Italian 01904 470221
Station Lane, Shipton by Beningbrough, York North Yorkshire, YO30 1BT

The Churchill Hotel - British 01904 644456
65 Bootham, York, YO30 7DQ

The Tanglewood - British 01904 468 611
Malton Road, York, YO32 9TW

Fox & Hounds - Langthorpe - International 0142 332 2717
Langthorpe, North Yorkshire, YO51 9BZ

The Garden Room @ Burn Hall - British 01347 825 400
Tollerton Road, Huby, York, YO61 1JB

The Inn at Hawnby - British 0143 979 8202
Hawnby, North Yorkshire, YO62 5QS

Listings are for **ILLUSTRATIVE PURPOSES ONLY**, please visit www.tastecard.co.uk for participating restaurants and offers

Scotland

Cargo
British — 0131 659 7880

129 Fountainbridge , Edinburgh , EH3 9QG

At the hub of one of the most up-and-coming areas Cargo's waterside location and sophisticated urban design found a place in the hearts of local residents some years ago.

Renowned for its superior level of service Cargo continues to offer quality food and drink and is recognised as one of the city's best venue for functions and events in Edinburgh.

Split over two levels with a spacious patio overlooking the Union Canal. The versatility of Cargo enables them to cater for any type and size of event including BBQ's, gala dinners, fashion show's and casino nights, all tailored to your own needs.

Bo'vine Restaurant
International — 0141 339 8811

383 Byres Road, Glasgow, G12 8AU

The Hilton Glasgow Grosvenor's West End location provides the perfect base for exploring one of Europe's most exciting cities. Just 2 minutes' walk from Glasgow attractions like the Botanic Gardens, the hotel is perfect for business and leisure.

Bo'Vine by Hilton is a new steak restaurant in the Hilton Hotel. Enjoy delicious steaks, fish dishes and salads in the comfort of this newly refurbished restaurant on the first floor of the Hilton Glasgow Grosvenor hotel. All steak come from grass fed, Caledonian Crown Scottish beef, aged for a minimum of 28 days. The wine list is extensive and there is a great selection of dishes for our vegetarian diners.

Scotland

Paperino's
Italian — **0141 334 3811**

227 Byres Road, Glasgow, G12 8UD

One of Glasgow's best loved restaurants, Paperino's offers great Italian food at affordable prices in stylish surroundings.

Situated in three locations; Sauchiehall Street, Byres Road and St Vincent Street, three of Glasgow's most lively areas, Paperino's is the place to go for affordable quality dining.

Paperino's has established a great reputation, often catering for families, office parties and cinema goers.

The menu principally offers pastas and pizzas, both of these are done with individuality and invention.

The pizzas are crispy and light, while pasta 'alla Paperino'; the house speciality, is more than a satisfactory medley of onions, bacon, peppers and chilli.

The general vibe is fun and informal, with much laughter and chatter filling the air: eating here provides the perfect atmosphere for any occasion and the service is second to none.

Hudson's Bar
British — 0131 247 7000

7-11 Hope Street, Edinburgh, EH2 4EL

Edinburgh has an amazing bar scene with more diversity than you would find in cities four times the size!

Reminiscent of a New York loft apartment Hudsons Bar in Edinburgh provides a lively vantage point to delight in Edinburgh's new cosmopolitan personality.

Open for breakfast right through to late supper, the food and drinks menus offer a superb selection of old favourites with a modern twist.

Scotland

Aberdeen

PizzaExpress Aberdeen Belmont Street - Pizza 01224 620 128
Caberstone House, 47 Belmont Street, Aberdeen, AB10 1JS

PizzaExpress Aberdeen Union Street - Pizza 01224 649 511
402-404 Union Street, Aberdeen, AB10 1TQ

The Athenaeum - Modern European 01224 595 585
5-9 Union Street, Aberdeen, AB11 5BU

Tiger Tiger Aberdeen - International 01224 252 434
1-2 Shiprow off Union Street, Aberdeen, AB11 5BY

Prezzo Aberdeen - Italian 0122 459 3009
Union Square, Aberdeen, AB11 5RG

Burnett Arms Hotel - British 01330 824944
25 High Street, Banchory, Aberdeenshire, AB31 5TD

Dundee

Deacon Brodies - International 0138 220 4137
15 Ward Road, Dundee, DD1 1ND

Playwright Restaurant - International 0138 222 3113
11 Tay Square, Dundee, DD1 1PB

All Stars - International 0138 220 1042
85-87 Commercial Street, Dundee Angus, DD1 2AB

Kennedy's Grill Room and Steak House - Steak 0138 220 0999
33 Castle Street, Dundee, DD1 3AD

Spice Restaurant - Indian 0138 220 4358
140 Perth Road, Dundee, DD1 4JW

Tally's - International 0138 222 4777
11-13 Old Hawkhill, Dundee, Tayside, DD1 5EU

Park House Hotel - International 0138 261 1151
40 Coupar Angus Road, Dundee, Tayside, DD2 3HY

Ashoka Shak Dundee - Indian 01382 858169
Camperdown Leisure Park, Dundee, DD2 3SQ

Bombay Joe's 0138 277 6448
44 Gray Street, Broughty Ferry, Dundee, DD5 2BJ

Dumfries

Blackaddie Country House Hotel - International 0165 950 270
Sanquhar, Dumfriesshire, DG4 6JJ

Edinburgh

Belushi's Edinburgh - American 0131 226 1446
9-13 Market Street, Edinburgh, EH1 1DE

The Bank Bar - Scottish 0131 556 9940
1 South Bridge, Edinburgh, EH1 1LL

PizzaExpress Edinburgh Northbridge - Pizza 0131 557 6411
23 Northbridge, EH1 1SB

Bella Italia - Italian 0131 225 2044
55 Northbridge, Edinburgh, EH1 1SB

Monteiths Bar - British 0131 557 0330
59 High Street The Royal Mile, Edinburgh, Midlothian, EH1 1SR

Henry J Beans Edinburgh - American 0131 222 8844
Caledonian Hotel, Edinburgh, City of Edinburgh, EH1 2AB

PizzaExpress Edinburgh George IV Bridge - Pizza 0131 225 9669
Victoria Terrace 59/63 George IV Bridge, EH1 2JL

Biddy Mulligans - Scottish 0131 220 1246
94-96, Grassmarket, Edinburgh, EH1 2JR

The Lot - International 0131 235 9924
4'6 Grassmarket, Edinburgh, EH1 2JU

9 Cellars Restaurant & Bar - Curry 0131 557 9899
1-3 York Place, EDINBURGH, EH1 3EB

The Street - International 0131 556 4272
2 Picardy Place, Edinburgh, EH1 3JT

Passage to India - Indian 0131 556 4547
20 Union Place, Edinburgh, EH1 3NQ

Pani Solinska - Eastern European 0131 557 6900
73 Broughton Street, Edinburgh, EH1 3RJ

Craig's Restaurant @ The King James - Scottish 0871 376 9016
107 Leith Street, Edinburgh, EH1 3SW

The King James Bar @ The King James - International 0871 376 9016
107 Leith Street, Edinburgh, EH1 3SW

The Wee Windaes - Scottish 0131 225 5144
144 High Street, Edinburgh, EH1 IQ5

Café Rouge - French 0131 225 4515
43 Frederick Street, Edinburgh, Scotland, EH2 1EP

Cafe Royal - British 0131 556 1884
19 West Register Street, Edinburgh, EH2 2AA

Bella Italia - Italian 0131 225 4808
9 Hanover Street, Edinburgh, EH2 2PL

Librizzi Restaurant - Seafood 0131 226 1155
69 North Castle Street, Edinburgh, EH2 3LJ

Ryans Cellar Bar - International 0131 226 7005
2 Hope Street, Edinburgh, EH2 4DB

Hudsons Bar - British 0131 247 7000
7-11 Hope Street, Edinburgh, EH2 4EL

gbk Edinburgh - Antipodean 013 1260 9896
137 George St, Edinburgh, EH2 4JY

PizzaExpress Edinburgh Queensferry Street - Pizza 0131 225 8863
32 Queensferry Street, EH2 4QS

Sygn Bar - British 0131 225 6060
15 Charlotte Lane, Edinburgh, EH2 4QZ

Iglu - International 0131 476 5333
2b Jamaica Street, Edinburgh, EH3 6HH

The Westroom - Scottish 0131 629 9868
3 Melville Place, Edinburgh, EH3 7PR

Papoli - Modern European 0131 477 7047
244a Morrison Street, Edinburgh, EH3 8DT

Filmhouse Cafe Bar - International 0131 229 5932
88, Lothian Road, Edinburgh, EH3 9BZ

La Bagatelle - French 0131 229 0869
22A Brougham Place, Edinburgh, EH3 9JU

Cargo - British 129 Fountainbridge, Edinburgh, EH3 9QG	0131 659 7880
Channings - International 12-16 South Learmonth Gardens, Edinburgh, EH4 1EZ	0131 315 2225
PizzaExpress Edinburgh Deanhaugh Street - Pizza 1 Deanhaugh Street, EH4 1LU	0131 332 7229
Prezzo Edinburgh - Italian 25 Pier Place, Edinburgh, EH6 4LP	0131 5524356
The Raj Restaurant On The Shore - Curry 85-91 Henderson Street, Edinburgh, EH6 6ED	0131 553 3980
Daniel's Bistro - French 88 Commercial Street, Edinburgh, EH6 6LX	0131 553 5933
Bond No 9 - International 84 Commercial Street, Edinburgh, EH6 6LX	0131 555 5578
PizzaExpress Edinburgh Waterview House - Pizza Waterview House, EH6 6QU	0131 5544332
Suruchi Too Restaurant - Indian 121 Constitution Street, Edinburgh, EH6 7AE	0131 554 3268
e:s:i Brasserie - British 46 Queen Charlotte Street, Edinburgh, EH6 7EX	0131 555 3103
Elbow Bar & Kitchen - International 133-135 East Claremont Street, Edinburgh, EH7 4JA	0131 556 5662
The Terrace Brasserie - International Terrace Hotel, 18'22 Royal Terrace, Edinburgh, EH7 5AQ	0131 557 3222
Love You Long Thai - Thai 20 Leopold Place, Edinburgh, EH7 5LB	0131 652 3987
Al Dente Restaurant - Italian 139 Easter Road, Edinburgh, EH7 5QA	0131 652 1932
PizzaExpress Edinburgh Holyrood Road - Pizza 111 Holyrood Road, EH8 8AU	0131 557 5734
Suruchi Restaurant - Indian 14a Nicolson Street, Edinburgh, EH8 9DH	0131 556 6583
Ann Purna - Vegetarian 44-45 St. Patricks Square, Edinburgh, EH8 9ET	0131 662 1807
Indian Mela - Curry 63 Clerk Street, Edinburgh, EH8 9JQ	0131 667 1035
Kings Balti - Indian 79 Buccleuch Street, Edinburgh, EH8 9LS	0131 662 9212
Manna Mahal Restaurant - Curry 111-113 Buccleuch Street, Edinburgh, EH8 9NG	0131 662 9111
The Murrayfield - Scottish 18 Corstorphine Road, Edinburgh, EH12 6HN	0131 337 1844
Prince Balti House - Indian 11 Seafield Road East, Edinburgh, EH15 1EB	0131 657 1155
The Sun Inn - British Lothianbridge, Dalkeith, EH22 4TR	0131 663 2456
Craigiebield - International 50 Bog Road, Penicuik, Midlothian, EH26 9BZ	0196 867 2557
The Grange - International 35 High Street, North Berwick, EH39 4HH	01620 893 344
Raj Poot Indian Restaurant - Indian 90 Uphall Station Road, Pumpherston, EH53 0L	01506 436611 / 431166
Classic India - Indian 3c Howden West Road, Livingston, West Lothian, EH54 6AA	0150 641 4683 / 0150 641 0786
PizzaExpress Livingston - Pizza 2 McArthur Glen designer outlet, EH54 6QP	01506 417 543
Ashoka Shak - Indian Unit 26 Livingston Designer Outlet, Livingston, EH54 6QX	01506 417799

Falkirk

FullStop - International 14 Lint Riggs, Falkirk, Stirlingshire, FK1 1DG	0132 461 1669
Behind The Wall - International 14 Melville Street, Falkirk, Stirlingshire, FK1 1HZ	01324 633 338
Ziggy Forelles - International 52 Port Street, Stirling, FK8 2LJ	0178 646 3222
River House Restaurant - Scottish The Castle Business Park, Stirling, FK9 4TW	01786 465 577

Scotland

Guy's Restaurant - Scottish 24 Candleriggs, Glasgow, G1 1LD	0141 552 1114
Thali - Indian 42 Albion Street, Glasgow, Lanarkshire, G1 1LH	0141 552 8332
Tiger Tiger Glasgow - International The Glasshouse, 20 Glassford St, Glasgow, G1 1UL	0141 553 4888
Café Rouge - French 20 Royal Exchange, Square, Glasgow, G1 2AB	014 1243 2055
PizzaExpress Glasgow Queen Street - Pizza 151 Queen Street, G1 3BJ	0141 221 3333
Waxy O` Connors - International 44 West George Street, Glasgow, G2 1DH	0141 354 5154
Fratelli Sarti Renfield Street - Italian 42 Renfield St, Glasgow, Lanarkshire, G2 1NF	0141 572 7000
Fratelli Sarti Bath St - Italian 121 Bath St, Glasgow, Lanarkshire, G2 2SZ	0141 204 0440
Fratelli Sarti Wellington St - Italian 133 Wellington St, Glasgow, Lanarkshire, G2 2XD	0141 248 2228
Annlann Restaurant @ Thistle Glasgow - International Cambridge Street, Glasgow, G2 3HN	0871 376 9043
Paperinos City Center - Italian 283 Sauchiehall Street, Glasgow, G2 3HQ	0141 332 3800
Topolinos - Italian 285 Sauchiehall Street, Glasgow, G2 3HQ	0141 332 2272
Torres - Spanish 327 Sauchiehall Street, Glasgow, G2 3HW	0141 332 6789
Kama Sutra - Asian 331 Sauchiehall Street, Glasgow, G2 3HW	0141 332 0055
Rawalpindi Tandoori - Indian 321 Sauchiehall Street, Glasgow, G2 3HW	0141 332 4180
CCA Bar and Café - International 350 Sauchiehall Street, Glasgow, G2 3JD	0141 352 4920
Indian Gallery - Indian 450 Sauchiehall Street, Glasgow Lanarkshire, G2 3JD	0141 332 3355

Listings are for **ILLUSTRATIVE PURPOSES ONLY**, please visit www.tastecard.co.uk for participating restaurants and offers

PizzaExpress Glasgow Sauchiehall - Pizza 0141 332 6965
436 Sauchiehall Street, G2 3JD

Sannino - Italian 0141 332 3565
61a Elmbank Street, Glasgow, G2 4PQ

Paperinos @78 - Italian 0141 248 7878
78 St Vincent Street, Glasgow, G2 5UB

Bella Italia - Italian 0141 2215321
96 Hope Street, Glasgow, G2 6PH

The Collage - International 0141 204 3333
301 Argyle Street, Glasgow, G2 8DL

Four Seasons - Chinese 0141 332 2666
87 Cambridge Street, Glasgow, Lanarkshire, G3 6RU

The Ashoka Glasgow - Indian 0141 221 1761
108 Elderslie Street, Glasgow, Lanarkshire, G3 7AR

Madras Palace - Curry 0141 248 8333
15-17 Kent Road, Glasgow, G3 7EH

Ashoka West End - Indian 0141 339 3371
1284 Argyle Street, Glasgow, G3 8AB

The Brasserie at The Menzies Glasgow Hotel - Scottish 0141 222 2929
27 Washington Street, Glasgow, G3 8AZ

City Cafe AA Rosette Restaurant - British 0141 227 1010
Finnieston Quay, Glasgow, G3 8HN

Lounge Bar @ City Inn Glasgow - Modern European 0141 240 1002
Finnieston Quay, Glasgow, G3 8HN

Tapas International - Tapas 0141 337 6378
1293 Argyle Street, Glasgow, G3 8TL

Ashoka at the Quay - Indian 0141 429 4492
Unit D2 The Quay, Springfield Quay, Glasgow, G5 8N

Bobar - International 0141 339 8811
383 Byres Road, Glasgow, Glasgow City, G12 8AU

Bovine Restaurant - International 0141 339 8811
383 Byres Road, Glasgow, Glasgow City, G12 8AU

Cail Bruich West - Scottish 0141 334 6265
725 Great Western Road, Glasgow, Lanarkshire, G12 8QX

Ashoka Ashton Lane - Indian 0141 337 1115
19 Ashton Lane, Glasgow, G12 8SJ

The Curry Leaf - Indian 0141 339 3777
192-194 Byres Road, Glasgow, G12 8SN

Paperinos West End - Pizza 0141 334 3811
227 Byres Road, Glasgow, G12 8UD

L'Aragosta - Seafood 01414 294604
213 Street Andrews Road, Glasgow, G41 1PD

Kebabish Original - Asian 0141 423 9988
677-681 Pollokshaws Road, Glasgow, G41 2AB

Camflava Bar and Restaurant - African 0141 440 7070
1006A Pollokshaws Road, Glasgow, G41 2HG

Bacco Italia - Italian 0845 226 7031
67'69 Kilmarnock Road, Glasgow, G41 3YR

Shezan Tandoori - Indian 0141 649 4776
1096 Cathcart Road, Glasgow, Lanarkshire, G42 9XW

Ashoka South Side - Indian 0141 637 0711
268 Clarkston Road, Glasgow, G44 3EA

Barbarossa Wine Bar - Italian 0141 560 3898
5 Clarkson Road, Cathcart, Glasgow, G44 4EF

Aishahs Indian Tapas - Tapas 0141 810 3914
10 Hillington Road South, Glasgow, G52 2AA

Prezzo Glasgow - Italian 0141 881 1467
Unit F1 Silverburn Shopping Centre, 763 Barrhead Road, Glasgow, G53 6QR

Ashoka at the Mill - Indian 0141 876 0458
500 Corselet Rd, Glasgow, G53 7RN

Ashoka Bearsden - Indian 0141 570 0075
9 Kirk Road, Bearsden, Glasgow, G61 3RG

Ashoka Brasserie - Indian 0141 776 7617
93-99 Cowgate, Kirkintilloch, G66 1JD

Irrocco - Modern European 0141 777 6655
Millersneuk Shopping Centre Lenzie, Glasgow, G66 5JD

Ashoka Shak Coatbridge - Curry 0123 643 7181
Showcase Leisure Park, Baillieston, G69 7TS

Blue Ruppee - Indian 0141 634 0019
163 Eastkilbride Road, Burnside, Glasgow, G73 5EA

Golden Star Tandoori - Indian 0138 972 1077
100 Main Street, Balloch, G83 8EP

Fratelli Sarti Balloch - Italian 01389 758247
Balloch Road, Balloch, G83 8SS

Cafe Lahore - Indian 01436 676 556
33-34 West Clyde Street, Helensburgh, Dunbartonshire, G84 8AW

Kirkaldy

Bella Italia - Italian 01383 729 133
Unit 7a, Fife leisure Park, Whimbrel Place, Dunfermline, KY11 8EX

Basils Restaurant - Modern European 01577 863 467
The Green Hotel, 2 The Muirs, Kinross, KY13 8AS

Monty`s Brasserie 0157 786 3217
Windlestrae Hotel The Muirs, Kinross Perthshire, Scotland, KY13 8AS

Maisha Indian Restaurant - Indian 0133 447 6666
5 College Street, St. Andrews, Fife, KY16 9AA

PizzaExpress St Andrews - Pizza 01334 477109
4 Logies Lane, St. Andrews KY169NL

Bella Italia - Italian 01334 476268
39 Bell Street, St Andrews, KY16 9UR

Motherwell

Pink Turban - Indian 0169 837 5566
157 Wishaw Road, Waterloo, Wishaw, ML2 8EN

Shimla Cottage - Indian 0123 643 6030
109 Sunnyside Road, Coatbridge, North Lanarkshire, ML5 3HR

Café Spice - Indian 0123 675 5123
76 Stirling Street, Airdrie, ML6 0AS

Paisley

Ashoka Shak Linwood - Indian 0141 889 4123
Phoenix Leisure Park, Linwood, PA1 2AB.

168 | Listings are for **ILLUSTRATIVE PURPOSES ONLY**, please visit www.tastecard.co.uk for participating restaurants and offers

Indian Scene Cuisine - Indian 82 Glasgow Road, Paisley, Renfrewshire, PA1 3PN	0141 611 9454
Brechin´s Brasserie - Mediterranean 2 Bridgend Street, Rothesay, Isle Of Bute, PA20 0HU	0170 050 2922
PizzaExpress Glasgow Braehead - Pizza 15 Xscape Centre, Renfrew, PA4 8XQ	0141 886 4996
Bella Italia - Italian Unit 14, Xscape, Braehead, Glasgow, PA4 8XU	01418 867 645
Ashoka Johnstone - Indian 3 Rankine Street, Johnstone, PA5 8AY	01505 336363

Perth

PizzaExpress Perth - Pizza 16/18 South Methven Street, PH1 5PE	01738 628 733
Lochside Restaurant at The Isles of Glencoe Hotel - Int Ballachulish, Nr. Fort William, Highlands, PH49 4HL	01855 811 602
Bulas Bar & Bistro @ The Ballachulish Hotel - Scottish Nr. Fort William, Glencoe, Scotland, PH49 4JY	01855 811 606
The Oak Restaurant @ Knock Castle Hotel & Spa - Scottish Drummond Terrace, Crieff, Perth and Kinross, PH7 4AN	0176 465 0088
The Stag's View @ Knock Castle Hotel & Spa - Scottish Drummond Terrace, Crieff, Perth and Kinross, PH7 4AN	0176 465 0088
Darjeeling Creative Cuisine - Indian 3-5 Atholl Street, Dunkeld, Perthshire, PH8 0AR	0135 072 7427 / 527

Inverness

Bella Italia - Italian 1 Bridge Street, Inverness, IV1 1HG	01463 230 138
PizzaExpress Inverness - Pizza B Eastgate Centre, IV2 3PP	01463 709 700

Eire & Northern Ireland

La Boca
South American — **02890 323087**

Fountain Street, Belfast, BT1 5ED

Named after the vibrant, Bohemian dockside district of Buenos Aires, La Boca is Belfast's first Argentine style restaurant. Located on Fountain Street it is a 3 minute walk from the front of the City Hall past the Linenhall Library. Its high ceiling and solid beech wood furniture create a stunning fifty seater dining room.

La Boca offers a delicious selection of authentic South American cuisine, prepared by their highly skilled chefs. In addition, La Boca have carefully selected their comprehensive and extensive wine list to complement the fantastic cuisine on offer.

The Grafton Lounge

International — (01) 679 6260
(00353) 1 679 6260

Unit 2, Royal Hibernian Way,
Dawson Street, Dublin 2

By day the Grafton Lounge is a buzz with local businesses on their lunch break and is very popular among shoppers and tourists in search of a break from the hustle and bustle of the city.

The Grafton Lounge is an ideal venue for after work drinks with an extensive cocktail menu, sunny terrace area, bar menu and upbeat tunes– what more could you want! A pool table perhaps?...

Tucked away on the lower ground floor this is Dublin's best kept secret..with a pour your own pint unit and comfy sofas...this area is a big hit.

The food is beautifully presented and delicious, with a cosmopolitan vibe to match the restaurant decor. Dishes include light bites as well as more hearty mains, with influences taken from international cuisine.

This venue oozes style and is perfect for any occasion.

Eire & Northern Ireland

Pacino's
Italian — (01) 677 5651
(00353) 1 677 5651

18 Suffolk Street, Dublin, 2 Co Dublin, Ireland

For over 15 years Pacino's has been a family run restaurant and is well known for its delicious 'Classic & Gourmet' Pizzas and Pastas, Steaks and Salads. Their aim is to serve traditional, fresh, quality Italian cuisine. Pacino's pride themselves on good service and well presented food with the emphasis on generous portions and value for money.

Pacino's has a capacity of 100 seats since its renovation in 2007 and can cater for large or small groups. They offer a modern dining experience, with an old world vibe – stylish brickwork, wooden floors and soft lighting all combine to create a relaxed, rustic, informal atmosphere.

Pacino's hope you enjoy your dining experience with them, as much as they enjoy welcoming you as a customer.

Northern Ireland

La Tasca Belfast VS - Spanish — 0845 126 2948
Unit SFC4 Victoria Square Shopping Centre,
2nd Floor 1, Victoria Square, Belfast County Antrim, BT1 4QG

La Boca - South American — 02890 323087
Fountain Street, Belfast, BT1 5ED

Kings Court Chinese Restaurant - Chinese — 0289 041 8961
756 Upper Newtownards Road, Dundonald, Belfast, BT16 1LA

Gingeroot Indian Cuisine - Indian — 0289 031 3124
73-75 Great Victoria Street, Belfast, BT2 7AF

Bokhara Indian Restaurant - Indian — 0289 124 0751
2 King Street, Bangor, Northern Ireland, BT20 3AH

Revivals Indian Restaurant - Indian — 0289 268 9624
41A Old Coach Road, Hillsborough, Co Down, BT26 6PB

La Tasca Belfast - Spanish — 0289 0738241
Unit 11 The Odyssey Pavilion, Belfast, County Antrim, BT3 9QQ

China Garden Ballymena - Chinese — 02825 648 368
6 Cullybackey Road, Ballymena, County Antrim, BT43 5DF

The Ginger Tree - Japanese — 02890 327 151
23-25 Donegall Pass, Belfast, BT7 1DQ

Rajput Indian Restaurant - Indian — 02890 662168
461, Lisburn Road, Belfast, BT9 7EY

Sonali - Curry — 02890 666833
703 Lisburn Road, Belfast, BT9 7GU

Eire

Isola Mia Restaurant - Italian — 01 675 3849
24A Erne Street Upper, Off Pearse Street, City Centre South, Dublin

The Grafton Lounge - International — 01 679 6260
Unit 2 Royal Hibernian Way, Dawson Street, Dublin 2

Punjab Balti Restaurant - Indian — 01 496 0808
15 Ranelagh Village, Ranelagh, Dublin 6

Boulevard Cafe - Mediterranean — 01 679 2131
27 Exchequer Street, Dublin 2, Co. Dublin, Ireland

Charming Noodles - Chinese — 01 872 9340
105 Parnell Street, 1 Co. Dublin, Ireland

Govinda's Vegetarian Restaurant Aungier Street - Vegetarian — 01 475 0309
4 Aungier Street, Dublin 2, Ireland

Govinda's Vegetarian Restaurant Merrion Row - Healthy Eating — 01 661 5095
18 Merrion Row, Dublin 2, Ireland

Indian Curry Club - Indian — 01 677 6873
6, South William Street, Dublin 2, Ireland

Indian Curry Club Kilbarrack - Indian — 01 871 2903
27/28 Kilbarrack Shopping Centre, Kilbarrack, Dublin 5, Ireland

La Caverna Italian Restaurant - Italian — 01 670 3110
12 Fownes Street, Temple Bar, Dublin 2, Ireland

Pacino´s - Italian — 01 677 5651
18 Suffolk Street, Dublin, 2 Co Dublin, Ireland

Purple Ocean - Seafood — 01 284 5590
St Michaels Pier, Dun Laoghaire, Co. Dublin, Ireland

Purty Kitchen Temple Bar - Seafood — 01 677 0945
34/35 East Essex Street, Temple Bar, Dublin 2, Ireland

Shimla Indian Restaurant - Indian — 01 824 9988
5 Weaver's Walk, Dublin 15, Co. Dublin, Ireland

Shimla Indian Restaurant - Indian — (0) 504 22444
Thurles, Co Tipperary, Ireland

Sinners - Lebanese — 01 675 0050
12 Parliament Street, Dublin 2, Co Dublin, Ireland

Taste of India Leixlip - Indian — 01 624 5899
Main Street, Leixlip, Co Kildare, Ireland

Taste of India Parliament Street - Indian — 01 675 9973
32 Parliament Street, Dublin, Ireland

Taste of India South William Street - Indian — 01 677 6873
6 South William Street, Dublin 2, Ireland

Rupsha Indian Restaurant - Indian — 01 836 3125
49 Lower Dorset Street, Dublin 1, Ireland

Vermilion — 01 499 1400
94 / 96 Terenure Road, North Dublin 6W, Ireland

Ameer Palace - Indian — 02 490 177
16 Sth Main Street, Youghal, Co. Cork

BD Spice Indian Restaurant - Indian — 01 495 4646
Eden House Grange Road, Rathfarnham, Dublin 16

Canters Restaurant - International — 01 833 3681
9 Fairview Strand, Dublin 3

China Garden - Chinese — 01 257 0364
Main Street, Saggart, Dublin

Dada Moroccan Cuisine Tapas Wine Bar - North African — 01 617 0777
45 William Street South, Dublin 2

Diwali - Indian — 01 475 0091
Unit 1 Castle House, South Great Georges Street, Dublin 2

Gojinka House of Teppanyaki - Japanese — 00353 01 840 0441
Swords Manor Brackenstwon Road, Swords, Co Dublin

Himalayo Tandoori - Indian — 01 4576023
Unit 6 Village Centre, Clondalkin, Dublin 22

Ming Court - Asian — 05 6772 2886
66 John Street, Kilkenny, Ireland

Ristorante Casanova - Italian — (21) 485 1111
88 North Main Street, Cork City, Ireland

Sardar Indian Restaurant - Indian — (061) 333915
56 The Orchards, Castletroy, Limerick

Spice Indian Cuisine Restaurant - Indian — (21) 437 5111
Mainstreet, Carrigaline, Cork

Tonic - International — 01 288 7671
5 Temple Road, Blackrock, Dublin

Washerwomans Hill Restaurant - International — 01 837 9199
60 Glasnevin Hill, Glasnevin, Dublin 9

Yo Thai - Thai — 00353 01 288 8994
Kielys Of Mount Merrion, Deerpark Road, Stillorgan, Co. Dublin

Shimla Indian Restaurant - Indian — (26) 43116
Fitzgerald Street, Macroom, Cork

PizzaExpress Killarney - Pizza — 00353 64 66 20620
16 Main Street, Country Kerry

Listings are for **ILLUSTRATIVE PURPOSES ONLY**, please visit www.tastecard.co.uk for participating restaurants and offers | 175

contact

Here at taste HQ we're always happy to hear from our customers, whether it's a general enquiry, restaurant recommendation, corporate enquiry or further information on one of our participating venues, the team would love to hear from you.

Our telephone lines are open from 9am-5pm, Monday to Friday. Out of these hours please feel free to email us, and we will contact you upon our return.

Many thanks for your continued support of taste, and we look forward to hearing from you soon.

Tel: 0800 5677 241
Web: www.tastecard.co.uk
Email: enquiries@tastecard.co.uk

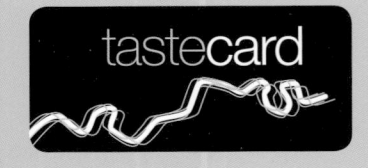

tastecard

www.tastecard.co.uk | it's a dining revolution!